GW01605451

Free is Cheaper

Free is Cheaper

Ken Smith

The John Ball Press Gloucester

Published in Great Britain by
The John Ball Press May Hill Gloucester.
Typeset by Tony Welch Gloucester.

Printed in Great Britain by
Billing & Sons Ltd, Worcester

ISBN 1 871240 00 X

British Library Cataloguing in Publication Data

Smith, (K. Rosser) 1922

Free is Cheaper.

1. Free economies

I Title

330. 12'2

Dedicated to

Sidney George Smith

Hanged Gloucester Jail 1903.

TABLE OF CONTENTS

PART II: Who does what, - a brief look at some of the principal employers.

Chapter 15.

The Manufacturing Industry.

PART III. Conclusion.

Chapter 16.

Parties from Left to Right

........offer no solution and are the real Utopians.

Chapter 17.

It's cheaper if it's free.

Chapter 18.

The real solution is all around us.

All we have to do is recover control of our lives.

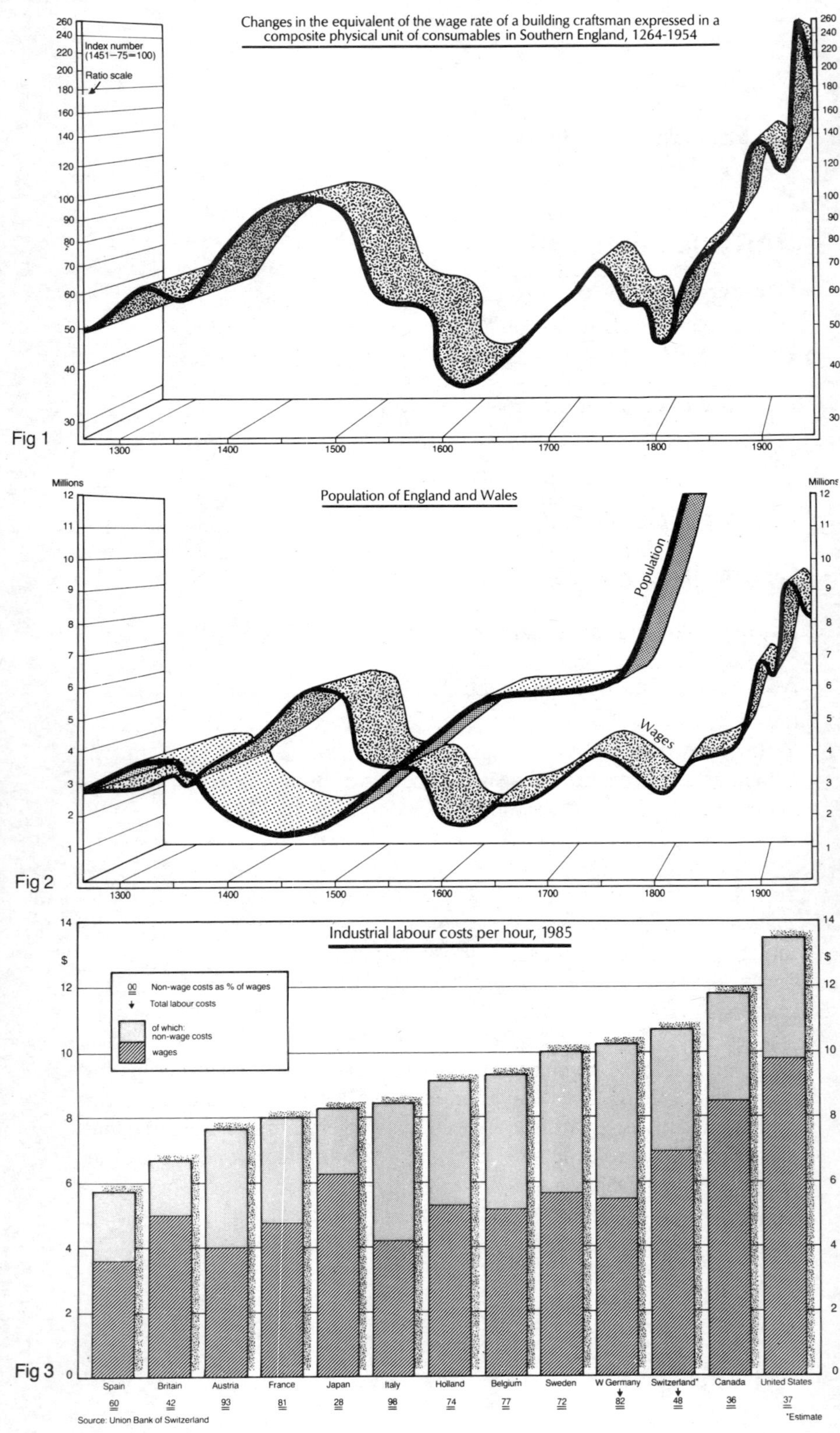

Changes in the equivalent of the wage rate of a building craftsman expressed in a composite physical unit of consumables in Southern England, 1264-1954
Index number (1451—75=100)
Ratio scale
260
240
220
200
180
160
140
120
100
90
80
70
60
50
40
30
1300
1400
1500
1600
1700
1800
1900
Fig 1
Population of England and Wales
Millions
12
11
10
9
8
7
6
5
4
3
2
1
Population
Wages
1300
1400
1500
1600
1700
1800
1900
Fig 2
Industrial labour costs per hour, 1985
14
$
12
10
8
6
4
2
0
00 Non-wage costs as % of wages
Total labour costs
of which:
non-wage costs
wages
Fig 3
Spain 60
Britain 42
Austria 93
France 81
Japan 28
Italy 98
Holland 74
Belgium 77
Sweden 72
W Germany 82
Switzerland* 48
Canada 36
United States 37
Source: Union Bank of Switzerland
*Estimate

INTRODUCTION

> "And some there be which have no memorial; who are perished as though they had never been; and are become as though they had never been born; and their children after them. But these were merciful men, whose righteousness hath not been forgotten. With their seed shall continually remain a good inheritance, and their children are within the covenant. Their seed standeth fast, and their children for their sakes. Their seed shall remain for ever, and their glory shall not be blotted out. Their bodies are buried in peace; but their name liveth for evermore."

Apocrypha. Ecclesiasticus XLIV.

Our Surreal World.

There have been many times in human history when men have lamented the state of the world: at the end of the great dynasties in China; with the collapse of the city states in Ancient Greece; the fall of the Roman Republic; the loss of Andalusia by the Arabs; the Thirty Years War; the Civil War in America. Yet in none of these nadirs in human affairs has there been such a feeling of unnecessary suffering as in these dying years of the twentieth century.

Upwards of half of all the scientific manpower of the developed countries, and up to half of the budgets are committed to war preparation. A quarter or more of the population is on poor relief, and at best, receives enough to keep body and soul together, yet there are real or threatened surpluses in every service and commodity from theatrical performances to cars, to wine lakes to wheat.

In the undeveloped countries the best land is devoted to cash crops for export while the native population starves. Everywhere the cry is for greater productivity, yet there is too much of everything. We are told that wages are too high yet people have not got the purchasing power to clear the stocks off the shelves. Millions are unemployed yet there is no-one to sweep the streets, mend the sewers, patch the roads, heal the sick, feed the hungry, repair the houses or protect the defenceless.

After several centuries of agricultural revolutions and industrial revolutions, during which time, we are assured, productivity has doubled every few decades, we appear to have stood still. Why are we not, all of us, up to our armpits in all the food, clothing, shelter and distraction that we could wish?

Insecurity affects everyone from paupers to millionaires. For the one, it is not knowing where the next meal is coming from; for the other it is in watching the share price disappear through the floor, the liquidator move into the office and hearing the bell of the ambulance racing to take him to the intensive care unit before the heart attack kills him. Apart from the relative poverty[1] that we see all around us, the endless worry and grubbing about, the enforced preoccupation with issues which should have been settled generations ago, why do we have no feeling of progress, of things getting better or of a more beautiful world? Quite clearly it is not as beautiful as it once was. The horrors of nineteenth century industrial blight are being replaced by the horrors of twentieth century poisoning of the land and water and air. The return to a green and pleasant land is being delayed by some mechanism we would do well to investigate. It would be bad enough if the war preparations, stress, pollution and ugliness were the price we had to pay for a prosperous and secure life. But we have the worst of both worlds. We could be poor without the hassle, without the worry whether the knock at the door is the debt collector or somebody else selling insurance or encyclopedias.

We would not be the first people to take that option. According to Professor Phelps Brown:

> "those who can stay on the land have seldom been willing, short of starvation to leave it for employment as wage earners; the poorest peasants have been reluctant to commit themselves to work in the factory even though they can earn more there, and in Africa and in Asia many of them still limit their commitment to a term of years. Wage earners who can get hold of land quit their employments - that was the experience of the colonists in America and Australia." ("The Economics of Labour")[2]

Dropouts.

From the eighteenth century with its communes and utopian settlements to the present day with its drop-outs and those who go to live the Good Life, there has been no shortage of people wishing to leave this world behind, but there is not, and never has been, any place to hide. The rich have to swim in the same polluted sea as the poor; the pacifist is just as likely to get killed as the soldier; we all have to breathe the same foul air. We are all in this together. There is no personal solution. There is no group solution. The solution has got to embrace everybody.

Tinkerers.

Not that we have ever been short of people with solutions. From the first half of the nineteenth century onwards, shoals of measures to curb child labour, provide education for all, health and unemployment insurance, the Welfare State, have been introduced to deal with at least some of the problems. No-one can claim that the measures have been an unqualified success. Like the hydra-headed monster of the Greek myth, as soon as one problem head is chopped off, another grows. Could it be on account of the piecemeal approach that has been used?

"Those who seek to manage economics or advise on their management are either tinkerers or structuralists."[3] But how structuralist should we be? Do West Germany, Japan, France, which seem to satisfy these researchers, offer us a real way out? West Germany, which we are told is a good place to earn money but a bad place to live. Japan? That society of "workaholics living in rabbit hutches" as some White House aide called them. Or the France of *dodo, metro, boulot; boulot, metro, dodo*? Is this all that life has to offer?

For the last century or more, parties of all shades of Left and Right, of interventionism and laissez faire have been appealing for our political support and have always left us feeling that the next time we shall say like the character in Balzac: "I know you my friend, you are as full of promises as a new made king!"

Loss of Control.

This is not to impute cynical motives to them. Prime Minister Callaghan was as surprised as anyone that his efforts to spend his way out of recession and reduce unemployment created more unemployment and more inflation. The Thatcher Government came to power aided by a poster showing a queue of unemployed with the caption "Labour isn't working". Pride alone would have prevented the Thatcher Government anticipating that nine years later inflation would be little better and that unemployment would have trebled.

Confusion.

A Cabinet Minister in the Callaghan Government expressed the view to friends that the Cabinet had completely lost all sense of direction in its last few months. David Howells, a Cabinet Minister in the first Thatcher administration was writing less than six years later:

> "Nor is it surprising that the Conservative Government in Britain, which has nailed its colours so firmly to the mast of liberal market economics, sometimes it seems to the exclusion of all other ideas and perceptions, has unmistakably begun to lose its bearings and directions." [4]

and Sir Alfred Sherman, ex-Communist, and guru for the Thatcher faction in the Conservative Party during the Seventies and early Eighties, co-founder with Sir Keith Joseph of the "Centre for Policy Studies" in the optimistic Sixties, was writing in the pessimistic Eighties:

> "Economic theory is in disarray. Rather like rival nuclear powers, each school of economic thought is far better equipped to annihilate its opponents premises than to defend its own." [5]

The Real Villain.

The assumption of all the adversaries from the extreme Left to extreme Right, from total laissez faire to apostles of the Corporate State, is that their approaches are collectively exhaustive of the possible remedies. The basis of the modern world since the sixteenth century, where a minority buys the energies of the majority to produce goods and services for sale to whoever has the money to buy them, is not questioned by these experts. Yet increasing numbers of people are indicting this market-based system itself as the root of most of our troubles: the enormous waste of the system, where nine out of ten employed are not producing any wealth at all but are simply dead-wood, economically speaking; the enormous callousness of the system where people are condemned to lives of drudgery with the alternative of enforced idleness; the enormous divisiveness of the system, where people's natural sociability and generosity are perverted by squabbling and competition over artificially created scarcity; the enormous destructiveness of the system with its periodic wars over markets and "spheres of influence", to the destruction of the environment caused by short cuts in the struggle for profits. These and other cancers in our lives have produced a number of Catos warning us of the dangerous drift: Louis Mumford, E.F. Schumacher, Leopold Kohr, warning us of the tendencies and dangers in thinking "big";Rachel Carson, Kenneth Allsop, Frazer Darling, Barry Commoner, The Green Movement, on the destruction of nature; Rene Dubois, Robert McNamara, Willi Brandt on impending disaster in the Third World; Ralph Nader, Hazel Henderson, The Campaign for Real Ale, on the "shoddy but ingenious" goods we buy (Wendell Berry's dismissive phrase.)[6]

But no less important were those warning us of the drift to bureaucracy and proliferation of non-productives identified by the Wilson Government in the sixties as money-making rather than wealth-creation, and by the Thatcher Government in the eighties as the need for "resource allocation" which might be summed up as not pouring good money after bad.

They were both right. An economy which favours middlemen and neglects producers is doomed. Likewise, an economy where bureaucracy, feather-bedding, mike-ing, ca-canny, is tolerated or even subsidised, is a crippled economy and a fair description of all of the world's developed nations. That is the point. None escape these maladies. Those enthusiasts for laissez faire who feel that Japan, for example, does not suffer from these defects have not done their homework. They might start their first night's task with a study of Japanese railways. They can follow that with a look at Japanese housing, pollution, sewerage etc. etc. And those enthusiasts on the Left for varying degrees of dirigisme from Sweden to Russia should ask themselves if the citizens in their particular Shangri La share their feeling of satisfaction with the regime. If not, the reason is surely because their country suffers the same defects as the others. And the cause of the majority of these problems arises, as I hope to show, from the Market Economy itself, be it as Free Enterprise as one likes, or as rigidly controlled as Mao's China, Hoxha's Albania, or Stalin's Russia.

1. "The greatest number of poor is not to be found in barren countries of amidst barbarous nations, but in those which are the most fertile, wrote John McFarlane in 1782. Giammaria Ortes, the Italian economist, pronounced it an axiom that the wealth of a nation corresponds with its population; and its misery corresponds with its wealth.......Adam Smith in his cautious manner declared that it is not in the richest countries that the wages of labour are highest." Karl Polanyi: The Great Transformation.

2. E.H.Phelps Brown: The Economics of Labour [Yale 1962]

3. Bacon and Eltis: Britain's Economic Problem - Too Few Producers. [Macmillan 1976]

4. Sunday Times 28/4/85.

5. Guardian 29/4/85.

6. Wendell Berry : The Unsettling of America (Sierra 1978).

Part I

Chapter 1

The Problem.

"As a young man I was very interested in how people lived in earlier times; how they got from place to place, lighted their homes, cooked their meals, and so on. So I went to the history books. Well, I could find out all about the kings and presidents; but I could learn nothing of their everyday lives. So I decided that history is bunk." Henry Ford[1]

Five hundred years ago an English building worker could earn the price of a steak or lamb chop,[2] a housebrick or rooftile in as little or even less time at work than he can today. This fact becomes even more surprising when we examine its implications. The position of building workers in the social order does not appear to have altered greatly in the intervening centuries. Meat, bricks, and rooftiles are as central now to a study of comparative wellbeing as they were then. Moreover our English building worker might well have been French or Italian, Dutch or Belgian, such was the mobility of labour at the time, so that he could be seen as a fair sample of fifteenth century European building workers, and by extension, of European society as a whole. By the same token, this data allows a comparison in real standards of living with the present in the countries of European colonisation.

There was a huge French labour force engaged in the construction of our cathedrals and larger churches. There were many Italian craftsmen engaged in the more exacting decoration. In the Eastern counties Dutchmen were working throughout the late Middle Ages on civil engineering projects. And outside the building industry the weavers from Belgium were bringing in their skills, the bankers from Italy their credit institutions. Our continental cousins provided the help and we can provide them now with the records. Britain is uniquely fortunate in possessing an unbroken series of economic records going back to the Norman Conquest. This is largely due to the fact that 1066 was the last time that this country was occupied by a foreign power. Mainland Europeans have had to endure endless campaigns being fought across their countrysides from Portugal to Russia, from Sicily to Scandinavia. The wonder is that anything is left there at all.

There was, then, a European market in building labour. There still is, but now the market has taken in a bigger area: Turkish workers in Germany, North African workers in France, Spanish workers in Belgium; West Indian, Pakistani and Indian workers in Britain; huge populations swilling about to the demands of the labour market, with all the attendant social problems.

No Help From The Historians.

If there has been no significant improvement in the material well being of working people since the end of the Middle Ages, where has the money gone? What has happened to the enormous increases in wealth which - according to the historians - have been piling up as a consequence of the revolutions in Agriculture and Industry since the sixteenth century? What of Coke, and of Turnip Townsend, Jethro Tull, John Kay (flying shuttle) Hargreaves (spinning jenny), Arkwright (water frame), Crompton (mule)? What, to go further back, of the huge increase in wealth allegedly created by robbing the peasantry of the Common Land and of the Glebe Lands; of the enclosures and engrossments from the Statute of

Merton in 1236 onwards? The period has been called by Professor Hoskins "The Age of Plunder".[3] Perhaps the increase in wealth refers to the plunderers only. Certainly, the conversion of millions of acres from arable to the more primitive economy of sheep pasture could only have resulted in a reduction of wealth in absolute terms. But if it were spread among a disproportionately smaller number of people, then, as in Al Capone's bit of Chicago, the benefits to them could be greater.

Similarly with the later, Industrial Revolution. The conspicuous consumption of a tiny minority which had begun with the Tudors continued while the living standards of the people plunged. The nadirs appear to have been around 1600 and again in the time of the Napoleonic Wars. But if the richness of the rich might provide a clue as to where a lot of the wealth produced in earlier centuries had gone to, it is not good enough today. This is not a plea to pity the poor rich. The rich have never had any difficulty either themselves, or through their apologists, in guarding their interests, and need no help from me.

But we have had enough of confusion and false trails from the historians and economists. If you start off with the premiss (as most of them do) that the world is flat and square, and your reasoning is sound, then you will end up with the manifestly stupid conclusions they offer us: that the answer to surpluses is higher productivity, that wage cuts lead to greater prosperity, that war preparation leads to peace, that more regulations lead to freedom.

A moment's reflection will convince that whatever statistics are produced to show that the rich are getting richer, the facts show otherwise. No-one is building stately homes now. Blenheim, Chatsworth, Longleat, the filthy rich are not even managing to keep them repaired let alone build new. The "J" class yachts of Tommy Lipton's era are rotting hulks; the big yachts today belong to Greeks and Arabs whose countries are only just passing through the Tommy Lipton era. And, moving down the social scale, the professionals: doctors, engineers, architects, lawyers who a century ago would be surrounded by ostlers, butlers, cook- generals and assorted skivvies, have been plunged into the ranks of the proletariat, to the chagrin of whingers like Paul Johnson,[4] John Vaizey, Patrick Hutber et al. (In 1982 the wealthiest 5% of the population owned 41% of marketable wealth compared with 52% in 1971)[5]

If they had done their homework instead of relying on a Reader's Digest level of study they would have discovered that Engels and Marx,[6] whom they abused for the wrong reasons, had predicted precisely this outcome.

Tweedledum And Tweedledee.

An increasing number of people are beginning to identify the system itself, the socio-economic set-up that has developed since the Tudors, as the villain of the piece. Production for the Market, with all its disciplines and rewards, has been held out as the guarantee of best return, social and personal, for any input. Certainly, compared with the alternative of interventionist capitalism, either half hearted on the social- democratic scale, or full-blooded Hitler or Stalin style, the argument is seductive. Its seductiveness increases with every extra bureaucratic straw placed on our backs. Until we come face to face with the reality of it, that is. Then the dole queues, the bankrupt little corner shops, the devastated industries, and the economic guerilla warfare reminds us that we have seen this film before. That, in fact, it has been showing since the early nineteenth century - the heyday of laissez faire capitalism. And so the pendulum of expert opinion and popular support swings back to intervention, but the bureaucrats have continued to multiply due to the ratchet mechanism built into the system. Vainly did Margaret Thatcher hand out Leslie Chapman's book "Your Disobedient Servant" on Civil Service Profligacy to her lieutenants. In vain did she complain[7] that there were more tax collectors than sailors in the Navy. Winston Churchill *nepos* put his finger on the problem when he complained in Parliament that the job of reducing the number of bureaucrats was in the very hands of the "pen pushers", i.e. the bureaucrats themselves, and dog does not eat dog.

The phenomenon of the "right wing" backlash, supported by popular revolt, against regulation, regimentation, bumbledom, high taxation and the money raised thereby disappearing like water out of a colander, was not restricted to Britain. Howard Matthews in California with his "Proposition 13", Mogens Glistrup in Denmark with his proposal to abolish income tax, Pierre Poujade in France as far back as the 1950's, for all their eccentricities, expressed feelings that were widely based and had their equivalents in every country of the developed world. Their ire, however was directed at the wrong targets. Like Paul Johnson they felt that Labour, organised and unorganised was the cause of their ills. This, again, is a film that we have seen before. The Lumpen Bourgeoisie of our own time got no further than that of Germany after the debacle of the Weimar Republic. Substitute the Labour administrations of Wilson, Foot and Callaghan for Ebert, Noske and Scheidemann, together with the money forging proclivities of both administrations and we can be relieved that the lumpen bourgeoisie - that class of life-insurance, secondhand car and knicker-elastic salesmen - delivered us into the hands of Margaret Thatcher and not another Adolf Hitler. The ruin of the British middle class during the last forty years can no more be laid at the door of the working class than it could in Germany in 1930. Inflation has been proceeding apace since 1527.[8]

It has merely accelerated in recent decades and, as Enoch Powell never ceases to point out, workers and unions don't print money, governments do. If we doubt that, we should ask the lawyers' question: Qui bono? It is in the interest of the governments to forge money. They can reduce wages without appearing to attack the working class. And they can appease the wealthy by not needing to raise taxes. But all pay in the end.

How We Got In This Mess.

Of the three pillars of the Market economy, two were created by driving the peasants off the common land; that is, capital in the form of privately owned land, and wage labour, in the form of the dispossessed peasantry. The third, production of goods for sale, Commodity Production, was ushered in by combining the first two.

The first of the Acts robbing the peasants of their land, the Statute of Merton was as early as 1236 and the last, the Great Enclosure in 1845. If anyone objects that the peasants' title to the land was defective, one can reply that it was better than anybody else's. It no more belonged to the Lord of the Manor[9] than it belonged to the King, title in their case being only a symbolic one. For the rest, the peasants had not only occupied their strips and grazing for more than the twelve years *nec clam, nec per vi, nec per consilio,*[10] as the Common Law required, but had done so since the dawn of time.

A noble lord was reported in the press in 1985 to be trying to get his hands upon a still unenclosed piece of common land in the Midlands, and a ten acre field at Elmstone Hardwicke near Cheltenham is one of the few plots still surviving from the Great Plunder. It is let out annually for grazing by the Parish Council - there are no real "owners". As I mentioned above, the rest of the looting was completed more than a century ago.

With this series of Acts passed by a parliament that represented nobody but the robbers themselves, the whole economy shifted over to a money base. The strangled cries of the peasants as they went under, the unctuous voices of the apologists as they surfaced: intellectual whores from Oxford and Cambridge, smoothing the ruffled waters, mopping fevered brows, saying a few prayers, singing a few hymns; all of this was repeated in the colonial empires. " When you came, you had bibles and we had the land. When you left we had the bibles and you had the land."

People who had, since the beginning of time, been accustomed to shifting for themselves: ploughing, seed-time, and harvest, were deprived of the means to fend for themselves and their families. Many were killed resisting the pillage. Many starved to death. Others were driven into exile. The remainder sought employment from the people who had robbed them and were now completely at their mercy.

The graph illustrates how, step by step, the yeomen of England were degraded. It also gives the lie to the sedulously peddled propaganda of the apologists that however hard times have been since the Tudors, they were worse before.

Living standards plunged from the time of Henry VIIIs' Accession, through his first attack on the currency in 1542 to the nadir from 1597 onward. The later part of that century was during the reign of Elizabeth I, Gloriana herself, so syphylitic, according to D.H. Lawrence, that she had lost all her hair and her teeth by the time she was thirty. This had come, with compliments from her father, Good King Hal himself.

The style of the ruling clique in those terrible years for the people was as splendid as unlimited wealth could make it. It can be said in their favour that they were not parochial in their ambitions. They plundered the Spanish abroad as they plundered their countrymen at home, and since the Spaniards had stolen the swag from the Indians in America they were not in a position to complain.

The apologists for the Market system from Hobbes onward have argued for its historical necessity. Some of them, e.g. Adam Smith and David Ricardo: "could not see that the bourgeois system had a beginning and a middle, because that required that it had an end. So with fearless honesty and great perception they rationalized the existence of the status quo." [11]

Unnecessary Unpleasantness.

The great contribution of Marx was to put the bourgeois system into its historical context; to show that society evolves just as much as animal and plant species evolve. He liberated it from the static world of Adam Smith, Ricardo, and their modern followers - there are none so blind as those who will not see. He insisted however, that it was contingent but also necessary. We now know that nothing is necessary in the world of experience; there is no amount of experience that will allow us to conclude that any historical event is necessary. Nature is full of blind alleys from the dinosaurs to Neanderthal Man.

The bourgeois system, Capitalism, the Market system, call it what you will is not an essential pre-condition of a free-society, of a world where people co-operate freely to produce all they need and then help themselves to the proceeds, be they porridge oats or Porsche cars. Marx's theory argues that the Market economy was a necessary stage to provide the machinery-for-abundance which could be used fully once the ownership of land and everthing on it and under it was restored to the people.[12]

But there never was a problem of machinery, either mechanical or social. The human race has been discovering needs and simultaneously satisfying them since time began, from the eyed needle to the flint arrow-head, from printing to the water-mill. To the charge that the Middle Ages didn't develop steam power, we can reply that the nineteenth century did not develop electronics and we ourselves have not developed who knows what?

The Market economy is a cul-de-sac leading nowhere. Much of that produced during the past five centuries, structures both physical and social, will be an enormous burden of garbage needing to be removed. Little of it could be used or adapted for a society producing only use-values.

Worthless Developments.

The megapolis: London, Paris, New York, for example, cannot be utilised by a society organised on a basis of free-cooperation, organised from the bottom up rather than the top down. The first call will be for the bulldozers to level the commercial districts, spread topsoil, seed, and plant trees. The villages and small towns swallowed up in the miasma of London during recent centuries will re-discover their identities. Camden Town will become a town again, with gardens and woods separating it from Highbury and Holborn.

More Correctives for the Historians.

The tendency of administrative centres and capital cities to develop tremendous centripetal forces is a feature of the Market economy wherever it develops, and is an important factor in the cancer-like growth which burdens the economy and simultaneously destroys it. But the phenomenon is not restricted to bourgeois society. Ancient Rome sucked the life blood, first out of Latium, then of Italy and finally out of the Empire, before the whole edifice collapsed in a cloud of dust when the Germanic "barbarians" blew on it. What was particularly barbarous about these latter people was that they exacted in taxes only a fraction of what the Roman state had been screwing out of the peasant farmers.

"A number of recent archeological publications provide evidence of a socio-economic transition that occured in the Roman Empire as it declined and fell ... As many as 40% of the bones in the early fifth century midden and 65% in the later fifth century midden are from pigs. The traditional balanced blend of meat consumption and stock rearing on rural lines seems to have been abandoned in favour of the short-term fast production of pork ... The major cities, in other words, were booming and attracting the rural poor, the recipients of the pork dole,[13] leaving agri deserti in the provinces, as Whittaker notes."[14]

Coming nearer to our own time, Third World countries entering the economy of the world market develop similar symptoms:

> "In Mauretania, says Rene Dumont, 400,000 people, one quarter of the population, now live in the capital Nouakchott, a city of no agriculture, no animal-raising, of no industry. It is an artificially created capital, a city of services, of bureaucrats and businessmen. It has factories that are closed and do not function. There is a possibility that there won't be enough water for it in 20 years."

But how can this all come about?

> "In 1983, when I delivered a report on Senegal to President Abdou Diouf, he told me, "Monsieur Professor, you are right. We must establish a better balance between the city and the countryside. But I cannot do it, because I do not have the organised political power in the rural areas to counter the organised political power of the urban areas."[15]

And on the other side of the world, the policy of the Pol Pot/Khmer Rouge regime in forcing the population of the capital Phnom Penh into the Cambodian countryside to grow food was an expression in rage and cruelty, of the frustration they felt with the leech-like character of the capital:

> "We had estimated the population of Phnom Penh at two million but we found almost three million people in the city when we entered it. The Americans had been bring-

> ing 30,000 to 40,000 tons of food into Phnom Penh daily. We had no means of transporting such quantities of supplies to the capital. So the population had to go where the food was. We had to feed that population and at the same time preserve our independence and our dignity without asking for help from any other country."[16]

The other aspect of bourgeois society which Marx thought was a necessary contribution to the future was "mass consciousness" of the need to bring it about. But this consciousness has been present since the beginning of class society.

Tiberius Gracchus proposed in his Land Act of 133 B. C. that the urban citizens of Rome be settled on the common land, the *ager publicus*:

> "The wild beasts of Italy have dens and holes to hide in; but when the wars are over and the brave men who have spilt their blood for her come home again, they find nothing that is theirs but the daylight and the air. Hearthless and homeless, they must take their wives and families and tramp the roads like beggars ... They fight and fall to serve no other end but to multiply the possessions and comforts of the rich. We call them Masters of the World and not a man among them all has a square foot of ground that he can call his own."[17]

Fifteen hundred years later the unfrocked priest John Ball argued the same thing in his sermon at Blackheath during the Peasants Revolt: "Matters will not go well in England until all things are held in common."[18] Thomas More also proposed the ending of servile labour in his Utopia, as did the Diggers during the English Civil War. "The Diggers agreed with the Levellers that wage labourers were unfree; but they drew the conclusion that wage-labour should be abolished."[19]

Marxists characterised all these movements as Utopian Socialism[20] because they were not rooted in the potential plenty[21] that they thought Capitalism had made possible. But they were suffering from a lack of information regarding the economic well-being of earlier societies as they suffered from a lack of information regarding the social organisation of primitive peoples until it was made good by the work of Henry Lewis Morgan in his "Ancient Society".

Thorold Rogers' "Six Centuries of Work and Wages," published the year after Marx's death, urged a rethink about poverty and earlier societies. The work of the research team led by Beveridge: "Prices and Wages in England, from the twelfth to the nineteenth century",[22] made it inescapable. Finally, modern archeology has pulled the rug from under the feet of most historians.

What is a new factor is the mounting impersonal chaos and pain created by the system. Whereas in the past, wars could be put down to kingly or imperial ambitions, and poverty to poor harvests or the greed of landlords and employers, the situation now is one where everybody is blaming everybody else and no-one is really to blame. "The notion of declining productivity of the American worker is a bum rap. Rather it is the declining productivity of capital investment in our mature economy, due to its rising social costs, the transaction costs of its complexity, the declining quality of its resource base."[23]

1. *Toronto Star reporter Ronald Frenburgh quoting interview with Ford in 1935 in letter to The Observer 3/8/86.*

2. *"For several centuries from the middle ages its (Europe) tables had been loaded with meat and drink worthy of Argentina in the nineteenth century. This was because the European countryside, beyond the Mediterranean shores, had long remained half empty with vast lands for pasturing animals." Fernand Braudel : Capitalism & Material Life (Fontana 1974)."In the German towns, according to Abel, the yearly consumption of meat declined from an average of 100 kilograms or more per person in the fifteenth century to not more than 14 kilograms in the nineteenth." Walter Minchinton : Fontana Economic History of Europe. (1974)*

3. *G. Hoskins : The Age of Plunder. (Longmans 1976).*

4. *"The economic decline of the middle class has been brought about by a combination of progressive taxation, inflation, and the power of the industrial unions." Paul Johnson: Enemies of Society, p. 189, et ad nauseam: "The proletarianisation of the British middle class, that leading creator and custodian of western civilisation is one of the most significant social changes of our times. Not only was the policy of promoting the embourgeoisment of society abandoned, not only was the effort to raise the moral code by introducing all to middle-class cultural privilege scrapped as impractical, but the whole process was put into reverse. The educated and cultured elite was positively stampeded by government policy into embracing the social morality of the industrial ghetto." p. 191 Johnson is clearly at odds with fellow conservatives like Professors Milton Friedman and George Stigler. According to Directors Law, formulated by Stigler: "Public expenditures are made for the primary benefit of the middle class and financed with taxes which are borne in considerable part by the poor and rich." And from Friedman: "Children from poor families tend to start work, - and start paying employment taxes - at a relatively early age; children from higher income families at a much later age. At the other end of the life cycle, persons with lower incomes on the average have*

a shorter life span than persons with higher incomes. Result is that the poor tend to pay taxes for more years and receive benefits for fewer years than the rich." Free To Choose, p.107. Johnson should know, having been kept at university by the taxes of the inhabitants of the industrial ghetto who started work at fifteen.

5." The share of personal wealth owned by the top 1 per cent of adults fell from about three-fifths in the 1920s to one- fifth in 1979." John Rentoul: The Rich Get Richer, Unwin Paperbacks 1987.

6. "The bourgeoisie has stripped of its halo every occupation hitherto honoured and looked up to with reverent awe. It has converted the physician, the lawyer, the priest, the poet, the man of science, into its paid wage- labourers." Communist Manifesto. (Penguin 1967) p.62.

7. Leslie Chapman : Your Disobedient Servant (Chatto 1978).

8. "The supply (of money) was augmented in the reigns of Henry VIII and Edward VI by a deliberate debasement of the currency in order to raise revenue for the Crown. Earlier monarchs had reduced the weight of the coins while maintaining the fineness of the metal; beginning in 1542, however, Henry VIII began reducing the silver content of the metal from the "ancient and right" 925 parts per 1000; this process was continued until, in the reign of Edward VI coins were struck from alloy containing only 150 parts per 1000 of silver, and the money remained in circulation until Elizabeth's re-coinage of 1560-1. E. Victor Morgan: History of Money (Penguin) 1965.

9. "The herbage was owned by a certain number of persons having stints or limited rights, the Lord of the Manor among them, being equally stinted with his tenants or any others." Elton: Commons p.64. "In England, for example, conveyances of most peasants' land had to be made through the local manorial court, with the peasant surrendering his rights in the land who then granted them out to his successor. Although the lord was in this sense superior to the peasant, he did not own the land either, for he could not disturb the peasant in his occupation of it, unless there was some breach of the customary obligations preserved either orally, or in a written form on the manorial court rolls. The lord was something less than an owner and the peasant was something more than a tenant." Frank E. Huggett: The Land Question (And European Society) Thames & Hudson 1977.

10. "Neither by stealth, nor by force, nor by agreement."

11. Michael Harrington : The Twilight of Capitalism (Macmillan 1977) cf also Paul Lafargue: "Political economists have laid it down .....that capital is co-eval with the world and that as it has had no beginning, so it can have no end." The Evolution of Property, p.1. (New Park Publications 1975). "The importance of these books (i.e. Bronislav Malinowski; Argonauts of the Western Pacific, and Marcel Mauss: Essai sur le don) in their successful propagation of the need for scientific examination of primitive economics, which had been the subject of "bourgeois ethnocentrism." Richard Hodges: Dark Age Economics p.13 (Duckworth 1981).

12. "It is now questionable whether the road to the carefree society runs through the market economy, dominated as it is by piecemeal choices exercised by individuals in response to their immediate situation. Unfortunately, individual liberation does not make them liberating for all individuals together." Fred Hirsch: Social Limits to Growth, p. 26. (Routledge & Kegan Paul.)

13. Richard Hodges: The Decline of Rome to a Fast-Food Empire. (Nature vol 309, 17/5/84)

14. C.R. Whittaker: Trade in the Ancient Economy, 1983.

15. Guardian 8/3/85

16. Ieng Sary quoted by Francois Ponchaud: Cambodia Year Zero, p.36. (Penguin 1978)

17. C.E. Robinson: History of the Roman Republic, p.235. (Methuen 1947).

18. Froissart's Chronicles.

19. Christopher Hill : The Century of Revolution, p.132 (Nelson 1967).

20. cf. Engels: Socialism Utopian and Scientific.

21. "It is obvious that hitherto the productive forces had not yet been developed widely enough to produce sufficiency for all." Communist Manifesto, Principles of Communism by Frederick Engels. p.80. (Progress Publishers, Moscow 1971).

22. Cass, 1939.

23. Hazel Henderson : The Politics of the Solar Age, p. 245 (Anchor Press Doubleday 1976).

Chapter 2.

How we got to where we are from where we were.

"It's every man for himself and God for us all," the elephant said as he danced among the chickens. G.B. Shaw.

What Really Happened in History.

The market now incorporates the New World. North and South America and Australasia were importers only, of labour, in the first place. Now there is a small but significant return flow, mainly of managerial grades. The consequence is that wages and salaries are tending to approximate more and more over the whole of the developed world, which is to say, the world of the Market. It is an imperfect market, but then perfect markets exist only in the imaginations of certain economists. It is still good enough to permit a comparison with the English medieval building worker, a comparison which is not flattering to our own time.

But why meat and housebricks? Medieval masons and carpenters did not have the compensations of television, freezers, motor cars or telephones. Quite true. But these things don't come free. They have to be worked and paid for. The medieval worker had the leisure instead.

Additionally, the need for food and shelter have to be satisfied first, which may explain why a lot of people today go without a decent diet and put up with substandard housing because social pressures require them to treat the television, video recorder, motor car, etc. on an equal footing with food and housing.

But why meat? Why not bread, fruit, vegetables? All first class protein - meat, fish, dairy products - was cheaper to our fifteenth century worker, and if there is anything that working people tend to forego in their diet it frequently includes animal protein - because of its cost. According to the 1986 Annual Digest of Statistics, the expenditure on animal protein accounts for about half of all household food expenditure.

Barring periods of actual starvation - extremely rare in the Western World, and equally rare in the Third World before the chaos wrought by Imperialism - there has always been enough cheap carbohydrate to fill stomachs with. But the fact that small stature and poverty tend to go together, demonstrates that many people have not reached and still are not reaching their physical potential. Pre-war British working class children averaged two or three inches less in height than their public school counterparts. And American-born descendants of Chinese and Japanese in California are frequently over six feet in height, as are overseas Chinese and Japanese in Malaysia, Indonesia and the Pacific. But if body size and weight is unquestionably a function of protein intake, there is another aspect which appears to be ignored.

Social Darwinism And False Premisses.

The fertility of the poor,[1] either in the Developed or the Undeveloped world is taken by the experts to be a function of their sloth and libidinousness. The poor just lie around and screw all the time while their betters' thoughts are on higher things - or so we are informed. There was a panic on some years ago in the West because it was thought that the intelligence of the race was going down; the same concern seems to be affecting the ruling elite in places like Singapore.

The syllogism runs:

The poor breed fast

The rich breed slow

The poor are intellectually (and otherwise) inferior

Therefore we are being swamped by cretins.

If one wanted to counter this social Darwinism one might argue that the more exacting the circumstances the finer the product, and that adversity sharpens the wits; therefore we should look to the historically poor for the finest genetic potential.

In the 1950's the great Brazilian biologist and first head of the F.A.O., Josue de Castro[2] exposed the canard of poor people's lust and pointed out what should not have needed pointing out, i.e. that fertility is closely connected to nutrition, that poor people have lots of children if their protein intake is low. The fact is well enough known to farmers. Only a fool "feeds" his tomatoes before the fruit has set. Fruit trees reluctant to fruit can be encouraged to do so by ring-barking, so reducing the amount of food they take up. Dennis Carter, a stockfarmer in the Vale of Gloucester tells me that if he has trouble getting a cow in calf he "puts her down in the bottom field. There isn't much feed there and it usually works after three or four weeks." And so with people.

Archeology Debunks History.

Historians have parroted the information for centuries that our ancestors were dwarfs, died young, and in the winter ate rotten meat because they could not afford to buy expensive imported spices to preserve it and disguise its flavour. The originator of this nonsense, Thomas Hobbes, was writing during the English Civil War, which explains his concern with "continuall feare, and danger of violent death; And the life of man, solitary, poore, nasty, brutish, and short."[3] Archeology which tends to deal more with facts and less with opinions has recently been producing evidence which does not support these public relations officers of the status quo. Numerous skeletons have been exhumed from half a millenium to half a million years old, which appear quite generously proportioned. A few miles from where I write, more than four hundred Romano-British skeletons were dug up in the 1970's at Cirencester.[4] The mean height of the males was five feet six and a half inches and for females five foot two. Bearing in mind that these were Ancient Britons i.e. the ancestors of the present day Welsh and Cornish and Bretons, their descendants don't seem to have increased in stature overmuch. And if the tallest of the Italo- Celts did not exceed six feet, the north of this county of Gloucestershire yielded the bones of a seven foot Saxon warrior in the decade before.

One does not have to invoke an arcadian paradise in earlier societies to counter Hobbes' judgement. He was writing during the Civil War, a turncoat, in fear of his life, and life could not have been much more nasty, brutish, and short, than it was for him in the 17th century.[5]

Those historians who have striven to point our the inconsistencies in the conventional view of earlier societies are being reinforced by the archeologists. Richard Hodges of Sheffield University, Colin Renfrew at Cambridge, are among many in Britain and on the Continent, citing the results from numerous digs which do not square with the prejudices of the majority of historians. Recent excavations at Southampton, York, East Anglia, and at Dorestad by the Dutch State Archeological Service have yielded evidence of levels of consumption that many would envy today:

> "...Six Dials site in Southampton ... The rubbish in these pits, like the rubbish buried in Dorestad and Ipswich shows that the community was well fed on livestock, presumably from the surrounding estates. Field surveys in Middle Rhineland and in various parts of Italy have begun to emphasise the modest scale of rural settlement at this time. There is, in fact, much to suggest that peasants had a comparatively high level of nutrition from maintaining mixed farming regimes in this pre-market environment as opposed to producing cash crops of one form or another."[6]

Professor Renfrew protests at the way the subject has been treated: "Dark Ages ... one of their characteristics is a slow development in the study of their archeology hampered both by the tendency among historians to accept as evidence traditional narratives first set down in writing some centuries after the collapse ... and by focusing on the larger and more obvious central place sites of the vanished state."[7]

One could understand tendentiousness in those scribes in the pay of princes of the church, or of the state, in earlier times. It is difficult to forgive historians who make great play with academic impartiality, detachment, freedom from bias, as a cloak for propaganda in defence of the status quo.

We have been told that in earlier societies, most of the animals were killed off in the autumn because of the difficulty of feeding them through the winter. Evidence from the digs shows that many of the beasts were four years old at slaughter - more *boeuf a la bourgignonne* than lightly grilled. But how did this nonsense ever gain credence anyway? Nonsense, because of the question: what had the human race been doing through all those yawning eons of evolution? It wasn't really necessary to wait for the archeologists to overturn this particular fiction. The Roman poet Horace, writing of the coming of spring says: "The beasts are no longer content in the stalls, nor the ploughman by his fire"[8]. This is nearly a thousand years before the period we are considering, and they were clearly stall-feeding their animals then.

No Money for Maintenance, Even.

One of the features which is said to distinguish mature developed countries from the recently arrived is in the richness of infra-structure. Northwest Europe and North America are well furnished with water and sewage systems, metalled roads, bridges and dams, railways and port installations. But this maturity shows increasing signs of developing into decadence and collapse. The newspapers are full of shock-horror stories of cracking bridges, and dams, potholed roads, collapsing sewers and water mains leaking up to a third of their water. Again, Britain, as front runner in industrialisation shows more signs of this than most countries.

With the progress of society economically and financially, one would expect that the mere maintenance of these installations should be easy enough. After all, previous generations had taken the original investment in their stride. Why do we find the maintenance beyond us?

Down through the ages society seems to have been able to spare people from the work of producing the necessities of life to build monuments, from the Pyramids at Gizeh to the Great Wall of China. It is no answer to say that these things were built by slaves, even if that were true of all of them, which it is not. Somebody had to be producing the food, clothing and shelter for the slaves, as well as guarding them. In any case, slaves are extremely inefficient producers and invoking the use of them only complicates the problem.

No-one has yet provided a satisfactory explanation of how bronze age people - and there could not have been many of them - were able to quarry the "blue stones" and transport them from Prescelly in West Wales 200 miles to Stonehenge, eighty of them, weighing some six tons each. And still in Wiltshire at about the same period:

> "The construction of Silbury Hill, which perhaps required as much as twenty million man hours from the builders, makes a convenient, as well as a prominent monument to the end of one era and the beginning of another. A C14 (radioactive carbon) date suggests that it was erected about 2,300 - 2,200 B.C."[9]

Some three thousand years later during the 8th century AD a dyke was engineered allegedly at the order of King Offa, one of the bewildering array of petty chieftains in Britain during the Dark Ages, with the apparent aim of keeping the Welsh out. One hundred and twenty miles long, as the crow flies, but nearer two hundred in actuality, sixty feet wide, twenty five feet deep, with an embankment surmounted by a palisade and with towers every few miles. It shows "a mastery of broken terrain" in the words of archeologist Sir Cyril Fox.[10]

The country in which it was built, between the mouths of the Wye and the Dee, was thinly populated. How many hundreds or thousands could be spared from ploughing, sowing and reaping, to carry out this enormous task?

BBC Television made a film about Offa's Dyke featuring the historian Michael Wood who reported:[11]"Britain's leading motorway contractors threw up their hands in despair when I asked them to cost it today." Our local civil engineers show more enterprise. I asked Peter Grimshaw of Grimshaw, Kinnear, Ltd. Cheltenham, to quote for rebuilding Offa's Dyke. His figure was 70 - 80 pence per cubic metre for excavation and £25 per metre for the security fence; roughly £50 million for the job, with the latest equipment. As for 8th century technology, iron picks, and wooden shovels? Windlasses to haul the wheelbarrows up to the top of the bank? They must have had an awful lot of free time after getting in what they saw as the necessities of life.

> "In the space of three centuries, from 1050 to 1350, France quarried millions of tons of stone to build 80 cathedrals, 500 great churches, and tens of thousands of parish churches. France quarried more stone in these three centuries than ancient Egypt in the whole of its history, even though the Great Pyramid alone has a volume of two and a half million cubic metres .... There was during the Middle ages a church for every two hundred inhabitants so the surface covered by the temples of the faith were considerable in relation to the modest dimensions of the cities. We know that in the cities of Norwich, Lincoln and York, - cities of 5,000 to 10,000 inhabitants, there were respectively 50, 49, and 41 churches."[12]

No Money for Developments.

In the last forty years of the 18th century more than a thousand miles of canal, complete with tunnels and locks, were completed in England. Many more were added in the 19th century together with thousands of miles of railways, with their embankments and cuttings. Yet plans to build a barrage across the Severn have languished for a century or more, and for a tunnel from Dover to Calais, even longer. The failure of the City of London to come up with the capital even for commencing the latter scheme in early 1987 brought an angry response from the Thatcher government. The failure to go forward on the Severn Barrage, estimated to produce up to a fifth of the entire electricity needs of the country, was not due to environmental sensitivity. Similar schemes to tap the tidal power of the Wash, Morecambe Bay, the Solway Firth, are wheeled out from time to time by the heavy newspapers when the political news gets slack.

The technology has been thoroughly tested and proven by the French in their tidal power station on the river Rance at St Malo, so that cannot be the cause of the hold-up. Might not the reason for the shyness of owners of investment capital be due to their preference for short-term gain, and might that not in turn stem from inflation, which as they well know, bears no relation to the official statistics? So what price the allocation of resources in the Market Economy?

Move On Debunking History.

Both *a priori*, and on overwhelming empirical grounds, we must reject the conclusion that primitive man was poor. The animals manage well enough. Has evolution been going backwards? Plenty never was a problem. The need for a thing and the means for supplying it arose simultaneously. But plenty is a problem for the Market economy. It threatens the collapse of the market mechanism. It has been justly said that Capitalism is the Organisation of Scarcity. Without a situation of scarcity, the entrepreneur has no reason for getting out of bed. In this way deprivation, poverty, is built into the system. Historical evidence is not lacking. Once the bourgeois system really got under way in the 16th century the poor appeared as a social phenomenon. The "flogging of sturdy beggars", the Poor Law of 1603, were the inevitable outcome of Henry VIII's seizure of glebe lands and the quickening pace of enclosures. For the first time in history, plenty was bad news. Harvest festival became harvest funeral.

There had been poor laws before, as early as 1349, but even the bourgeois apologists do not pay them the attention they are obliged to devote to the catastrophes beginning a couple of centuries later under Henry.

With regard to age, the Bible tells us that threescore years and ten was par for the course of life in the Middle East three thousand years ago. Modern research confirms that life expectancy is little greater now but the reduction in child mortality flatters today's figures. A less flattering comparison between ancient Greece and Eighteenth Century Europe, admittedly not our very own day and age, is contained in the classic study "The Greeks" by H.D.F. Kitto, a Gloucester scholar:

> "From a recent century I take down at random the following names: Haydn, Mozart, Beethoven, Goethe, Schubert, Mendelssohn, Wordsworth, Coleridge, Keats, Shelley. From a Greek Century a comparable list of names: Aeschylus, Sophocles, Euripides, Aristophanes, Socrates, Plato, Isocrates, Gorgias, Protagoras, Xenophon. The age of death of the first list is respectively 77, 35, 57, 83, 31, 38, 80, 62, 26, 30; of the second 71, 91, 78, at least 60, 70, 87, 98, 95(?) about 70, 76."[13]

As for eating rotten meat; whatever happened to smoking, and salting, drying, pickling and preserving? These arts seem to have been practised by people from the earliest times and by primitive peoples in our own time. In fact the most devastating reply to those who see the past as one long nightmare from which the Market system has rescued us is contained in "Stone Age Economics - The Original Affluent Society" by Marshal Sahlins of Chicago University.[14] By gathering together the fieldwork of many different anthropological researchers from the earlier decades of this century, Professor Sahlins was able to demonstrate that palaeolithic people surviving into our own century in the Australian and Kalahari Deserts, in Papua and New Guinea did not make heavy weather of the work of acquiring what they saw as the necessities of life. Two or three hours a day sufficed to collect the berries, shoot the game, dig the roots. The rest of the time was spent in socialising, gossiping, telling stories. And from what we know of the caves at Altamira, Lascaux, and thousands of lesser galleries of art which have survived the millenia, that was not the limit of their distraction.

Of course the danger of exposing oneself to the charge of being just another *Laudator Temporis Acti,* of whingeing on about the good old days, is great. To question the basis upon which the world since the Tudors has been developing is to invite the condescension that people reserve for brain damaged children. Marx left no doubt about where his sympathies lay. He said that the Bourgeois System had rescued the population of England from the idiocy of rural life.[15] The great critic of bourgeois society ranged himself on the side of the bourgeoisie when it came to considering earlier societies. But this is understandable. The first and arguably, still the greatest work of research into wages and prices from the thirteenth century onwards, that of Professor Thorold Rogers, M.P., was not published until 1884, the year after Marx's death. "Six Centuries of Work and Wages"[16] compressed into one volume much of the material gathered into his seven volume "History of Agriculture and Prices in England" begun twenty years earlier. The conclusions of Professor Rogers were reinforced with the publication of the first volume in 1939 of a series entitled "Prices and Wages in England, from the Twelfth to the Nineteenth Century", [17]by Lord Beveridge and his research team.

In the 1950's Professor Phelps Brown and Miss Sheila Hopkins of the London School of Economics published graphs in the journal "Economica"[18] (Fig 1 referred to earlier) accompanied by two articles drawing on these and other researchers which showed that living standards of building workers measured by a "unit of consumables" were no higher at the end of the Nineteenth Century than they were at the end of the Fifteenth Century. The L.S.E. researchers showed commendable academic restraint; it could be argued that they settled for a weakened conclusion. A more rigorous approach might provide even less comfort for those who hold that we have never had it so good. The "unit of consumables" compares potatoes with barley, cod with sheep, tea and sugar with malt, and so transgresses the first rule of statistics: that you can only compare like with like. Which brings us back to housebricks and roof tiles.

Houses now and five centuries ago are not comparable. People's ideas of their needs have changed - indeed they are different in different parts of the world today - but bricks have not. The reason is that the brick's dimension is determined by the strength and size of the average man's hand, an objective consideration. And the quality of the product - the brick has to be "burned" to resist the climate. Clearly we are not discussing the sundried brick of near-desert countries.

The medieval brick was what today's building industry would call a "hand-made brick". These are still available at premium prices. A nearby brickworks producing them at Cinderford is busier than ever. Thorold Rogers claims that the medieval bricks were premium products and points to Eton College and other buildings where they seem to have exhibited remarkable durability. But even if we equate them with the "common" or "fletton" brick today, the comparison still sees the medieval mason or carpenter better off.

The prices of houses in the Fifteenth Century are available. That is not the problem. John Burnett cites a 1400 square feet house being built in Gloucester "all the wood of oak" in 1483 for £14.[19] This was less than two and a half years take home pay for our building tradesmen. Lucky the bricklayer or carpenter who could buy the same today. The house would almost certainly have been a timber frame structure on stone or brick foundations.

This is the prevailing architecture today in North America and Scandinavia. Many of the medieval houses are still standing and worth a small fortune, not entirely on account of their historic interest. Their modern equivalents, frequently bring to mind Pete Seeger's song : "Little people in Boxes, all made out of ticky tacky." But we still cannot permit ourselves the luxury of comparing the modern house with its medieval equivalent. Glazing and plumbing barely existed then, neither did floor covering and chimneys. The interior resembled the cottages of many Mediterranean peasants even today, almost bare of any fixtures and fittings. It was clean, nevertheless. "In general very few peasant houses have any accumulated rubbish on their floors, and the general impression all over the country is of houses swept clean with the rubbish deposited in the yard. This is a most important point as it explains why medieval village sites have such thin deposits and why there is no thick build-up of accumulated rubbish leading to well stratified levels. This evidence must clearly affect very strongly our views about the dirtiness of the medieval peasant as still presented in history books."[20]

And what of other goods available both then and now? Clothing was different and cloth is a long way from what it was even sixty or seventy years ago when a man might be buried in his wedding suit. Still, our modern mason would seem to have the edge on clothing. With drinks, on the other hand, he is very much worse off. Beer, cider, wine, were drunk in enormous quantities and were very much cheaper in terms of work than they are today.

In the centuries between 1500 and our own era, potatoes have come to supplement bread as a cheaper source of carbohydrate - to the rage and chagrin of writers like Cobbett.[21] And tea and coffee, both real and ersatz, have replaced beer to a great extent. But lean meat is still an essential part of our diet and the first to suffer in any belt tightening. A purely vegetarian diet is simply a defective one for human beings, lacking among other things, vitamins of the B group. Vegetarian propaganda, motivated usually by what are called "humanitarian considerations" for animals, thereby simultaneously betraying anthropomorphism and unconcious humour, emphasises the health giving qualities of vegetables. This simply muddles the issue with food reform, i.e. the need to avoid too much fat, sugar, salt, additives, and to seek freshness, fibre, variety and exercise. The problem is, of course, greater in the Anglo-Saxon countries with a wretched tradition of cuisine. Travellers will have noted that a street sweeper in Paris, a bus conductor in Barcelona, a mechanic in Rome, eats infinitely better than a stockbroker in London or a brain surgeon in New York - unless the latter has ethnic traditions to call upon.

There is still a cultural dimension to poverty, often the product of generations of poverty, of separation from the land, which is most evident in countries like Britain but is beginning to affect even those countries with a great tradition of good food. Junk food, T.V. dinners, fast food, the snacks which are claimed not to interfere with your appetite, are urged upon us everywhere. Equally depressing are the efforts of the better-off in the countries without a tradition of good food to embrace the good life with equal rubbish, but this time on account of its pretentiousness: steak with Grand Marnier, salmon stuffed with lobster, and so on. One could say with confidence that the great dishes of the world are the food of poor men, made by their equally poor women; Tripes a la mode de Caen, Bouillabaisse, Callos a la Madrilena, Paella a la Valenciana, Risotto, Pasta, Goulash - every country with a peasant population could supply its own list.

There's the rub. With the destruction of the British peasantry, whatever culinary traditions there were in these islands disappeared. Later British cooks could have turned the Last Supper into an even nastier affair than it was. A good cook can make the most innocent ingredients into a feast but cannot turn vegetables into meat, which is where we return to our muttons.

1. All discussion about population begins, and for some ends, with Malthus: "Population, when unchecked, increases in geometrical ratio. Subsistence increases only in an arithmetic ratio." He goes on to argue that population movements rise and fall with real wages. The evidence is that they vary inversely (see graph fig. 2) at least until the nineteenth century, a fact that was not lost on Adam Smith and Karl Marx. "Poverty, although it no doubt discourages, does not always prevent marriages. It seems even to be favourable to generation. A half-starved highland woman frequently bears more than twenty children, while a pampered fine lady is often incapable of bearing any and is generally exhausted by two or three. Barrenness, so frequent among women of fashion, is very rare among those of inferior station." "Wealth of Nations" Vol.1 p.70. Also Marx : Capital; "Not only the number of births and deaths but the absolute size of the families stand in inverse proportion to the height of wages, and therefore to the amount of means of subsistence of which the different categories of labourers dispose. This law of capitalistic society would sound absurd to savages, or even civilised colonists. It calls to mind the boundless reproduction of animals individually weak and constantly hunted down." Vol. I, p.643 (Lawrence & Wishart 1954).

2. Josue de Castro: Geography of Hunger (Faber 1951) "It is known that there is a direct connection between the functioning of the liver and the ovaries; the role of the liver being to inactivate the excess oestrogens which the ovaries throw into the blood stream. Fatty degeneration of the liver and the tendency to cirrhosis are, as we have previously seen, some of the characteristic results of protein deficiency, and are very common in the Far East and in certain tropical areas of other continents. When degeneration of the liver occurs it begins to operate less efficiently and is less effective at its job of inactivating excess oestrogens. The result is a marked increase in the woman's reproductive capacity...the supporting facts are at hand and we can risk a collision with Victorian prejudices and neo-Malthusian theories. It is high time to challenge a point

of view which, inspired by economic or political interest, regards as a natural human condition, what is in fact the result of social factors." p.140.
Malthus is afraid that "vice" is the only factor curbing population growth apart from starvation though it is not clear whether he means sodomy, masturbation or contraception by this word. Professor Chambers thought that disease played a large part in limiting population growth and also wrote: "The population was able to recognise economic opportunities when it saw them, and ready to adjust marriage and child-bearing propensities more quickly and to a greater extent, than is commonly allowed by those who assume that in the pre-industrial world birthrates were more or less constant at the limit of biological potential." (Population, Economy and Society in Pre-Industrial England, p.65)
The tunnel vision arising from the job-demarcation rules between university departments seems to have prevented the historians calling down the corridor and getting the biology department to come and explain how species maintain homeostasis. It recalls the old squabbles between the boilermakers and shipwrights. Although he shows no awareness of de Castro, Professor E.A. Wrigley seems to have worked out for himself what is, after all, a platitude among biologists: "Dr. Wrigley has assumed the former (i.e. regulated their own birthrate) although he suggests that it may have been instinctive, a form of automatic self- adjustment to external circumstances derived from our animal ancestry which reduced fertility in such a way as to produce a point of balance between births and deaths some way short of the maximum possible." (Professor J.D. Chambers op. cit.) In Wrigley's own words: "...south of the Beauvaisis in the pays de Bray. This was an area of mixed agriculture with an important pastoral element in the total rural economy. Here there were large areas of woodland and meadow. The more diversified the agricultural base of a community the less likely it is to be crippled in years of distress and harvest failure. The same summer of constant rain which brings ruin to the wheatfields may yield a rich growth of grass and a larger production of meat and dairy products than usual. In the north of the Beauvaisis on the other hand, on the high plains of Picardy where Breteuil is situated, a system had developed which might almost be called cereal monoculture. Here there were few beasts and very little of the countryside was uncultivated. Population was dense..." (E.A. Wrigley: Population and History, Weidenfeld 1969).

3. Thomas Hobbes : Leviathan (Penguin 1980) p.186. "We live in a market society. Our behaviour, our values, are largely shaped, directly or indirectly, by the requirements of the market. We are bourgeois men. So were the men Hobbes described and analysed." - C.B. McPherson, Introduction p.11. Also: "He was so impressed with the divisive and destructive force of the competition for power which he put into his model (and rightly put in, for this force is indeed present in the capitalist market society, to which we have seen, his model closely corresponded), that he failed to see that the model also generates a class differentiation which can be expected to produce a class cohesion, at least in the class which is on its way up to the top." (p.56)

4. Alan McWhirr, Linda Viner, Kelvin Welff: Romano-British Cemeteries at Cirencester (Cirencester Excavation Cttee. 1982)

5. Hobbes "convincing apologia for the emergent seventeenth century market society," (McPherson) is qualified by his awareness of the "lucrative vices of the men of trade or handicraft such as feigning, lying, cozening, hypocrisy or other uncharitableness,"

(Behemoth p.25) also: "merchants whose only glory is to grow excessively rich by the wisdom of buying and selling and by making poor people sell their labour to them at their own prices." (Behemoth p.126)

6. Richard Hodges and David Whitehouse : Mohammed, Charlemagne and the Origins of Europe.

7. Colin Renfrew : Systems Collapse as Social Transformation; Catastrophe and Anastrophe in Early State Societies (1979) quoted by Hodges and Whitehouse, above. Renfrew's concern has been voiced elsewhere: "Historians prefer to work with ample documents such as have been left to us by merchants, bankers, and landowners, - those who manipulate the goods. Unfortunately the peasants, craftsmen and engineers who produce the goods have generally provided spare words. The state of records and the tastes of historians have thus combined to distort past activities," to which observation Frank E.Huggett (The Land Question and European Society) provides a postscript: "Without the peasants, the gentlemen would have had to soil their hands or starve; but dependence is no cause for love." (p.9)

8. Horace Odes Book 1: Nec iam gaudet stabulis pecus aut arator igni.

9. Keith Branigan : Prehistoric Britain (Spurbooks Ltd 1978)

10. Sir Cyril Fox F.B.A. : Offa's Dyke (OUP 1955).

11. Michael Wood: In Search of the Dark Ages (Ariel Books 1984)

12. Jean Gimpel: Les Batisseurs de Catedrales (Editions du Seuil 1973)

13. H.D.F. Kitto : The Greeks (Penguin 1957).

14. Marshall Sahlins: Stone Age Economics; The Original Affluent Society (Tavistock Publications 1974)

15. Marx & Engels: Communist Manifesto, p. 36. (Progress Publishing, Moscow 1971).

16. James E. Thorold Rogers : Six Centuries of Work and Wages (Swan Sonnenschein 1903)]

17. Lord Beveridge : Prices and Wages in England, from the Twelfth to the Nineteenth Century (Cass 1939)

18. Economica 1955 p.195 and Economica 1956 p.296.

19. John Burnett: History of the Cost of Living, p.44 (Penguin 1969).

20. Beresford & Hurst : Deserted Medieval Villages; a Review of Archeological Research to 1968. p.99.

21. William Cobbett : Cottage Economy, for example.

Chapter 3.

More Confusion from the Experts.

*"Green to green, red to red; perfect safety, go ahead.
When on red, green appears, pull your foreskin over your ears."*

[Mnemonic for navigators.]

So, to repeat the question: what has happened to all the increased wealth which should be available as a consequence of the enormous increases in productivity in recent centuries? We are assured that productivity has been doubling every few decades for much of the time. I shall endeavour to prove that the increase in the on-costs of the Market System, (or of the overheads of the Capitalist System, if you prefer, although I don't) since it evolved at the end of the Middle Ages, have kept pace with productivity growth and have simply absorbed most of the difference. Marxists might call the phenomenon the increase in the cost of the realisation of Surplus Value[1] but none, to my knowledge, have shown an awareness of it.

In The Country of the Blind.

Others have, to a greater or lesser degree. In the 1970's two Oxford researchers, Robert Bacon and Walter Eltis published their diagnosis of Britain's ills: "Britain's Economic Problem: Too Few Producers." They pointed out that there had been a great move from industrial employment to non-industrial employment in the period 1965-75 amounting to 14%. The trend they identified is continuing:

> "Between 1979 and 1983 the number of employees in the metal goods, engineering, and vehicle industries fell by 22% and the number in the construction industry by 19%. In the service industries, which expanded by almost 2 million between 1971 and 1979, the number of employees fell slightly between 1979 and 1983 although in banking, finance, insurance business services and leasing, the number increased by 10% over this latter period."[2]

The portmanteau expression "service industries" used above, highlights the confusion which is almost universal in conventional thinking about economics. It rolls together activities which are pure on-costs like money transactions, advertising and most clerical activities, with activities like health care and education. These last two are inseparable from, and part of, the productive process. A doctor or a teacher are as much production workers as are tool-makers or universal grinders. Dead or sick or illiterate or innumerate people cannot produce, in any kind of world. But people from monks to housewives to St. John's Ambulance and thousands of voluntary groups have produced and continue to produce without involving any transaction costs. "Social Trends 1987" lists a few of them including: Age Concern, Leagues of Hospital Friends, Round Tables, Rotary, Red Cross, Royal Society for Mentally Handicapped, R.S.P.C.A., Lion Clubs, N.S.P.C.C., Women's Institutes, Scouts, Girl Guides, Youth Clubs, Duke of Edinburgh Awards, Civic Trust, Conservation Society, Friends of the Earth, National Trust, Royal Society for the Protection of Birds.

> "Activities (of voluntary groups) include fund raising, visiting and assisting the lonely, the sick, the old and the disabled, providing transport, arranging holidays and

> running resthouses, and running canteens, shops and trolley services in hospitals. In 1983 St. John Ambulance provided over 3.75 million hours of cover and treated more than 375,000 cases at public events. More than 180,000 people are trained in first aid and related subjects every year. In the year ended September 1983 the Womens Royal Voluntary Services served nearly 17 million meals (Meals on Wheels)..."[3]

An interesting sidelight on the above is that the voluntary groups tend to be Right Wing politically, people who set their faces firmly against the idea of something-for-nothing, of a Free Lunch (*pace* Milton Friedman),[4] yet they provided 17 million free lunches, not to mention other acts of sociability and kindness. Left Wingers, on the other hand, committed to the idea of fulfilling needs, regardless of the ability to pay, are thin on the ground here.

Confusion from the Economists.

Apart from the confusion created by expressions like Service Industries, the whole of Economics and Politics is beggared by a lack of intellectual discipline. Words are used as things rather than as symbols - to borrow an idea of Sartre's. These things, bouquets if one likes them, bludgeons if one doesn't, are understandable if used by propagandists of either side. But they are unpardonable when used by people claiming the least amount of detachment. Expressions like "The Socialist Economies of the Communist Countries" (Friedman) are the sort of rubbish up with which we should not put. The word "Socialist" was pretty well synonymous with "Communist" in the 19th Century and meant a world with free access to goods and services, without money, with voluntary labour, "everything for free" etc., as can be seen in Morris' "News from Nowhere", Engels "Socialism Utopian and Scientific", Oscar Wilde's "The Soul of Man under Socialism" and many others. Exactly the same ideas, whatever we may think of them, are expressed in the "Communist Manifesto" of Marx and Engels, particularly after the later prefaces where all ideas of bureaucratic intervention were dropped. Similar ideas are expressed in "Mutual Aid", and "Fields, Factories and Workshops" by Kropotkin and the works of other anarchist writers.

But what of the word "Socialist" today? Does it mean anything at all? Hitler's "National Socialism", Lenin's "Socialism on the way to Communism", Gaddafi's "Islamic Socialism", Ben Gurion's "Jewish

Socialism". Perhaps it simply means government intervention in economic affairs, like the Conservative nationalising of the pubs in Carlisle during the First World War or Prime Minister Edward Heath nationalising Rolls Royce in 1974, or President Reagan intervening to bail out the Continental Illinois Bank and Chrysler Motors. We may yet see the Conservative Socialist Party of Britain and the Republican Socialist Party of the United States.

A further misuse of the word was made when, in the 1940's, the press baron Lord Beaverbrook instructed reporters on his Daily Express to substitute the word "Socialist" in any reference to the Labour Party, even to forging the word when anybody wrote or said the word "Labour". He was, of course, convinced that the word "Socialist" would be a liability. His error may well have helped the Conservatives to lose the 1945 election. Only a brave person would predict the same result today. Such words have all the impermanence of women's fashions and the ambiguity of Chinese syllables, as conveyed in a "Times" report:

> "To the astonishment of scholars, the Oxford University Press seems to have sold out to the Russians. "The Oxford Advanced Learner's Dictionary of Current English" has just been reprinted in Russia, and with the full blessing of O.U.P. The Russians have altered ideologically unacceptable definitions without indicating that they have been changed. The Soviet edition - which bears the Oxford Crest - leaves Russian readers with the impression that the Oxford definition of capitalism is "the last antagonistic social and economic system in human history, based on the exploitation of man, replacing feudalism and preceding Communism! Socialism, the dictionary says, is the first phase of Communism, a social system based on public ownership of the means of production which "is now replacing capitalism".[5]

What should astonish us even more than the "scholars" is the assumption that they have a monopoly on the interpretation of these words; that their definition is less rubbishy than the Russians. Here we have the nub of the problem: they feel that the definition of the words should be prescriptive rather than descriptive.

All of the developed countries: Russia and its satellites and the United States and its satellites have a common feature - their economies are based on the Market, i.e. goods and services are produced for sale with the hope of a profit. This distinguishes them from the undeveloped countries and from Medieval Europe, where most goods and services are, and were produced and consumed by the producers themselves, with only a small surplus being produced to exchange for items like salt, tools etc. The enormous confusion produced by the propaganda machines of both blocs has led people to believe that their economies are fundamentally different. Stalin's daughter Svetlana expressed her shock at the discovery that the United States ressembled Russia more than it differed from it. There was an even closer resemblance between "Left Wing" Russia and "Right Wing" Hitler's Germany. Here again the Market was the aim of production but with a great deal of State intervention in both cases. Not that the United States has always eschewed State intervention, even in the twentieth century. As mentioned above many companies like the Continental Illinois Bank, the Chrysler Motor Corporation, have been shielded from the disciplines of laissez faire when it suited the Government.

During the nineteenth century, while American producers were economically weak and terrified of British low prices, the American Government intervened with the highest tariff wall in history and only lowered it when its own producers had got their production runs into a competitive condition. Powerful economies are always in favour of "free trade". The weaker ones cannot afford the luxury. But all governments will intervene if the interests of their producers are seriously menaced. The difference between State Controlled or interventionist economies and Free Market economies is one of degree and not of kind. The important feature is that they both produce for the Market.

The consequence of this fact is that behind the confusion created by economists and journalists we find common features and common problems. Presiden Eisenhower's identification of an American "military industrial complex" applies equally to Russia and all other developed countries, as do crime, corruption, labour unrest, capital shortages, shoddy goods, pollution, stress and insecurity.

Wealth and Non-Wealth.

The same is true with the falling proportion of productive workers and the increase in on-costs of the state-controlled economies. They may not have to support the same burden of advertising and transaction costs, of armies of salesmen trying to persuade people to buy goods or services they would not otherwise buy. They do have to support a huge and growing bureaucracy which is not subject to the checks and controls of the balance sheet and the shareholders meeting.

Bacon and Eltis point to Adam Smith's awareness of the burden of unproductive labour: "The Sovereign, with all the officers both of justice and war who serve under him, the whole army and navy, are unproductive labourers. They are the servants of the public and are maintained by a part of the annual produce of other people".[6] Adam Smith then goes on to show his confusion by adding doctors, writers, musicians, actors, comics and dancers to the list of non-productives, and Bacon and Eltis comment that it is a mistake to assume that only physical goods represent "tradeable" wealth. They then make confusion worse confounded by saying that an opera singer who works in the Metropolitan Opera and brings home dollars is an exporter and therefore, presumably, productive. But why only when working abroad? Does something happen to them in mid-Atlantic? Do they not create similar wealth on the stage of Covent Garden? Bacon and Eltis go on to say that "more substantially" bankers, insurers, and "other specialists" are exporters, and are also, productive. This is, of course, true, when they become part of another country's on- costs and are paid for it. At home they are simply overheads, with nothing to show for it. Bacon and Eltis almost concede this: "There are of course, service activities that make virtually no contribution but the same is true of some industrial work." Then they continue : "Concorde, for instance has taken far more resources out of the economy in the form of consumer goods for the workers who make it, and plant and machinery specifically needed for it, than will ever be recovered when it starts to be sold. Other successful firms, and even some in the City of London, have therefore had to give up some of the results of their fruitful activities to make it possible for the workers who make Concorde to continue to produce something that will hardly sell enough to recover more than a small fraction of its costs."[7]

Now I have no intention of pulling the chestnuts out of the fire for the politicians and businessmen responsible for Concorde. I doubt if I shall ever get to fly in it. But surely there is some end product, if only fast transport for a handful of wealthy people. And there must be some technological spin-off. The people designing and making it must know some things now they didn't know before, which is more than can be said for people shuffling the pack in the City of London.

For a long time the increasing cost of running the system was masked by conspicuous consumption beginning with Henry VIII and his cronies: vast palaces and estates, enormous banquets, and fortunes spent on clothes. This coincided with plunging living standards of the common people culminating in famine at the end of the sixteenth century. But the huge fortunes spent on foreign wars, on building the navy, were a token of what was to come, of what would dwarf all personal consumption.

> "By contrast with its limited role as producer the Government was the greatest consumer in the country. In the late 16th century total expenditure by the crown was probably between £500,000 and £600,000 a year. By the first decade of the 18th century Government spending averaged £6 millions a year of which two thirds was military expenditure."[8]

Towards the end of the 17th century Sir William Petty drew attention to the tendency "for the proportion of the working population engaged in services to increase as the economy develops."[9] Petty was clearly not thinking of personal services like haircuts, or poetry, or the comforts of religion.

Non-Wealth.

These services are found more abundantly in pre-bourgeois societies, as can be witnessed today in the Third World. In the developed countries the haircutting is as likely to be done by the wife or the friend, with shaving you are strictly on your own, and poetry is for the birds. What Petty had in mind was the growth of banking, law, the military; all those instruments for controlling, or attempting to control the system.

Various writers since that time have drawn attention to the growth of non-productives in the labour force, notably William Cobbett at the beginning of the nineteenth century, but the conspicuous consumption of the ruling class distracted most observers from the increasing cost of the non productive sector. This was still marked until the First World War. "While there was a decrease in the consuming powers of the people, and while there was an increase in the privations and distress of the labouring classes and operatives, there was at the same time a constant accumulation of wealth in the upper classes and a constant increase of capital."[10]

A great deal of this disappeared in the war of 1914-18. The armies of servants, the big houses, valets, butlers, head gardeners, survived only in the anachronistic world of P.G. Wodehouse. The rich were still very rich, but not as rich as they had been. The continuing depression of the '20's and '30's did not restore the world as it had been ante bellum. The Second World War added some more costs to running the system. The First World War had taken up the services of a mere 28% of the population; the Second World War took up 34%.[11] These costs naturally fell upon the people who owned the country. The 99% of the population who owned only the right to hawk their skills to the highest bidder had nothing at stake.

The costs are rising exponentially. On the one side are those calling out for reduced taxation, for tight budgetary control of spending, and on the other, those who point out the neglect of the poor and sick. Both are right, given the premisses. But are the premisses right?

> "Unanticipated social impacts, environmental depletion, and proliferating bureaucratic attempts to regulate and co-ordinate the situation add to the general transaction costs, until the social costs of the system begin to exceed actual production. Since the social costs are added to the gross national product instead of subtracted, the G.N.P. goes up, while inflation begins to mask the declining situation."[12]

But what are the social costs referred to here by Hazel Henderson? Well, in Britain, for a start, Banking and Finance are calculated to contribute 6.1% of the Gross Domestic Product and growing at a hairy 20% per annum. But what sort of product are bank charges? What businessman puts bank charges on the income side of his ledger?

And advertising, according to official figures, contributes 1.2% to the GDP. But are soap adverts on television, are junk mail, are those pages upon pages of adverts in the magazines and newspapers, are they all wealth? Somebody should have told us.

And insurance? The official figures assure us that its contribution to the GDP is 1% and growing at 10% per annum. But can householders, can motorists, can businessmen count the insurance premiums they pay out as additional income? Aren't these the economics of the madhouse?

James Bellini estimates that "roughly 60% of the activity of Britain's economic system is taken up with the gathering, storage, processing, and distribution of information", and adds that for the U.S. the figure is between 65% and 70%.

Information is a rather flattering word to describe the overwhelming majority of activities in the bureaucratic sector, almost all dealing with the ultimately meaningless activity of buying and selling, but in a world where almost everything is being devalued, we should not be surprised to see language go the same way. What is important is that Bellini has identified the trend, unlike the majority of his fellow economists.[13]

1. Fred Hirsch: Social Limits to Growth (op.cit.) says: "The recent shifts from the production of things to the doing of things can be interpreted in a wide variety of ways. For (Daniel) Bell, Herman Kahn, and other enthusiasts of the postindustrial cornucopia, they are the source of the enlarged surplus over what would be available from primary and secondary production alone. For neo- Marxists the prime significance of the expansion in the tertiary sector lies in the absorption of the surplus." But who are the neo-Marxists? Hazel Henderson, who is much too eclectic to be called any kind of Marxist, gets nearer to the heart of the matter than anyone else I know:

"The proportion of GNP that must be spent in mediating conflicts, controlling crime, protecting consumers and the environment, providing ever more bureaucratic co-ordination, and generally trying to maintain "social homeostasis" begins to grow exponentially." - Creating Alternative Futures, p.84.

Others have seen parts of the picture, e.g. Sweezy & Baran, in Monopoly Capital on the "sales effort"; Bell, in Post-Industrial Society, William Kapp, in The Social Costs of Private Enterprise, join with J.K. Galbraith and many others in pointing out the burden that the rich (industry) throw over the wall (externalities) for the rest of society to clean up. But the cry of "private wealth and public squalor" is only a translation of the complaint made two thousand years ago by Cato nepos: "Habemus publice egestatem privatim opulentiam." The problem we identify is of a little more recent origin.

2. Social Trends 1985 (HMSO)

3. Social Trends 1986 (HMSO)

4. Milton Friedman - There's No Such Thing As A Free Lunch (Open Court Publishing 1977)

5. Times 27/3/85

6. Adam Smith : The Wealth of Nations : Vol 1, p. 295 (Everyman 1947). Karl Marx in his notebooks writes: A.Smith was essentially correct with his productive and unproductive labour, correct from the standpoint of bourgeois economy. What the other economists advance against it is either horse-piss (for instance Storch, Senior even lousier etc.) namely that every action after all acts upon something, thus confusion of the product in its natural and its economic sense; so that the pickpocket becomes a productive worker too, since he indirectly produces books on criminal law (this reasoning at least as correct as calling a judge a productive worker because he protects from theft). Or the modern economists have turned themselves into such sycophants of the bourgeois that they want to demonstrate to the latter that it is productive labour when somebody picks the lice out of his hair, or strokes his tail, because for example the latter activity will make his fat head - blockhead - clearer the next day in the office. It is therefore quite correct - but also characteristic - that for the consistent economists the workers in e.g. luxury shops are productive, although the characters who consume such objects are expressly castigated as unproductive wastrels. The fact is that these workers, indeed, are productive, as far as they increase the capital of their master; unproductive as to the material result of their labour. In fact of course, this 'productive' worker cares as much about the crappy shit he has to make as does the capitalist himself who employs him and who also couldn't give a damn for the junk. Grundrisse p.273 (Pelican 1973).

7. Britain's Economic Problem p.25.

8. L.A. Clarkson: Pre-Industrial Economy in England 1500-1750, p.161.

9. Sir William Petty : Political Arithmetic; "as trades and curious Arts increase, so the trade of husbandry will decrease; or else the wages of husbandmen must rise and consequently the rents of lands must fall." p.25.

10. W.E. Gladstone quoted by Marx : Capital, vol 1, p.651.

11. M.M. Postan: History of the Second World War, British War Production, p.222.

12. Hazel Henderson : Politics of the Solar Age.

13. James Bellini : Rule Britannia (Cape 1981).

Chapter 4.

Are There Any Producers At All Out There?

"This frenzied activity which has us all, rich and poor, weak and powerful, in its grip - where is it leading us? There are two things in life which it seems to me all men want and very few ever get (because both of them belong to the domain of the spiritual) and they are health and freedom. The druggist, the doctor, the surgeon are all powerless to give health; power, money, security, authority do not give freedom. Education can never provide wisdom, nor churches religion, nor wealth happiness, nor security peace. What is the meaning of our activity then? To what end?

Henry Miller: Good News! God is Love (Nicholson & Watson 1945)

The costs of controlling, policing, recording, mediating and otherwise dealing with the system take up the energies of nine tenths of the working population. Only one tenth is producing wealth, and many of those would have their jobs phased out in a rationally ordered economic system. Out of a working population of some 26 million, less than one million produce all of our food, clothing and shelter, and distraction. Add in medical and educational services and the total is less than ten per cent of the whole.

A third of the entire population, more than half of the labour force, were absorbed in the war effort in 1939-45, yet a substantial proportion of the non-productives remained undisturbed. Admittedly, only a third of a million remained unemployed but there was a great expansion of bureaucratic activity: ration cards, identity cards, regulations governing every aspect of life.

During the Three Day Week of the miner's strike in 1974 production scarcely fell. It was 6% lower thirteen years later, despite the claims made for higher productivity! Nobody working for a wage or salary gives of his best. One volunteer is worth ten pressed men. And people forced to sell their energies for a living can hardly be called volunteers. Would a man do for his employer what he does in his amateur rugby team, the risk to limb if not life, and all in the freezing February rain? Do the women in the typing pool have the same dedication as those in the Voluntary Services, and if not, why not? Sometimes they are the selfsame people.

Even that ten per cent of the working population who are concerned with creating wealth are not putting heart and soul into their work, not unless they are self-employed farmers for example. And in those cases we cannot be sure that what they are producing is not faulty in some way. After all, what they have in mind is sale, and not necessarily satisfaction.

Smith's Law.

Adam Smith[1] propounded the doctrine that if everybody adopted the attitude: "Up ladder, I'm inboard", everything would be fine in the long run. "An invisible hand" would see that we were all taken care of. Ken Smith is now propounding the doctrine that where the prevailing mode of production takes the form of commodities, the bad drives out the good and the worse drives out the bad. Thus the nut and bolt is replaced by the spot weld, which is replaced by a self-tapping screw, which is replaced by a dab of adhesive, which is why everything we buy falls to pieces and can't be repaired.

Gresham's Law.

This law of downward progression in quality which affects every good and service supplied by the Market is implicit in Gresham's Law[2] concerning bimetallic currency. Gresham argued that bad money, i.e. inferior metal, drives out good. If this law holds good for money, which is a substitute for all commodities, then it holds good for all those commodities.

Adam Smith's other enthusiasms, the Division of Labour,[3] for example, are also mixed blessings. The division of the job into little repetitive actions is no better for the quality of the product than it is for the quality of life for the operative. One has only to compare a Chippendale or simple Windsor chair with its factory- made equivalent to see the results. As for the psychic, not to mention physical wellbeing of the machine-minder, Charlie Chaplin's classic film, Modern Times, or Alan Sillitoe's novel Saturday Night and Sunday Morning, remind us of the "nine hundred and ninety eight, nine hundred and ninety bloody nine" syndrome, as the finished widget falls into the pallet, and the one he was looking for, the end of the shift, looms up, and life can begin once more.

For the rest, the division of labour means the end of craftsmanship, of pride in work. It means the beginning of ca- canny, go slow, sabotage, absenteeism, psychosomatic illness, industrial injuries, union battles, strikes, lockouts, police as strikebreakers, gas (C.S. or plain teargas), watercannon, rubber bullets. In less namby-pamby countries the bullets are lead. In all countries the Governments are arming themselves against the people, and the Army itself stands ready to break strikes and force workers to accept lower wages or worse conditions if all else fails. Meanwhile the radio, television and press keep up a steady drumming to create the maximum confusion.

To compare the life of a craftsman with that of a machine-minder is not to argue hand tools against machines. No one wants to cut mortices or dovetails by hand. Spinning or milling of metal by hand is impossible. But hi-tech craft workshops involve no contradiction, even with computer-programmed milling, boring, grinding, swaging or welding machines. Trends are developing even within the Market ecomomy attempting to deal with psychic, physical and quality-control problems thrown up by assembly line production. The Volvo car company has built a factory at Kalmar in Eastern Sweden, for example, where groups of not more than 25 men complete each stage in the building of the cars.

Another negative aspect of the division of labour is the diseconomy of scale that it involves. Once again the bourgeois system is being driven by the hard facts of the balance sheet to question the Big is Beautiful philosophy of the 1950's and '60's. Hazel Henderson again:

> "A recent paper by Belgian information theorist Jean Vòge, "Information and Information Technologies in Growth and the Economic Crisis" in Technological Forecasting and Social Change 1979, Voge verifies that the logic of efficiencies of scale in production are meeting diminishing returns and bogging down in the even larger information and co-ordination costs they incur, resulting in increasing bureaucratic sectors."[4]

Ricardo's Law.

David Ricardo's Theory of Comparative Advantage[5] is to a great extent the same division of labour extended to nation-states, colonies, geographical and metropolitan areas, and produces ills parallelling those of manual division. These range from the waste involved in the exercise of taking in each other country's washing, to trade wars, monoculture, struggles for control of cash crops, plundering of natural resources instead of husbanding them, Colonialism, Imperialism, War, Tariffs and "Non-Tariff Barriers", as economic gamesmanship is called.

Many of the troubles of the undeveloped world, and the reason why it remains underdeveloped can be traced to the chimera of international trade. Clearly nobody is going to argue in favour of trying to grow bananas and pineapples in Newcastle, although an Indian community in Leicester stunned the Ministry of Agriculture in the'70's by persisting in growing exotic fruit and vegetables in their backyards, in polythene tunnels, which the laws of agriculture said could not be grown. This is reminiscent of the bumble bee, which according to the most sophisticated model of aeronautical theory, cannot fly.

Gloucestershire Again.

But foreign trade has always appealed to governments for the opportunities it offers to control or profit from economic activity. Very little of the Black Economy involves foreign trade, for example, except drug smuggling. In the Middle Ages, this Vale of Gloucester was more thickly planted with vineyards than any other part of England and Wales, and the 14th century Bishop of Gloucester, confusingly named William of Malmesbury, wrote that the product compared well with French wine and was less tart. After a thousand years of English viticulture, ways were found to discourage its production, and encourage French imports which were easily taxed as they came into Bristol.

In the 17th century the remaining peasants hereabouts hit upon another good wheeze and that was tobacco growing. Like wine growing, if it could be done the returns were very good and the activity boomed. The Government of the period had a good wheeze too, and that was to tax tobacco. But tracking down the patches of cultivation were difficult and collecting the taxes even more difficult. Three hundred dragoons were sent out from Gloucester along the road to Cheltenham to suppress the cultivations but they were met by six hundred peasants who were armed, if only with makeshift weapons, who had different ideas. The dragoons withdrew, but then began a war of attrition, galloping through the plants at sundry times and places, the peasants went back to cabbages and leeks, and tobacco came from Virginia through Bristol where it was conscientiously taxed.

Paper Blizzards.

With the development of chaos on the shop floor as size of the production unit increases, there is reciprocal growth in paperbashing which threatens companies and the country in a paper landslide. Computers, word processors are rushed in to deal with problems and these in turn produce a tide of paper-borne facts which no-one has the time to read, and the world would not be much better off if they read them anyway.

Transport Mazes.

Bigger units require more transport facilities for the workers and their products. The end result is a nerve-racking drive home as can be seen during the rush hour in any city in the developed world. The alternative is waiting for a bus or train in February as the finale to a trying day at the factory or office. T.S. Elliot caught the feeling with "J. Alfred Prufrock":

> "Under the brown fog of a winter dawn,
> A crowd flowed over London Bridge, so many
> I had not thought death had undone so many
> Sighs, short and infrequent, were exhaled,
> And each man fixed his eyes before his feet."

Homogenised, Uniform, Undifferentiated, Characterless.

Bigger units result in a loss of regional products and lower quality in those that are made. Regional cheeses give way to the mousetrap variety; the Wensleydale, Stilton, Cheshire, that we buy is all made in the same factory from the same pasteurised milk; no wonder one is indistinguishable from another. Even Camembert is made from pasteurised milk now, except for a few small dairies in Normandy. With a little effort in tracking one of them down, sceptics can discover for themselves the difference between what we have now and the real thing. The reason why, for all this loss of quality is not anybody's wickedness but the need to ensure longer shelf life for centrally distributed products.

It means houses countrywide built of Bedfordshire brick, and Kentish concrete roof-tiles, as opposed to vernacular houses of granite, limestone, flint or timber frame. And if it is argued that we cannot afford to build in such labour-intensive materials, how did the allegedly so-much-poorer societies in the past manage to afford it? In any case how can that argument be sustained at a time when millions are looking for something to do. If labour were the problem, we could set about levelling the Pennines with toothpicks!

The vast amount of traffic generated by those centrally produced cheeses, bricks, cornflakes, beer and sausages, is responsible in turn for the hideous things that have been done to our towns and countryside. Some people have blamed the architects and civil engineers:

> "The Team Who Brought You Ronan Point has been in a panic ever since, fearful that it will no longer have the power to impose its megalomaniac follies on our environment, and be richly rewarded for doing so. If £19 billion is needed for public housing repairs, this is largely because of that unholy alliance of planners, architects, contractors, and developers who laid much of Britain waste ... respect the laws of harmony? Surveying the High Rise jungles, shopping megastructures, and windswept concourses of post-war Britain, most people would agree that this is precisely what the architectural establishment has most conspicuously failed to do.It has also produced an environment that is bad for both mental and physical health, as scientific study is now beginning to demonstrate clearly."[6]

But the contractors are instructed by the architects, who are in turn instructed by the developers, who are in the grip of Market forces, and the planners can do nothing but make the best of a bad job.

Backs To Basics.

I repeat: Wealth consists of food, clothing, shelter, and food for the mind-distraction, call it what you will. Man does not live by bread alone. Wealth consists of nothing else but it does consist of these things. It is easy to forget this in the bedlam the salesmen have created of our world. The appeals to greed, keeping up with the neighbours, to instant gratification, to the pure and simple desire for possession, are all part of the poverty of our lives. This is not an appeal for self-denial, for a more puritanical outlook. Only people who have access to everything can decide how little they really want. The nouveau riche go in for conspicuous consumption. The really rich have been through and out the other side. Eating two dinners every day is unhealthy, wearing two shirts at a time is uncomfortable, one needs godlike qualities to be in two rooms at the same time.

In short, the human capacity to consume is extremely limited, and to believe otherwise is to betray one's poverty, material and spiritual; a beggar's eye view of the world. We betray this in the junk with which we surround ourselves; we betray it even more with the periodic clear-outs which adorn the local rubbish tip.

Who Is Doing What?

Once we are clear in our own minds what wealth is, we can move to a consideration of who is producing it. British farmers produce the bulk of our food. Indeed, during the war, they produced almost the whole of it. "In the early stages of the War the British War Effort was more or less self-sufficient" (Official History of the II World War)[7]. Although items like bananas and oranges were absent, diet in general improved as was demonstrated by the increased body weight of British children. Wheat was imported, but now under the stimulus of Common market prices we have a surplus for the first time in two centuries.

The total number of people engaged in agriculture, forestry and fishing is less than 300,000 including part timers. This is not much more than 1% of the labour force.

The total number of people engaged in the construction industry is nearly 800,000. These are clearly not all building homes for people. What proportion is taken up with work for the war machine, for new office blocks to house yet more bureaucrats, for more marble halls to house people moving money about, is difficult to untangle. Even companies devoted exclusively to house-building will be carrying their complement of non-productives - wages-clerks, salesmen, bumf-bashers of various disciplines. What is certain is that carpenters, architects, bricklayers, tilers, surveyors, plumbers, decorators, comprise only a proportion of the above number. For a further discussion, however, see the chapter on the Shelter industry.

The clothing constituent of our wealth categories is even more difficult to calculate. A part of the clothing we buy in Britain comes from overseas so that estimates of the number of workers involved in its production could only deal with the U.K. part of the total. On the other hand, there are exports from Britain of large quantities of synthetic yarns and cloths and small quantities of fine quality woollen cloths and clothing.

And food for the mind? Adam Smith's catalogue of musicians, actors, comics etc. whom he mistakenly calls non-productive, must be added to. Priests and rabbis, psychiatrists and gurus create wealth by their counselling (I write as a devout atheist); teachers by expanding our consciousness. We must distinguish this last from education as instruction which is simply part of the chain of production, as is medicine. A sick or uninstructed person cannot work. A doctor or educator is as much a part of production as a surface grinder or scaffolder.

The total number of workers in production industry is given as just under 6 million.[8] Once again, only a proportion of these are engaged in wealth production. Substantial numbers - and usually the best paid - are in war industry. Many more are in industries which, on the face of it, are peaceful enough but in fact are distorted in their development by the requirements of "Defence". For example, nuclear power stations have been built, and are continuing to be built surplus to requirement to supply plutonium to the American War Machine. And we can be sure that the Russian economy is being distorted in a similar way by their military/industrial complex.

Although as much as a quarter of people's incomes in the developed countries is spent on the motor industry, seven out of ten new cars are bought not by people but by companies for their employees. Millions of miles are clocked up each week by the reps who pour onto the roads on Monday mornings in the struggle to sell their firms' products. Would the world be any worse off if they stayed in bed?

Even when we get down to the bedrock of engineering companies which are engaged in the production of undeniably useful and necessary products, we still have to deal with the non-productives we find there.

I carried out a company search some time ago of a small highly productive company making equipment for the building industry - cement mixers, small cranes, dumpers. Three quarters of the labour force worked in the office. They were, no doubt, being kept busy by correspondence from various officials, by the need to keep advertising their products, by the need to keep an eye on the men producing the goods. The factory, on the other hand, was a lonely place. Endless efficiency drives had brought them to the point where one man could do the work of many. But instead of this being of general benefit the men displaced seemed simply to have been transferred "upstairs" thereby fulfilling for some the urge felt by all for a "clean" job, to wear a suit to work and not overalls, and not to come home smelling of lathe suds or grease, or machinery.

And above all, to enter the charmed world of people who do not work with their hands, with the low status and relative poverty associated with manual work.

> "While America's real business output grew by 18% from 1978-85, American businesses cut the number of blue-collar workers on their payrolls by 1.9m, to about 30m. During the same period, the number of white-collar workers in America rose by 10m to about 58m. As the 21% rise in white-collar employment outstripped the growth in output, the implication is that dismal white-collar productivity dragged down a respectable showing by blue-collar workers."[9]

But if panning out the real wealth producers from the silt of our society is difficult, there are other means of separation open to us. We can begin at the other end with those who are clearly part of the on-costs, not productive. Subsequent chapters will deal with industries and activities in greater detail, productive and non-productive. Of the latter, however, we can note the more conspicuous examples.

The Unemployment Industry is the most compelling. In the year of 1987 the official figure was 3.25, the real figure was 4.5 million, and we have to add to this the 102,000 clerks, managers, etc. who serve the men and women engaged in the industry. Its turnover in 1983 was £38,391 million i.e. nearly a third of the entire budget. There are those who will say that it is not an industry because there is no product. A moment's thought will show that there are many industries which have no product; Banking, Insurance, - the "Defence" industry, if there is no war. Many other industries have only the tiniest product content: beauty preparations, patent medicines, pop music; the promotion is the greater part of what one pays for.

Competing with unemployment for the number of its participants is Bureaucracy. For most economists this is synonomous with the Civil Service but anybody who has worked for a large company will know that it doesn't really end there. Nevertheless the 1986 figures show local and national bureaucrats totalling just over a million. This is exclusive of services like Fire, Law, Police and Social Security. But it also excludes the Ministry of Defence with 232,000 civilian employees. After 1979 the Thatcher Government hived off many bureaucratic activities to the private sector, so that fact, plus the natural shyness of bureaucrats, makes it certain that we shall underestimate this number. The sale of Telecom for example, got rid of 227,000 workers and they were not all telephone engineers. Then the Health and Education services hide vast armies of bureaucrats. Behind every nurse (1/2 million) and doctor (30,000) lurks two pen pushers, and behind every teacher and professor (400,000) lurks another. The total so far approaches 3 million bureaucrats and this should not surprise us. Bacon and Eltis, mentioned earlier, had drawn attention in 1975 to the shift from production to non-productive employment. Robert Bacon returned to the subject later and was reported in the Sunday Times as confirming the continuation of the trend.

In 1980 the Financial Times drew attention to the growth in public sector employment from 3.6 million in 1961 to 5.3 million in 1978 and pointed out that Britain was the most heavily administered country in Europe, having twice as many civil servants as Italy and 2.2 million more that France. The French writer Rene D'Abernat in his book "Messieurs Les Anglais"[10] published in 1974 argued that Britain had administered an Empire covering a quarter of the globe, then lost the Empire but retained the administration. It is easy to see how this administration, based mainly in London is sucking the life-blood from the wealth producers in the rest of the country.

1. *Wealth of Nations: Book 1, chapter 5. (Everyman)*

2. *Sir Thomas Gresham ; Chancellor to Elizabeth I.*

3. *Wealth of Nations, Book 1, Chapter 1,*

4. *Politics of the Solar Age, p.101.*

5. *Political Economy and Taxation p.81.*

6. *Professor Hugh Freeman, Editor, British Journal of Psychology, letter to Guardian 3/12/86.*

7. *M.M. Postan op. cit.*

8. *Annual Digest of Statistics 1987 (HMSO)*

9. *Economist 13/12/86 : Is American Business Being Managed to Death.*

10. *Rene D'Abernat : Messieurs Les Anglais (Hachette 1974)*

Part II

WHO DOES WHAT, A BRIEF LOOK AT SOME OF THE PRINCIPAL EMPLOYERS.

CHAPTER 5

The Food Industry

"Labra profundo y echa basura y cágate en los libros de agricultura."
[Dig deep and spread manure and shit on the books of agriculture.]
Traditional Spanish saying.

"Fifty million flies can't be wrong. Eat shit!"
Inscription on wall of British Museum toilet.

In 1986 the total number employed in British agriculture and horticulture was 298,000.[1] The number had been falling for many years and there is no reason to believe that it has not fallen still further.

British agriculture is notable for being the most mechanised in the world. There are more tractors than farm workers. A small proportion of the working population - about one per cent as opposed to four per cent in the United States - works on the land and is responsible for two thirds of all our food and drink. Yields are among the highest in the world; wheat at more than five tons to the acre, for example. This compares with North America where one ton is the norm, curiously enough, not much more than the average yield in Medieval England. But this arises from the extensive agriculture of Canada and the U.S. with their limitless plains. Europeans have to squeeze more out of their plots.

Ill Fares The Land, To Hastening Ills A Prey.

Historically this yield was effected by good husbandry; manuring, marling, liming. Now it is achieved by spreading ever increasing amounts of chemical fertiliser on the fields. Equally increasing amounts are washed off into the watercourses creating new problems, causing the Health Ministry to warn mothers in East Anglia, for example, not to make up their babies' feed with tap water on account of the sodium nitrate in it.

> "Britain is facing legal action from the Common Market for regularly supplying at least a million people here with polluted drinking water. Very high levels of the pollution can cause infantile methaemoglobinaemia, or 'blue baby' syndrome. Lower levels are suspected by some scientists of setting off a chain reaction in the body which causes stomach cancer. The European Commission announced last week that it had decided to start formal proceedings, which could lead to the Government being hauled before the European Court. The Department of the Environment said it had no idea legal proceedings were planned."[2]

In the middle 1980's Britain again became after a gap of two centuries, a net exporter of grain. British agriculture had, during those two hundred years, been the plaything of governments. The split in the ruling oligarchy between the landed interests and the new industrial magnates, between the old Tory interest (which incorporated the State Church) and the new Whigs, had made agriculture a political football. The most outstanding expressions of this struggle were those Corn Laws which were passed from 1815 onwards and repealed after a bitter struggle in 1846.

The Tories favoured protection: high tariffs on imported corn, so guaranteeing them as landowners a high price. The Whigs wanted free trade in corn so that bread and beer for their workers was cheap and would result in cheaper labour. After the repeal of the Corn Laws, imported grain from North America, but also from Russia, Argentina and Australia kept British agriculture in an almost permanent state of depression.

It is interesting to examine the nature of this competition that British farmers faced from overseas:

> "The very cheapness of our public lands, and the facility of purchase and transfer, tended to a system of bad farming, or strip and waste of the soil, by encouraging short occupancy and a speedy search for new homes, entailing upon the first and older settlements a rapid deterioration of the soil, which would not be likely to be arrested except by more thorough and scientific knowledge of agriculture and by a higher education of those who were dedicated to its pursuit." [3]

So much for the doctrine of Comparative Advantage of David Ricardo [4] in which each nation is supposed to concentrate on what it does best. The Americans, once the Red Indians were got out of the way, took over a continent stuffed with good things: thousands of square miles of timber, some of it centuries in the growing; oil in the South West so abundant that a pipe had only to be banged into the ground and oil would gush out; mountain ranges of high grade iron ore in Minnesota; and the loess soil of the great plains, wind blown alluvium which had build up over geological time to the equivalent of a topsoil thirty and forty feet deep in places.

Agricultural Chaos and Social Disaster.

Most of these comparative advantages have lost some of their edge. The soil was the first to go. From the first settlers on, the technique of farming was little different from the crudest slash-and-burn agriculture of primitive peoples. The land was "pumped" as the French say. It was cultivated until exhaustion set in, often no more than four harvests, and culivators moved onto a fresh patch. It was cheaper to do this than replace the nutrition in the soil as European farmers had been obliged to do for thousands of years. It followed the doctrine of Comparative Advantage as enjoined by the new Market-based economics with highly satisfactory results - in the short term. European - particularly British - agriculture could not compete and the result was the economic destruction of small and medium peasant farmers. The continuing Enclosure Acts scooped up the small farms into the properties of the big landowners and social disaster was added to agricultural chaos.

Third World Disaster From Market Economics.

In our own time the process is being extended to the Thirld World, in this case Brazil:

> "The big trouble is a steady flow of migrants from the countryside. Squeezed off the land by the rapid advance of mechanised crop farming and by the spread of huge ranches raising beef cattle, millions of families swarm into the cities. Under pressure to survive, they turn to crime and so provide more than their share of the jail population. The civilian Government that took over in Brazil last year, after 21 years of military rule, is trying to clinch a programme whereby millions of acres of land still sloppily farmed by big landlords are to be split up into family small-holdings. That way, the human tide flowing into the cities would be reduced to a trickle, even reversed, Ministers hope. But many landlords are digging in their heels against the scheme, some using gunmen to keep wandering landless families from settling on estates where they try to build huts, plough and plant. Landless squatters are being murdered by paid triggermen at the rate of about four a week across Brazil. But you don't see many of the gunmen, or their bosses, in jail."[5]

Needless to say the majority of the huge ranches are owned by foreign-based multinationals and the bulk of the meat is intended for junk-food in the West - hamburgers, hot dogs, sausages. Agronomists have predicted ecological catastrophe in the cutting down of tropical rain-forest and replacing with grazing on the fragile soil of the area. In the United States the catastrophe has already been visited upon huge areas. The soil was deprived of the organic material which bound it together and the wind and weather just blew it or washed it away again. The dust bowls and dust storms of the United States are part of world history and the process is continuing. Chemical fertilisers, herbicides and pesticides are being rushed up into the battle to get food out of the land, yet every time the solution seems short lived, the cure worse than the disease.

The chorus of warning from biologists and agronomists fills the reading lists and the newspapers. Massed against them is the power of the multinational agrochemical industry and the stubborness of farmers who are struggling to avoid foreclosure by the banks. Thousands of farmers in the Mid-West were turned out by the bailiffs in the late seventies and early eighties depression, and the big interests took over.

Deja Vu.

There was a major crisis in British farming in the late 1870's and 1880's. Many small farmers went bankrupt and they and their labourers emigrated - the majority from England going to the South Wales coal and steel industries where they re-emerged a generation or two later as Welsh speaking, chapel-going Welshmen named Smith or Brown.

When in the slump of the 1920's they once more broke camp to return to their ethnic brothers in Wilts, Oxon, Dorset and Worcester, they were abused by English men named Lloyd and Llewelyn and advised to get back to Wales. But to return to food and agriculture.

Wartime Agriculture.

The agricultural depression was interrupted by World War I when foreign food imports were almost cut off by German U boat attacks. The stimulus to cultivation and stock rearing did not last much longer than the end of the war, however. By the middle 1920's there was less land under the plough in England than there had been in the Domesday Book, nearly 900 years before, when the population was one thirtieth of the size![6]

Those who do not learn from the lesson of the past are doomed to repeat its errors, says George Santayana,[7] and the British Government again found itself in World War II with the prospect of starvation for the people. All talk of market forces was forgotten. Backyards, tennis courts, lawns, public parks and golf courses were dug up and planted. A medieval cottage economy took over great areas of the country with people keeping pigs, chickens, ducks and rabbits in back gardens and, in London, even on their roofs.The well-to-do had to hustle almost like the poor. Money itself was of less value so the poor were reluctant to sell their eggs or chickens to the well heeled.

The tendency to import Britain's food and drink requirements rather than rely on home-produced goods had begun early. Large quantities of wine were imported in the Middle Ages but it was not a staple of diet, despite the quantities involved, three million gallons annually in the fifteenth century, one for every man, woman and child in the country.[8]

From the eighteenth century on, however, exotics like cane sugar, tea, and coffee were imported to join potatoes as new and important items of diet, to the chagrin of commentators like Cobbett. He felt that tea and potatoes were no substitute for the bread and ale of old England.[9]

Bad Food and Bad Teeth.

The deleterious effects of sugar in the diet were far greater, especially when cane sugar from the West Indies met competition from the new home-grown beet sugar. The greatly reduced cost, together with advertising and the confectionery industry, have produced the highest sugar consumption and the worst teeth in the world. The dental profession's efforts to do something about it are stultified by the fact that the Government is corrupted by the power of pressure groups like the sugar and confectionery interests who dominate all food committees and ultimately Parliament itself. He who pays the piper calls the tune, and the sugar interest pays a lot to politicians, particularly Conservative politicians.

The move to the steel-roller milling of flour in the latter half of the nineteenth century reduced still further the quality of the average British diet. The new mills could not deal with the germ and the bran of the wheat as the old stone mills had done and these elements were disposed of as animal feed or sold to the public as cures for the diseases created by the deficient flour.

The resistance which might have been offered to the continuing debasement of British diet by a peasant population was missing; the remaining peasantry had finally been got rid of by the General Enclosure of 1845. The "allotments" offered as a sop might have enabled a worker to survive on a lower wage; they would not enable him to thumb his nose at an insufficiently generous wage offered by a prospective employer. As Thorold Rogers wrote of earlier Enclosures:

"Two acts of government had effectually delivered the English labourers into the hands of their employers and left them helpless. These were Henry's crime of base money and the confiscation of glebe lands."[10]

The period between World Wars I and II must be reckoned among the worst years for British diet. True, there was not the picturesque squalor of Victorian England nor the comedy of the Union-Jack-waving freaks who offered themselves for service in the Boer War, two thirds of whom were rejected as unfit even for the army. The scraps and leavings with which Dickens' characters fed themselves had been replaced by a diet of weak tea, turnip jam, and a bread which might have been made from Plaster of Paris for all the nutritive value it contained. The consequence was a race of dwarfs with blackened teeth and rickets. When the Second World War broke out a vast industry was called into being to fit up these degenerates with sets of false teeth and spectacles and to sew up their piles and hernias. As Mayhew, Engels and the Hammonds had exposed the terrible diets of the nineteenth century, so another group of reformers: Sir Albert Howard, Lady Eve Balfour, Sir Jack Drummond,[11] and John, subsequently Lord, Boyd Orr were calling attention to the condition of British agriculture and the terrible diets of British citizens in the twentieth century.

War Improves Diet.

The Second World War brought death to forty million Europeans and privation to the survivors, but to the British working class the war-time rationing of foodstuffs meant, paradoxically, an improvement in diet, so bad had standards been before. Official statistics reported increased height and body weight of children, and dental decay was reducing. This was despite a generous ration of confectionery - at the end of the war it stood at seven ounces per person per week. The conclusion this suggests is that the body can deal with a certain amount of sugar and other rubbish provided general levels of nutrition are kept up - which had not been the case pre-war.

The end of sweet-rationing was strongly opposed by the trade - another paradox. But they knew what anarchists and libertarian Marxists have always argued : that free access to a good or service, or to all goods and services does not mean increased consumption, but usually the opposite. The illusion or reality of limited supply creates a false demand. At all events, sweet rationing was ended, average consumption fell from seven ounces per person per week to five ounces and the confectionery trade went into recession. Limitation of demand by price was never an issue; sweets were and still are comparatively cheap in Britain.

Worse To Come.

During the 1950's a new group of factors entered the diet of people over the whole world served by The Market. Artificial fertilisers were brought in to replace the animal manures which were disappearing with the move to a mechanised agriculture. Chemical herbicides were introduced to eliminate the need for hoeing and good tilth which had always been regarded as the sine- qua-non of good agriculture. Insecticides were being increasingly used to deal with problems created by, among other things, monoculture:- the giving over of large areas to a single crop with the consequent build-up of huge concentrations of parasites: potato eel-worm, carrot-fly, codling-moth, aphids. This problem was not entirely new. In the nineteenth century the phylloxera vine-louse from N. America had devastated the European vine-yards. After desperate attempts to deal with the invader by chemical means had failed, the growers decided to go natures' way. The European vines were grafted onto N. American roots. These had evolved along with the phylloxera and were unattractive to the insect, interrupting its life-cycle.

No such wisdom has taken hold of the world's cultivators in the twentieth century. According to the Economist, a study of 3,000 Americans revealed only 30 of them without at least one kind of insecticide in their blood.[12] And that is the good news. In Britain, while Labour governments have been complacent about such matters, the Thatcher administration was active in conspiring to prevent public health action on the subject and even to deny information to those outside Government and the Agrochemical Industry. The final horrors are reserved for the Third World where chemicals are freely used which are banned even in slovenly Britain. The consequences are that up to 10,000 people a year there die from pesticide poisoning.[13]

> "Three trade unions representing 250,000 agricultural and public service workers, said yesterday that they would boycott pesticides after February unless secret safety data on the pesticides were disclosed. The unions want the Ministry of Agriculture and the pesticide manufacturers to disclose the data used to approve the safety of the 400 pesticides. They intend to send the data to independent scientists to test whether pesticides in common use are responsible for many ailments, acute illnesses which include cancer, and birth defects. February has been set as

> the deadline to coincide with the start of the planting season. The Ministry of Agriculture has always refused to make public the animal studies and other toxicological data used to assess pesticides safety on the grounds that the data are 'commercially confidential'".[14]

But where warning voices from the 1930's onwards have not been heeded, the disciplines of the balance-sheet are beginning to be felt. To quote the Economist again:

> "Chemical solutions are expensive. Those that come from fossil fuels cost a small fortune to develop. Third World countries spend huge sums subsidising their use. In Egypt, for instance, agrochemical subsidies work out at an annual $5 a head. Recently the pace of agrochemical invention has slowed, while the evolution of resistance has accelerated. In the 1940's the United States lost 7% of its agricultural crops to insects. Today it loses about 13%."[15]

Hopes For The Future.

Exeter University has a number of fast selling lines in insects which eat other insects - name your enemy and they will try to supply you with an enemy of your enemy and therefore your friend. In Essex, an octogenarian, Lawrence D. Hills, who had been sending out warnings for decades about the way farming was going, and being ignored or denounced as a fool for his pains, acquired a new intellectual respectability and was being listened to. Apart from his research into nature-based means of combating pests, Hills drew attention to the dangers inherent in concentrating agriculture on too narrow a genetic base, allowing thousands of plant varieties to disappear. On the Cotswolds near here farmer Joe Henson has set aside a reserve for rare and disappearing animal breeds. They will be needed.

A glance through any of those magnificent Victorian gardening manuals will remind the interested person of the specimens which have been lost, leaving only those varieties which fit the needs of the Market - fruit and vegetables which travel and store well and look good on the supermarket shelves, never mind that when you get them home they taste terrible. Nasty things happening on the agricultural front have been paralleled by equally nasty things in animal husbandry and poultry keeping.

Britain : A Nation Of Greaseballs.

During the latter part of the last century unwelcome amounts of fat were being urged on the public by the meat trade. The drive to intensive rearing of birds and animals had increased fat by decreasing mobility. At the same time the move from candles and rushlights made of animal fats to lamps fuelled by mineral oil increased the surplus. During the 1930's sausage maker Thomas Walls and Company solved the problem of mounting surplus fat by converting it into ice cream. Fifty years later nutrition experts were complaining that British sausages contained as little as five per cent meat, the rest being made up of fat and "rusk" - a flour based absorber for the fat.

The problem of animal fat surpluses was brought to a crisis point by the development of petroleum derived synthetic soaps - detergents - after World War II. This virtually ended the career of animal fats which for thousands of years had provided mankind with uses ranging from lighting, soap, and grease for axles to waterproofing for clothes and boots.

Involuntary Castration.

Another development of the decades following the War was the dosing of poultry and animals with chemicals, first to control disease, later to increase body weight. In the 1950's a number of Swiss men had gone to their doctors complaining of strange symptoms: loss of facial hair, incipient breasts. These were found to derive from canned chicken imported from the U.S. which contained significant residues of female hormone used to promote growth. The Swiss promptly banned a wide range of American goods and a bitter commercial squabble developed. Since then the use of hormones has been extended to beef cattle and similar symptoms have shown up in places as far apart as Italy and Puerto Rico including, *horribile dictu*, mature breasts on baby girls of four years.

A corn and beef farmer of Truro, Cornwall, explained the circumstances to me like this:

> "If you inject a hormone pellet into the ear of a bullock, you can bring him to market in twenty months. If you don't, it will take twenty four months to bring the animal to market, you will go bust and the bank will send the bailiffs in. The cost of feed will wipe out what you get for

the beast. But I know a man who puts a pellet in each ear and one up the arse. He markets his animals in eighteen months and he is making a fortune!"

Are The British Really Europeans?

A significant development for British agriculture at the beginning of the 1970's was the U.K. entry into the Common Market. This economic union which began after the war with the linking up of some of the smaller countries into the Benelux (Belgium, Netherlands and Luxembourg) agreement was then joined by Germany, France and Italy. At the beginning it was mainly an agricultural arrangement - the Common Agricultural Policy, CAP. British Governments first ignored it, then tried repeatedly to sabotage it, then finally applied to join it. They were humiliated by General de Gaulle who, in vetoing British entry, said that the British were bad Europeans. He was right, of course. British governments since the turn of the century had been living in a cloud cuckoo land of past glories and De Gaulle exacted bitter revenge for slights he had suffered during the war when exiled in Britain.

The European Economic Community, to give its correct title, set about stimulating its agriculture to ensure European self- sufficiency, but also to protect its smaller farmers and thereby reduce social chaos. This ran counter to the trend of British thinking, which was that the Market must decide and if the remaining peasants were driven to the wall, too bad. But the British were outvoted and an endless series of financial squabbles ensued.

Another consequence was the build-up of huge surpluses of every imaginable foodstuff: in 1986 nearly a million tons of beef, fifteen million tons of grain, butter mountains, wine lakes, olive oil lakes, the dumping of millions of tons of fruit and vegetables. This was not new. In the thirties wheat was being dumped in the sea and fish was being dumped on the land and the Brazilians were firing their trains on coffee beans, but the surpluses were not on anything like the same scale. What was not new was that these surpluses were building up alongside massive deprivation.

Just Like Mother Makes.

Good food was being destroyed while people were driven to consume junk food, because it was cheaper, and because more housewives were being driven out to work because of economic pressures - unemployed husbands, debt, mortgages etc. By 1987 a million more women were at work than a decade earlier. The boom in junk food cannot be unrelated.

Canned, frozen, or dried soups, TV dinners, instant mash, ready hash, custard without eggs, ice cream without cream, lemonade without lemons, fruit jelly without fruit, meat loaf without meat. And to make this rubbish palatable - and saleable - a veritable witch's cauldron of chemical dyes, flavourings, and smells, entered the food industry. This, with the accompanying publicity has created a scene more surrealist than the landscapes of Salvador Dali, with all his breasts and sagging clocks.

More money is spent on the advertising and packaging than on the food itself. More money is made on processing the food, devitalizing it, than is made in growing it. While the natural element is progressively removed from nutrition, the advertiser's message positively throbs with assurance: "countryside", "farmhouse", "homecooked", for goods that have just emerged from a processing tube.

Tristes Tropiques.

The consequences for the undeveloped world of the trade in food have been no less disastrous. In the Great Famine in Ireland of the 1840's people starved while wheat was being exported to England. In the Great Ethiopian Famine of the 1980's, fruit was being exported to Europe, fruit which could have saved lives.

Throughout the Thirld World fruit and vegetables are being produced by multinationals like United Brands of Boston, Massachusetts, and Unilever of Holland and Britain, on the best land in Central America and Africa for export to North America and Europe, while the local population is forced to survive on poor land, or worse, to become labourers on the latifundia of the big foreign companies. The power of these companies to influence, form, or destroy governments led in the inter-war years to the phenomenon of the Banana Republics, governments which were mere puppets of western multinational fruit companies.

It is difficult to find any aspect of food production in the modern world where the Market can be said to exert a good influence. The mere fact of production for sale and not to satisfy needs, promotes an urge to grab the money and run in all industries and services, but in food the results seem to be more catastrophic than anywhere else. Unfresh vegetables containing toxic chemical residues, meat with dangerous levels of antibiotics and hormones, fruit and vegetables which do not taste like fruit and vegetables used to taste, chocolate where the cocoa content has been reduced to the point where the Common Market Commissioners will not allow it to be called chocolate. The list is endless and depressing.

Disturbing Developments.

Another revealing development in this connection is a growing tendency for stock farmers to keep a particular animal for their own family which is raised the old way, without chemicals, and for fruit and vegetable growers to raise plants for their own consumption separate from those they send to market.

The revival of a critical interest in food has brought garlic back into some British kitchens and one smart cultivator on the Isle of Wight sensing, dare one say smelling, the possibilities has gone in for large scale cultivation of the plant, even exporting it to France. It had been absent from British cooking for centuries but was widely used in the Middle Ages; the word is Anglo-Saxon, meaning spear (shaped) leek, and there was a wharf on the Thames in those times called Garlick-hithe where a market was held dealing with the stuff. But hundreds of other food plants which could be found in a peasant's kitchen have disappeared and we can only guess at their range from the traces that remain. Sorrel, used by French peasants to make the delicious soupe d'oseille, has disappeared almost entirely as permanent pastures have been replaced by leys, for example.

And saffron, the herb that gave Saffron Walden its name, and the saffron cake they say used to be sold in Devon? It can only be found in poor countries now, it is fast disappearing in Spain, for example. Rich countries could not afford to cultivate crocuses just for the exquisite flavour, colour and perfume of their stamens.

Light Amid The Encircling Gloom.

Is the picture then, one of unrelieved gloom? By no means. As in so many other sectors of the Market economy, there are growing, contrary currents. Balkan countries, Hungary, Bulgaria, were pleasantly surprised a decade or two ago to find that their jams and preserves were being sought out by middle class British housewives because, in their naivety, and because they couldn't afford the chemicals, they were still manufacturing from fruit and sugar and nothing else. More recently there has been a rush by supermarket operators to find products they could label "No additives", or "Natural products only", and more recently "Organically grown", "Free Range". On the supply side these developments have been driven forward by the higher prices such goods command, and on the demand side by the enormous increase in what people believe to be allergic reactions to the non-natural materials and processes involved, apart from their fears for their health.

There has been a considerable increase in the number of cookery articles and supplements in the newspapers, and writers of books on cookery are enjoying a boom not seen since the days of Mrs. Beeton in the last century - whose works were aimed at the servants, not, as today, at the middle class housewife. Cookery experts on television enjoy superstar status, as do gardening experts - another boom subject in newspapers and book publishing.

Figures show gardening to be the biggest leisure activity of all, the growth in the number and ambitions of garden centres reflect this. While the pressures of the Market are driving farmers to restrict their range of products more and more, home cultivators are looking increasingly for new items: those lovely yellow waxy potatoes the French use for potato salad, the huge, shapeless, but superb tasting tomatoes the holidaymakers have brought abroad. They are looking for the hams of Parma, the hams of Bayonne, the Jabugo of Spain. Not yet, but who knows? Perhaps some idiot is planting saffron, about to hit a huge jackpot.

1. *Annual Digest of Statistics 1987.*

2. *Observer 1/2/87.*

3. *Wendell Berry : The Unsettling of America, quoting Justin Smith Morell, p.145.*

4. *David Ricardo op. cit.*

5. Observer 11/5/86

6. M.M. Postan : The Medieval Economy and Society (Penguin 1975) : "the aggregate acreage represented by the Domesday ploughlands was at least as great as, and in most Midland counties greater than, the areas under plough during the periods of high farming in the nineteenth century."

7. George Santayana, The Life of Reason, vol. 1, chapter 12

8. John Burnett, History of the Cost of Living, p.32.

9. William Cobbett: e.g. Cottage Economy.

10. Thorold Rogers : History Of Agriculture and Prices in England volume 5.

11. In fact Drummond with A. Wilbraham (The Englishman's Food, 1957) traced the decline to a long time before the twentieth century : "Standards of food consumption deteriorated for the rural poor in the second half of the eighteenth century to a predominantly bread and cheese diet because the system of enclosures had taken away their pasturages and the land where they collected the fuel for cooking their hot meals." p.206.Could not this low-protein diet be part of the explanation for the staggering rise in population from 8 million to 10.5 million in the twelve years between 1788 and 1800? (Sir John Call, cited by Wrigley and Schofield: Population History of England 1541-1871, p.406) And could not a continuation of this diet for the poor through the nineteenth century be the explanation for the population rise rather than a theoretical rise in living standards? See fig.2.

12. Economist 12/4/86.

13. Ibid.

14. Guardian 12/12/86.

15. Economist 12/4/86.

Chapter 6.

The Clothing Industry.

Few Producers of Clothes.

By the middle of the 1980's there were less than 200,000 people employed in the clothing industry and some 40,000 in the footware industry, with little more than 200,000 engaged in textiles - these being materials of every variety, from suit lengths to car and furniture upholstery materials, carpets and fishing nets.[1]

A century ago there were more than 2.5 million so employed - five or six times the above number. They were producing the cheap goods which, in the words of Karl Marx, the English capitalists used as artillery to batter down the Chinese walls of feudalism. Surely, the most mixed metaphor of all time, but Adam Smith would have understood and agreed.

A huge proportion of the textiles produced, and a lesser proportion of the clothing were exported, right up to World War I in fact. But then the markets collapsed, and the industry went into a long decline. In the middle 1980's more clothing was being imported than exported. This was funded by the Rake's Progress of the Thatcher administration, using the proceeds of North Sea Oil to finance a consumer boom. In the 12 months following the Falklands War imports rose by 26% in value, clearly a policy of togas and circuses if not bread and circuses.

Large Scale Textiles; Small Scale Clothing.

The textile industry has been characterised since the early part of the last century by large companies; the names J. and P. Coats, Courtaulds, ICI Fibres, are synonymous with large scale manufacturing. The clothing industry, on the other hand, has often been identified with small firms, sweatshops, low pay, appalling conditions and industrial diseases.

Much of this has now been transferred to the Third World - Hong Kong, Korea, Taiwan, Singapore, India, and the trade moves on elsewhere as wages and conditions improve as a consequence of the inevitable rise in consciousness and militancy of the operatives. Nevertheless, there is still a lot of Third World style manufacture in the developed countries themselves, i.e. labour-intensive with terrible wages, using immigrant labour, almost always female: Cypriots, Indians, and Pakistanis in Britain, North Africans in France, Turks in Germany, Sicilians and South Italians in Milan and Turin. A century ago it would have been Jews in London and New York: cutters, fellers, button- holers and pressers, who in their struggles for a tolerable life wrote some of the most moving chapters in the history of labour.

Low labour costs have acted as a brake on technical development in the clothing industry since its earliest days. Why bother to buy sophisticated machinery when people are so cheap? In the event of a turndown in trade you can always fire them and let the community at large look after them.[2] With machines lying idle, on the other hand, there is always the reproach that you over-traded, that you didn't see the storm clouds, that the liquidator is selling the machines too cheap.

There is little doubt that the clothing industry - and almost all the other industries - could manage on one tenth of the labour if advantage were taken of state-of-the-art technology. With a bespoke industry, it would be more difficult, although computer- controlled cutting and sewing machines could handle constantly changing instructions. But the made-to-measure business died in the '60's and '70's anyway, and there is nothing in current clothing manufacture which could not be handled by available technology, since, unlike the making of false teeth, the work involves simple repetition.

Skirts Up, Trousers Down.

Another factor excercising a great influence upon the industry is fashion. This is simply the industry's efforts to make last year's clothing obsolete so that the factories do not have to close down. Skirts go up or down. Dresses are tight or loose fitting. Puce is this year's colour. Efforts have been made to bring men's clothes within the ambit of fashion, with varying degrees of success. Trousers are drainpipe or flared. Coats are long or short etc. But men tend to drag their feet in fashions. They have less need to market themselves, put frills on the ham-bone as it were. At other times and in other places it was different. Men were the peacocks and women the dun coloured hens.

Expenditure on women's clothes today accounts for twice that on men's clothes. The fact that they are much more flimsily if not shoddily made increases the discrepancy and shows the extent to which fashion controls expenditure. How much of it is intrinsically elegant or attractive - *de gustibus non disputandum* - can be gauged by looking at women's fashions of five or fifty years ago. Somebody in the twenty-fifth century, say, might find it less attractive than the dress of ancient Egypt, Greece, or Rome.

Just how many people a high-tech, fashion-free clothing industry producing for desire and not sale might require in the future is impossible to say. What is certain is that it could only be a tiny fraction of today's labour force.

In the hotter parts of the world clothing has rarely been necessary: Australian Blackmen, Amazonian Indians, Kalahari Bushmen, Dinkas of the Southern Sudan, people of Papua New Guinea or our own ancestors, managed or still manage without clothes. In the colder areas it was different. James Laver writes: "The Persians overran the Babylonian civilisation in the sixth century B.C. Since they came from the colder climate of the mountains of what is now called Turkestan they wore warmer clothes but soon abandoned these for the fringed tunics and overmantles of the conquered race."[3]

The first clothes for cold climates seem to have been the furs of animals, whose use goes back certainly tens and possibly hundreds of thousands of years. It is only during the past decade or two that their use has almost totally ceased due to the campaigns of animal-rights movements. No film star, no duchess, of 30 or 40 years ago would think her wardrobe complete without a mink coat. And lower income group women would regard a lamb, sealskin, or rabbit fur (called coney) coat as something to strive for. But the fashion seems to be in decline due to the campaigns, and age-old customs have halted.

According to Laver the first fabrics were in the forms of felts, this is, animal or vegetable fibres wetted and placed in layers on a mat. The mat is then rolled up tightly and beaten with a stick. The strands of wool or hair are thus matted together, and the felt produced is warm, pliable and durable, and can be cut and sewn to make garments, rugs and tents.

For the sewing itself the technology was already to hand. The "eyed needle" was in Laver's opinion "one of the greatest technological advances in human history, comparable in importance to the invention of the wheel and the discovery of fire." This tool had been available since palaeolithic times. Weaving into fabric followed, at what interval it is again impossible to say; the whole process belongs to pre-history, and everything is much older than we thought it was.

Even when we come into recorded history problems remain. History is written by the winners. The Carthaginians got a bad press. No wonder; the Romans wrote it. We do not know what the Saxon ruling class thought of the Norman invasion. They were silenced, often in the most unpleasant way.

So with the ordinary people throughout history.

> "Books on the history of European costume generally concentrate on aristocratic and bourgeois fashion, which, because of their rapid rate of change provide a graphic index to the ideals and fantasies of successive generations, successive decades, and even of successive years and seasons. The present book (Alma Oakes, Rural Costume) treats of a very different subject, that of rural dress, which followed a quite different timescale, since here the flux of fantasy was checked by practical considerations, by the

> slower rhythms of country life and the innate conservatism of country folk, perhaps by poverty, or by sumptuary laws, or the weight of local traditions. In its own way, however, rural dress was no less rich and varied than aristocratic and bourgeois dress."[4]

Another authority writes : "Little has been written up to the present on the costume worn by people at work, since compared with high fashion its documentation has always been scanty."[5]

The efforts of the ruling class to make the common people into non-persons, or at least as unobtrusive as possible, go back a long way. Sumptuary laws attempting to control the use of colour and decoration in peasant clothing were widespread in Europe during the late Middle Ages, and Herodotus mentions an Athenian decree forbidding the lower classes to appear in dyed clothing at the theatre and in other public places.[6]

The Sumptuary Laws were eventually repealed in 1603 in Britain; it is doubtful whether they ever really worked, although one writer thinks they had an effect on colour.[7] If this is so one wonders why they were repeatedly passed. At all events another authority writes: "English rural clothing remained on the whole simple. The general impression is that it was neat and well cut, of good material."[8]

On *a priori* grounds alone this should not surprise us. People had been making clothes for thousands of years, every person was the heir to a wide range of refined skills, and there was also a limited division of labour. Women made the clothes. Men were out getting in the meat and the crops. Women were turning them into meals. It is only in the last generation or two that a vast range of needleworking skills has been lost by the majority of women; ruching, smocking, pleating. These skills were not developed recently or during the last millenium. The superb rugs of Bokhara, the needlework in the Egyptian tombs were not the product of Adam Smith's division of labour but were made by the adepts of pre-Market economies.

Modern and Maladroit.

Not long ago a British television company attempted to re-create a Bronze Age settlement in the south of England and make a series of programmes around it. A dozen or so candidates to attempt to live the life of Bronze Age people were selected - mainly young academic couples. Local carpenters and thatchers were engaged to construct a group of huts in what the archeologists imagined were Bronze Age style and the candidates settled in.

The vanity of all concerned was breathtaking. None of the participants appeared to have any particular skill let alone a collection of them. They couldn't farm, hunt, preserve food, cook, make clothes - certainly not from the raw materials. There were efforts at making pots, weaving, making hurdles etc. But real Bronze Age people would have done the lot and done it well, beginning with the house-building, as people still do today in Africa and did in England in Cobbett's youth.

Upper Class Clothing.

When we come to the clothes of the ruling classes, on which entire libraries have been written, we can see that different influences have been at work. Where the common people sought to reconcile comeliness with comfort at work the aristocracy emphasised their distance from any kind of effort. Sleeves cover the wrists and part of the hands which ultimately come to resemble seal's flippers. Nowhere is this more emphasised than in the portrait of Phillip II by Velasquez and in the superb and decadent poem of Manuel Machado beginning:

> "No-one more polished and courtly
> Than our King Phillip
> (Whom God preserve)
> Always dressed in black
> Down to his feet."

Evolution of Clothing in Europe.

Dress of all classes during the Middle Ages had been relatively sober, consisting mainly of a tunic - long for the women, short for the men - and breeches, with a cloak for extra protection. Kings and Princes of the Church had magnifient ceremonial costumes but they were no more in everyday use than they are today.

With the Renaissance and later, the Reformation, the Age of Plunder began and the clothing of the Aristocracy began to show it. The "slashed effect" (the practice of cutting slits in the garment and pulling the lining through) spread from Switzerland and Germany through France and to England. Slashed doublets and breeches were the uniform at court, but for the men only. "Slashing spread to women's clothes but was never prevalent. This extravagant fashion was more suitable for breeches than for large areas of fabric such as skirts. Indeed, female dress at this period is much more modest than male costume. Skirts, however, were ampler and more richly embroidered than in earlier reigns."[9]

Then in the middle of the 16th century came the Spanish influence, as sombre as the German influence had been gaudy. Almost all of the Spanish aristocrats wore black, due to the growing power of Spain, according to Laver. It could have been due to piety and clerical influence; the Spaniards had spent seven centuries driving the Moslems out of Spain and the ideological justification was Christianity complete with warrior-bishops. But the economy they won from the Arabs which had exported fine cloths and leather to Europe and the East was crumbling. The discovery of gold and silver, particularly the latter, in America had distorted the Spanish, indeed the whole European economy through inflation. Four centuries later the process was to be repeated. This time it was not the flood of precious metal, but the absence of it, in relation to the paper dollars being printed in the 1950's and '60's, which allowed American governments to cause European and other governments, some of them the poorest in the world, to pay for the Space Race and the Vietnam War.

The Spaniards stopped manufacturing, the young men went off to "Indias", as they called the New World, to make their fame and fortune, and Spain was content to import, using the silver from Potosi, the goods she had previously manufactured herself. Europe was awash with doubloons and pieces of eight.

Spanish literature of the early seventeenth century like Cervantes' "Exemplary Novels" contain reference to "Holland sheets", "scissors from France" and "fine English cloth." When the gold of the Incas and the silver of Bolivia finally ran out, the roof of the Spanish economy fell in and the most powerful country in the world disappeared from the political scene for three hundred years.

Fur Coats and No Knickers.

The "pride, pox and poverty" of the Spaniards' position expressed itself in a "rigidity and hauteur", reflecting the stiff and proud etiquette of the Spanish Court. "Gone were the easy flowing lines of the costume of the early part of the century, when clothes seemed to express a man's own personality, even his own fantasy. Instead men now seemed to be indicating their membership of an aristocratic caste."[10]

An example of this was the development of the ruff. "It goes without saying that the ruff was the mark of aristocratic privilege. It is an extreme example of the tendency of men's clothes to show that their wearers do not need to work, or indeed to engage in any strenuous pursuit; and as the (sixteenth) century progressed, ruffs grew larger and larger until it is difficult to see how their wearers could have conveyed food to their mouths."

During the next century, the contending parties for power in England are known in popular image as much for their differences in clothes as for their ideologies: the dashing Cavaliers and the soberly dressed Roundheads, the Royal party and the Burgesses. To generations of British school children the sentimental painting of a small velvet- clad Cavalier boy confronted by a committee of Roundheads dressed in fustian and titled: "When did You Last See Your Father?" summed up most of what they had learned about the Civil War. The subject is one big provocation to Marxist interpretation of historical costume, but perhaps more Groucho than Karl.

The Royalist side obviously owed much to French influence although they were not as thoroughgoing as the real thing, immortalised for a later generation by the inventions of that black Frenchman Alexandre Dumas. The historical model for his Three Musketeers with their side slung capes and bucket-top boots was too much even for King Charles' retinue.

The Roundheads took their dress and haircuts from Holland. Protestantism, the Work Ethic, and no jokes please; the whole ethos seemed the inevitable result of thirty years of war for the Dutch to free themselves from the weakening grip of Spain.

The Restoration of the Monarchy in England brought an upper class fashion even dafter than the ruff; this was the periwig. Astonishingly, this bizarre fashion lasted a century. Even more astonishing is that it is still worn as part of the clown-costume of the British legal system.

The 18th century saw the three-cornered hat, the "cocked hat", added to the conspicuous consumption of the ruling class. The "cocked hat" says Planche was considered as a mark of gentility, professional rank, and distinction from the lower orders who wore them uncocked.[11] It was at the end of this century that the quality of life of the ordinary people of England reached its nadir. As the enclosures of the peasants' lands continued and their living standards plunged, the dress of the ruling class reached ever greater heights of extravagance and absurdity.

The French Revolution brought a changed mood and more sober fashions on the Continent. The French Wars which followed did the same for Britain; business was depressed, agriculture too, and for a decade or so extravagances were muted.

Then after Waterloo the last burst of upper-class hocus-pocus in men's dress took over. The Age of the Dandies, Beau Brummel, the Prince Regent, Daniel Mendoza; gentlemen-pugilists and aristocratic layabouts occupied the scene for the last act of ruling class conspicuous consumption in dress.

No More Male Peacocks.

It was all finished by the middle of the century and a world more like our own took over. "The dominant figure in English life was now a respectable bourgeois, who had no desire to make himself conspicuous, but wished merely to present a gentlemanly appearance, both in his counting-house and at home."

A world safe for Pooters to live in.

A jacket or trousers, matching or contrasting, have been normal dress for men ever since, with a modified jacket, the battledress blouse or "bomber" jacket the only variant. The clawhammer coats and top hats of the last century now only survive as the folk- dress of the rich or socially ambitious in weddings, at Ascot, or the Honours List presentations.

Frills on the Hambone.

Women still remained overdressed and victims of fashion masochism: corsets, flattened chests or breasts raked like anti- aircraft guns, billowing skirts or hobbles, endless nonsense until World War II.

Wartime regulations stipulated "sensible" clothes and solid shoes, and these were continued after the War by the Labour Government. But the clothing trade was chafing at the bit and Paris got the French fashion business going again. The Conservative administration which followed again in 1951 got rid of the controls but Fashion was never quite the same as pre-war. The Debs had lost their charm.

Hollywood, whose influence on clothes since the '30's had been growing (and in other matters too, one noble lord said that at least Hollywood had taught the British working class how to use a knife and fork) and whose populist appeal made much more sense to the new mass market than Paris's avowedly elitist approach, became the arbiter in the 1940's and '50's. Clothes were all the time becoming more casual. Jeans, the uniform of the American farm worker, became the uniform of a great part of the world, women as well as men. Sex differences in clothing were becoming less marked. And class roles had been reversed. The bourgeoisie, who had set the fashions were now content to imitate working class youth and it became more difficult to distinguish class differences through dress.

Mawkishness was disappearing too. The Victorians who were so modest they draped the table legs, were a long time ago. Brassieres were burned by enraged feminine liberators, pre-war swimming costumes which had little skirts to mask the mons veneris were followed by skin-tight costumes, which were followed by the bikini, which was followed by the mono-kini, which was followed by swimming and sunbathing in the nude. We had found our roots.

What can we anticipate about clothing in a society freed from the fashion-hysteria of the Market? Supply-push will clearly disappear whatever demand-pull remains. Nobody will depend on shifting a quantity of schmutter wholesale or retail in order to keep the bank happy and the mortgage paid. But the disappearance of flash and trash should not lead us to think that the future must be dowdy. A glance through the geographical magazines at people who dress themselves, from Lapland to Liberia, and who have dressed themselves in the past, from Portugal to Poland will suggest that the future of dress can be bright and perhaps even beautiful.

1. Annual Digest of Statistics 1987, (HMSO).

2. Fred Hirsch : Social Limits to Growth, points out that the Market Economy could not survive without the backup provided by the Informal Economy.

3. James Laver.

4. Donald King, Deputy Keeper Dept. of Textiles, V & A Foreword to Alma Oakes, Rural Costume.

5. Cunnington & Lucas : Occupational Costume in England Eleventh Century to 1914.

6. Laver : ibid

7. McLintock: Old Irish and Highland Dress.

8. Alma Oakes : Rural Costume.

9. Laver : ibid.

10. Laver :ibid.

11. Laver: ibid.

Chapter 7.

Shelter.

The Building Industry.

There are more people employed shuffling the money about for the housing industry, building societies, banks, insurance companies, and other assorted loan sharks, than there are engaged in the actual building and maintenance: bricklayers, carpenters, plasterers and plumbers. The wealth the money changers consume can only come out of that created by the building workers.

Small Number Employed.

The numbers employed in the "construction and repair of buildings, demolition work, installation of fixtures and fittings, and building completion", according to the official figures are nearly 800,000. Yet there were only just over 200,000 houses built in 1986. At the going rate it takes about 40 man-weeks to build a three bedroom house, so that, at the most, there could only have been a quarter of them engaged in house building, i.e. 200,000. Perhaps the War Department, office block construction, banks and shops, can account for the activities of the other three quarters.[1]

Property Booms.

There has certainly been nothing like the same degree of excitement, of effort, of capital investment, and of gigantic fortunes made, in house-building as in commercial property, since the Second World War. It began with the boom unleashed by the abolition of commercial building licences in 1954, and chronicled by Oliver Marriott in his classic The Property Boom 2 written ten years later. It was followed by the boom under the Heath Government of the early seventies, provoked by Chancellor Barber's attempt to stimulate the economy, manufacturing in particular, by typical Keynesian tactics, i.e. printing money.

Ted Heath and Anthony Barber did not foresee the reaction of their friends in the City who were dealing out this largesse, although Heath as a former banker should have known better than most. The money, or most of it, ended up in the hands of the property boys, there was another mushroom growth of office blocks and shops, additionally it diluted the stock of money which lost four fifths of its value before the decade was out, exceeding by a wide margin the inflation set in train by Henry VIII sweating and clipping the coinage in the sixteenth century. There was another crop of millionaires, some of them with a minus sign before their fortunes.

One, William Stern, went personally bust for more than a hundred million, but continued to live in Millionaires Avenue, Hampstead, and drive his Rolls Royce, showing once again that when you deal with money in telephone numbers it doesn't much matter whether there is a plus or minus sign before it. In any case his record has been broken by even bigger personal bankruptcies since that date.

A third boom was set in train in the 1980's by the Thatcher Government's disdain for and discrimination against manufacturing industry. Those with money got the message and apart from the hundred billion pounds shipped abroad, much of it lent to dodgy dictatorships in the Third World and lost for ever, the rest went once more into commercial property, principally in the City, but with an additional trough for them to get their snouts into in the old and derelict London Docks. The "de-regulation" of the City, mentioned in the chapter on the Money Industry, only added to the frenzy.

Housebuilding was languishing, the number of housing "starts" fell by a third from the 300,000 necessary to barely maintain the stock,to not much more than 200,000. But this part of the industry still had to pay Danegeld to the already over-endowed City.

Houses are a favourite form of collateral security for lenders.[3] They cannot be spirited away and are growing, not wasting, assets like cars or yachts. But they can be snatched back in the event of default, as the twenty thousand families dumped on the pavement outside their homes with all their possessions found out in the year 1986.

Increasing Real Cost of Houses.

The snowstorm of credit offers had other consequences. Inflation of house prices - which are not included in the Government's Cost of Living Index - combined with a 40% cut back in house building, reached more than 20% per year during the middle '80's in London and the South East. Unemployed workers could not move from the North to the South to find work, even assuming such a gypsy existence was desirable; there was no accommodation available at a price they could pay.

According to David Gilchrist, General Manager of the Halifax Building Society, house prices were well above four times average annual earnings in London. And the average earnings in London would be higher than the wages of a bricklayer or carpenter. Yet as mentioned earlier, five centuries ago a house of 1,400 square feet was built to order in Gloucester, "all the timber of oak" for the sum of £14.[4] At the going rate of sixpence to eightpence per day, this was little more than two years take-home pay for a building tradesman.[5] And according to Peter Moreton, chief surveyor of the Anglia Building Society, the average floor space of a two bedroom inner-city town house built before 1919 is 800 square feet. In the modern equivalent it is around 550 square feet. This is smaller than a post-war pre-fab.

In the 1930's three-bedroom semi-detached houses were selling in Cheltenham for £375 newly built. Tradesman's wages, including carpenters and bricklayers averaged £3 per week and labourers £2.10 shillings. The tradesmen could buy the houses for little more than two years take-home pay; even the labourers with three years pay. Remember, the gross pay was subject to very little in the way of tax or insurance deductions at that time.

Those same houses, which were typical of millions built between the wars were changing hands at over £50,000 in the 1980's which was a lot dearer in take-home pay to our tradesmen than they were half a century ago.[6] *Ou sont les neiges d'antan?*

The consequences of the increased cost of housing, or the lower incomes measured by housing, which comes to the same thing, has had a number of consequences.

One is the increased part of the family budget taken up by accommodation, despite the fact that it does not figure in the Government Cost of Living and Inflation statistics.

> "... if a married man earning £12,500 a year (the average income of a building society borrower) takes on a mortgage of 3.5 times his income - about £44,000 - then his monthly mortgage payment of £369 absorbs more than half of his disposable income (after tax, national insurance, and pension contributions). This leaves the couple with only £334 to live on for the month, and with no cushion if interest rates rise." [7]

Matters seem little better on the other side of the Atlantic:

> "In 1981, according to International Currency Review, a leading financial journal, the median price of houses in the United States was $68,200 and a median family income was $23,500. With mortgage interest rates of approximately 14 per cent, a 30 year mortgage with a 25 per cent down payment yields annual interest payments of $7,400 or about 32 per cent of gross income, a huge amount even by American standards. "Thus", concludes the International Currency Review, "the average American family can no longer afford the average American house." [8]

Falling Standards.

Another consequence of the increased real cost of housing is the trading down by both builders and residents in a quest to balance the budget. Cheaper forms of construction are being forced upon builders : roof trusses are now made of 75mm x 30mm battens - the dimension does not merit the word timber.A generation ago it would have been 100mm x 50mm. Tongue and groove flooring has been replaced by particle-board or chipboard, which is sawdust pressed into a board with plastic adhesive - there is a lot of built-in obsolescence going into present-day housing. The private sector has also experimented with 'timber frame' housing surrounded with a skin of brickwork. Again, the flimsiness has brought swift response from the insurance and mortgage companies who are wary of such innovations. After all, they are being asked to lend for 35 years.

Until 1981 Parker Morris standards controlled building quality in the public sector at which date they were abolished by the Thatcher Government in an effort to reduce bureaucracy. Many believe that this accelerated the trend to smaller rooms in the private sector. Anne Jacobs in the Sunday Times quoted a man in the prosperous South East whose second bedroom was a mere 9 feet square - barely enough room to move around once the bed was in it. Another group of houses on the same estate had kitchens just 8ft 6ins x 6ft 3ins. Anne Jacobs[9] cited the concern of the Institute of Environmental Health Officers who feared that overcrowding in small rooms could be a health hazard, allowing rapid spread of infection.

According to the 1986 Government publication Social Trends, in 1981 there was a total of 19.1 million dwellings in England and Wales of which:

1.2 million were considered unfit for habitation

1.1 million needed repairs costing more than £7,000 at 1981 prices

1 million lacked basic amenities.

The Homeless.

These three categories amounted to 11% of the total dwelling stock. They do not, however, represent the worst off. There are many with no dwelling at all. According to the Sunday Times.[10]

> "Nobody knows the real extent of homelessness in Britain but all across the country official records are showing a rise. In the last five years households who presented themselves to councils as having nowhere to live has gone up from 160,000 to 203,000 a year. A survey by the Department of the Environment in 1982 said there were 330,000 concealed single homeless."

Housing Minister John Patten was quoted as saying: "I am deeply offended by the amount of empty property there is in this country. We have some 120,000 council houses and flats of which 20,000 have been empty for more than a year." [11]

The Environment Department thinks there are also between half and three quarters of a million empty houses in the private sector. This highlights more than anything the fact that houses are built to make a profit for somebody rather than to house people. Meanwhile, local authorities who are under a legal obligation to provide shelter for these people, are forced to put them into bed and breakfast accommodation, often at enormous cost to the taxpayers. The attraction for slum landlords is irresistible, as frequent press revelations disclose: "A convicted extortionist is earning up to half a million pounds a year from Manchester City Council for housing the homeless."[12]

Housing in the Past.

The reaction of historians and politicians from Left to Right to criticisms of failure to house people has always been that however bad things are now, in the past they were even worse.

"Cold, isn't it?"

"It was a bloody sight colder in the Ice Age."

When we recover our breath and start to examine the conventional wisdom on the subject of housing, now and in the past, doubts start to creep in. The subject is slippery. Houses long ago were mainly made of perishable materials like timber and thatch. But when the neolithic houses made of granite at Skara Brae in the Orkneys were excavated, the inhabitants were clearly seen not to have gone short of the glory of making themselves as comfortable as they might have done.

Granite bed and chair frames, granite sideboards; can we not assume that when people had much more easily handled material like timber available they would have made themselves equally comfortable? Were the people who built Stonehenge incapable of building themselves a decent shelter? One man's mud hut is another man's cobwalled cottage, complete with heat-conserving thatch. It is difficult to believe that people so housed were much worse off than the 16,000 more people who died during the cold winter of 1985 than in the previous year.

Energy Efficiency.

These figures from the Office of Population Censuses in 1986 were accompanied by warnings from doctors and pressure groups that people, particularly the old, were dying because they could not afford to heat their homes. It could be argued that many houses in Britain are incapable of being maintained at a reasonable temperature anyway. The pre 1914 houses with their 9 inch solid walls, the houses built between the wars with their 11 inch cavity walls, could only be kept at a reasonable temperature during a cold (for Britain) winter by enormous expenditure on fuel.

Older houses like the cob-walled types could manage on a fraction of the heating; likewise Cotswold cottages with their two foot thick random-rubble stone walls, rendered inside with a thick, spongy, lime plaster and not the modern hard plasters which sweat with condensation.

The problem is not that the modern technology to produce energy efficient houses does not exist. Twenty or thirty different houses have been built at Milton Keynes by different companies to prove that it does. A school was built at Wallasey, Cheshire, 25 years ago without any heating system at all. The designer, Hemslie Morgan, relied on solar gain and heavy insulation for his effect, with stunning success. He did not get any architectural prizes. They were reserved for the more conventional architectural whimsies.

Caveat Emptor.

The problem is that there is no profit in building energy-efficient houses. By the time the purchaser discovers that heating his house costs an arm and a leg, the builder has moved on. The oil, gas and electricity companies are not going to press for efficiency. They have a built-in interest in houses that leak heat in every direction. The Government could insist on high K (insulation) values for every new house that is built. But that would simply add to the thicket of regulations which set out minimum standard for house construction at present: staircase tread and riser dimensions, room heights, window sizes, toilet construction, drainage etc.

Nevertheless:

> "The National House-Building Council is tightening up its inspection and disciplinary procedures to try to cut down on the £10 million it is paying out each year to buyers of defective houses. The NHBC gets about 5,000 complaints a year from purchasers, accepts about 3,000 of them, and strikes about forty builders off its register for failing to make repairs or comply with the council's regulations." [13]

Do it Yourself.

Meanwhile, those who "own" their houses, some 63% in Britain at the last count, get on with fashioning to their own needs and tastes, putting shelves up, fitting new kitchens, building conservatories and extensions. Giant out-of-town Do-It-Yourself stores have spread to cater to the new market. Many techniques have been taken out of the hands of the experts. Plumbing is no longer a business of wiping lead joints, benching-up inspection chambers, tamping joints on LCC piping. Those manual skills have been replaced by solder-ring or compression joints for copper piping, and the rest is a matter of push-fit plastic pipes and fittings.

A similar approach has produced a huge range of kitchen and bathroom furniture; cupboards, cabinets, units, much of it, alas, in the ubiquitous chipboard. After a few years the drawers drop, the doors fall because the hinges come away with parts of the cupboard wall. One company, Habitat, was enormously successful through offering plain but solid wood fittings to its trendy, up-market clientele. But shoddy or solid, the development has given tremendous satisfaction and happiness to many people. To put a shelf up in your own home satisfies very deep urges. To build your own home, or to extend it is ecstasy, as those who have done it know well.

A Home of One's Own.

The Thatcher government judged the public mood brilliantly with its commitment to a "property owning democracy" and left the Labour Party hopelessly out-flanked. The latter was talking about building more council houses, more council maintenance of existing stock. The Conservatives were meanwhile selling off the council houses and leaving people to do the maintaining themselves. Never mind that the home ownership was largely bogus; the average couple were in a race to pay for the house before the undertaker called on them. It still left them feeling entirely different about the place. I recall growing up in a council house between the wars. You needed the permission of the Housing Inspector to bang a nail in the wall for a picture. Although invariably dreadful kitsch, the picture was one of those things which make a home.

Git Off Mah Land!

Be it ever so humble, there's no place like it, and most people's wishes are modest enough. Get them to draw their ideal and they will come up with the same cottage. Same bit of lawn in front and vegetable garden at the back. Vandalised, graffitti-ridden estates have been transformed by being sold-off, in some cases virtually given to their tenants. Try a bit of vandalising or writing on walls then and one of the people inside will come out and break your legs; try pissing in the the lift and you'll come out singing falsetto.

(1) e.g. C.G. Powell : Economic History of the British Building Industry 1815 - 1979 (Butterworth 1980) :

"The value of housing output as a percentage of all building and construction was slightly over 30% in the later 1950s falling to a little under that figure by the early 1970s." p.138. But between 1975 and 1985 the number of houses built fell from 312,600 to 203,000, (Sunday Times 15/06/86) so the number of men employed on housebuilding at the latter date could not have been many more than one fifth of the total engaged in construction.

The activities of the rest appear to have been a continuation, if slightly varied, of those carried on in the nineteenth century:
"Other recipients of heavy public expenditure were the workhouses which appeared as a result of the Poor Law of 1834. The buildings were often substantial, consisting of chapel, administrative block and several wings of accomodation, graced with the popular name bastilles ... All too closely associated in the public mind with workhouses were lunatic asylums and gaols. Both were expensive buildings ... Perhaps the bluntest of all instruments of social control were the barracks. One at Portsea was estimated at £35,000 in 1848 and another on a ten acre site at Newport was estimated five years ear-

lier at between £40,000 and £50,000.
Hospital building relied on philanthropy and appears to have been moderately large in volume. "Powell, p.18

(2) Oliver Marriott : The Property Boom (Hamish Hamilton 1967)

(3) "Not long ago, houses were homes to live in and building societies were part of a public spirited movement, dedicated to lending money to those who most deserved to buy them. Today houses have become investment commodities, societies and banks compete to lend money and social conversation tediously and inevitably drifts round to the housing market. Many peoples lives and careers are wildly distorted by the pressures created by rapidly rising prices." Peter Rodgers and Margaret Hughes in Financial Guardian 22/8/87.

(4) John Burnett : History of the Cost of Living.

(5) "West Germany, where a house usually cost eight times the average annual income, as against 3.3 times in the U.K." - Giles Merritt : World Out of Work (Collins 1982).

(6) Yet according to C.H. Feinstein : Statistical Tables of National Income and Output of the U.K. 1855-1965 : "National product grew by only 10% between 1920 and 1932 in spite of an increase in fixed capital formation of over 60%. Output per worker increased by 22% in the same 12 years, but income from wages declined, as did personal disposable income per capita." (Cambridge University Press) Tables 7, 17, 20, 21, quoted by Bill Jordan : Automatic Poverty.

If in the richest country in Europe - Germany, houses are eight times annual earnings and in Britain they are four, but in the Thirties they were two and a half times average annual earnings when wages were lower than they were in 1920, then there must be a lot of wealthy, homeless people about.

(7) Economist 16/08/86.

(8) Michael Moffitt : The Worlds Money (Joseph 1984)

(9) Sunday Times 27/07/86

(10) Sunday Times 15/06/86.

(11) Sunday Times : 3/08/86.

(12) Sunday Times : 3/08/86.

(13) Guardian : 8/08/86.

Chapter 8.

Food For The Mind.

"Man does not live by bread alone."

In earlier societies, faith and entertainment, art and spectacle, counselling and comforting, moulding and moralising, were all aspects of the same thing - Religion. In modern society they are frequently but not always separated. They have also suffered different fates in recent centuries.

The Loss of Faith.

Traditional religions in Europe have entered the last stages of crisis. Roman Catholics have left the Church in droves because of unacceptable teachings on, amongst other things birth control, divorce, abortion, priestly celibacy, or the bodily assumption of the Virgin (the logical possibility of a fast space vehicle finding her is too much). Protestant sects have finally split into the myriad schisms that the Council of Trent predicted, and many of them cannot declare themselves believers of the Thirty Nine Articles of the Anglican persuasion, of the predestination of the Calvinists, or the more exotic exegeses of the Free Churches. Jews are reduced to less than 100,000 of the Orthodox who hold it *rassenschande* to marry a *goy* or a *schickse*. Many of the rest have 'married out' and abandoned themselves like the majority of the population, to the worship of fashion, concern with their diet, and furnishing the house nicely.

To the extent that the void left by traditional beliefs has been occupied, and this for a tiny majority, the new faiths are mainly exotica imported from the East via the United States, or a retreat into Old Testament Fundamentalism - they know that the moon is made of green cheese and that pigs can fly, and they can prove it.

Missionaries Among The European Tribes.

Saffron robed monks, and sharp-suited Mormons, Pentecostal sects, Christian Scientists, and Jehovah's Witnesses, wave after wave of these spiritual kamikazes launch themselves upon Europe, particularly Britain, and on to populations which are clearly underwhelmed: Frank Buchman, Judge Rutherford, Billy Graham, L. Ron Hubbard, The Rev. Myung Moon, and all the swamis and gurus; but although there is clearly a section of the population which wants to believe something, but is not sure what it is, the vast majority have become more hedonistic than the Ancient Greeks.

The situation appears to be different on the other side of the Atlantic, particularly in California. Perhaps there, the problem lies in the region's proneness to earthquakes although even in the rest of the United States the spiritual climate ressembles 19th or even 18th century Britain in its rampant sprouting of religious growths. The Canadian, Tom Hawthorn, writing from Vancouver, is close enough to observe what is going on without being affected by the strange cults further south along the Pacific coast:

> "Nobody seems to like cults, except cultists. And then they don't like any other cult but their own. This is a shame. I think cults are part of what makes America great. People have spiritual needs, and cult leaders promise to

> fulfill them - for a price. It's unfettered free enterprise. What's good for your average swami is good for the country, I say. My guru, right or wrong.
>
> Try this one out. Imagine yourself to be the doe-eyed eldest son of a wealthy Indian family, who tires of teaching philosophy at universities in India. Years later you find yourself heading a commune in the USA which, at last count, owned 68 Rolls Royces. Every day at 2 p.m. you take a spin down Nirvana Drive in one of the Rollses. The faithful, all clad in sunrise reds and purples, leave your fields, your shopping mall, your casino and your local outlet of the 35- unit Zorba the Buddha restaurant chain to line the road as you go by, all the while singing: 'Bhagwan's our master, we love life's laughter.'
>
> Such is the heart-warming tale of Bhagwan Shree Rajneesh. Mind you, he's no Bhagwan come lately. A decade ago he opened an ashram in India, blending ancient Eastern religions with pop psychology and a healthy dose of free love. Thousands of the rich used to vacation with Bhagwan (literally, Blessed One) until India revoked the ashram's tax-free status. Then it was into the ashcan with the ashram and sayonora to the subcontinent."[1]

For the majority in Europe the opium of the masses has been replaced by new hallucinogens. The Church fought a rearguard action and at various times during the past century or two, held its ground. The short papacy of John XXIII was such an occasion. The gentle and kindly old peasant disarmed a lot of the fear and hostility which the Juggernaut of the Catholic Church aroused, but he died and the retreat continued. The present incumbent, John Paul, is a bigot from Poland, entirely out of sympathy with the easier going tendencies of the times, and is hastening the end.

The Death of Religion.

France was declared '*pays de mission*' a century ago by the Church, but the mission has not got very far. The disappearance of militant anticlerical writers of the style of Anatole France across the Channel, and Pedro Antonio de Alarcon in Spain, with their equivalents in Italy, Germany and the Netherlands, is a measure of how little clericalism there is left to attack.

In Britain, as in Continental Europe, the extent of the decay of religious faith can be seen in the parallel disappearance of the great atheist figures of the past: Chapman Cohen and (ex)Father Joe McCabe thundering away from the editorial chair in The Freethinker; H.G. Wells, Bernard Shaw, Julian Huxley, Bertrand Russell, all sapping and mining the foundations of faith. The arrival of Freddie Ayer back from Vienna with the forces of the Vienna Circle: Rudolph Carnap, Moritz Schlick and the other philosophers of Logical Positivism, like Blucher arriving at Waterloo with the Prussians, ended the battle. Henceforward you could not derive an ought from an is; the meaningfulness of a statement was limited by how you tested it, and if you couldn't test it, it was meaningless; a truth could not be both contingent and necessary, therefore 'God' was either a hypothesis to be tested like any other scientific statement or was a mathematical equation telling us nothing about this or any other world.

The Dying Anti-Religion.

The surviving atheist institutions: the Secular Society, The Humanists and the Rationalist Press Association have little left to do but go round and shoot the wounded. These mainly take the form of hopeful people who have 'intuitions that point to God', or those whose hands are desperately held out to clutch at straws that modern physics are imagined to offer. They are dispatched by intellectual provost marshalls like Nicholas Walter of the Rationalist Press Association (if the presentiments of God are not merely referred pain, masking something like constipation, for example, there must be some experiences capable of rendering them truer or falser. Failing that, all statements about the case, this case being God, are of equal value, including contradictory statements).

But these matters concern only the tiniest fraction of the people, Godbashers and Godpeddlers together, and, it must be said, they have a lot more in common with each other than they have with the population at large. They are united by their concern with the-day-after-tomorrow. Most people live from day to day. The old feasts and fasts, the baptisms and barmitzvahs, the engagements and weddings, the religious Christmas and the observance of Yom Kippur, are fast disappearing. All that is left is a few mumbled words to comfort the living before the race to the crematorium; a sort of 'Eloi, Eloi, Lama Sabachthani!' when confronted with the corpse.

The New Opiates Of The Masses.

For the rest, television turns every living room into a chapel. Several decades ago Hollywood provided the opium of the masses. The hushed congregations in the Egyptian temples of the film distributors sat looking through the smoke haze at the flickering altars while the priests and priestesses - Clark Gable, Errol Flynn, Bette Davis and Betty Grable - of the most banal cult in human history, performed their rites.

Earlier still, the subversive, socially aware, anarchic world of silent pictures, the world of Chaplin, Keaton, W.C. Fields, had given way to the money-bags, to people who really did know the price of everything and the value of nothing; people of truly awesome vulgarity, full of pettifogging business tricks. Order was brought into the industry. Policemen and immigration officials, or any other officials were no longer figures of menace or ridicule. They were to be looked up to. The baddies were the little men who broke ranks, raised doubts about the status quo:

> "As for films, the curve of its development has rapidly ascended, only to sink into an immediate decline.Stuffed to bursting, tricked out with an absurd and meretricious pomp, with every kind of frill imaginable, it has hypertrophied into a monstrous industry. The attraction was merely potential, the magic contained the seeds of an unpardonable decay until, with the abruptness of a volcanic eruption, the huge shambles collapsed beneath the weight of its own emptiness."[2]

The dream factories of California turned thousands of fine writers, directors, actors and musicians into whores, so that after half a century or more of production that swamped the world with their cheap products, all is forgotten, as memorable as yesterday's newspaper.

> "Hollywood, the great industrial centre of world cinema, had for more than five decades accommodated its geniuses, if only by attempting to remove half their brains. It even brought them over from Europe in boatloads. But it would now deliberately avoid any such talents. It's the moderate they actually want, not the brilliant. That is far too dangerous these days when the fast buck is imperative."3

All that is left are a few clips that escaped the producer's scissors, and the one work of incontestable genius that Hollywood sponsored by mistake and then screamed that it had been robbed, that it had been unwittingly nursing the viper, Orson Welles, in its bosom, that the ungrateful boy had libelled one of its noblest citizens, the yellow press baron Randolph Hearst, with his film Citizen Kane. Fortunately for Hollywood the film was a commercial failure.

The Bad Drives Out The Good.

Meanwhile the world wide success of 'Getting Gertie's Garter' and other masterpieces was a vindication of David Ricardo's Law of Comparative Advantage for the American film capital. Students of Economics will know that this law states that if we have world free trade and every country produces and sells what it does best, we shall all be richer and happier. The long production runs, the huge home market, the vulnerable English-speaking markets abroad who could be undercut to little more than the price of the celluloid, contributed to the bad driving out the good, and the worse driving out the bad.

Behind the Linguistic Barriers.

Non English-speaking cultures had a better time of it. In the shadow of the Stalin dictatorship, Eisenstein did what he could not do in Hollywood. From the great innovations of the 1920's he moved on to *Alexander Nevsky* and *Ivan the Terrible*. Dmitri Donskoi turned out his trilogy on the life of Gorky. In Germany the actors and directors of the UFA studios, and the people who had made The Blue Angel, and Emil Jannings, Marlene Dietrich and Fritz Lang fled from Hitler to the United States, where they disappeared down the drain of Hollywood.

France fared better. Even under the German occupation Marcel Carne produced the sumptuous *Les Enfants du Paradis* against all the principles of the Market. Every actor and actress in Paris was put on the books to help them avoid forced labour in Germany. To say that the result was not economic is like saying that the life of Shakespeare was not cost-effective.

After the war the French cinema took up the thread again at the level of pre-war masterpieces: *La Kermesse Heroique*, the Pagnol trilogy and *Le Jour Se Leve*. They now faced new challenges, among others, the Italian cinema with directors like De Sica and Rosselini. The Japanese appeared on the scene and awed everybody by the sophistication and stoicism, the realism and nihilism of *Rashomon* and the *Seven Samurai.* A one man industry in the person of Luis Bunuel, exiled from his native Spain and moving from Mexico to Argentina and back to France, continued his disturbing parables, *Los Olvidados*, *Viridiana*, *The Discreet Charm of the Bourgeoisie*. Less obvious producers demonstrated their cultural vitality; Sweden, with the films of Ingmar Bergman: Yugoslavia awoke to find the anarchic Makaveyev in the bed and screamed 'Rape!' The director was trying to make a point with his '*Wilhelm Reich and the Function of the Orgasm*' but few people could make out what it was. And Australia, the last place on the planet to claim aesthetic sensitivity, moved centre stage with not one but a series of films of such ambiguity and tentativeness that they stunned the critics.

Back To Banality.

Meanwhile, back at the ranch, television was offering Hollywood a chance to go even further downmarket with a degree of triteness that eclipsed the cinema. American television, arguably the worst in the world, still relies on Hollywood's products for a lot of its time filling, but Europe and the rest of the world make their own contributions to producing the syrupy sentiment, shallow emotionalism, and skin-deep grief that characterise the medium.

The homogenising of experience has shocked people coming in from harsher cultural climates, like Solzhenitsyn. Two more refugees from the Soviet bloc: Peter Vail and Alexander Genis who 'escaped' from Latvia in 1977 and now edit a weekly paper, The New American, expressed their anguish and disappointment in the Washington Post:

> "The American dream seems to have no room for the intellectual side of life. There is prosperity, freedom, and justice (sic.). The Founding Fathers believed that a person possessing these virtues would automatically become an intellectual who would read Horace in the original.
>
> They were wrong. America has no time for Horace. The average American family watches television eight hours a day. Eight! One third of the time is spent sleeping, one third working, and one third watching T.V. Television no longer competes with other forms of recreation. It has replaced them."[4]

Some thousands of Jews who had got out of Russia in the late 1970's were subsequently reported to be congregating in Vienna and Amsterdam where they were trying to get back into the Soviet system, expressing the same shock and disgust at the lack of seriousness in the West.

> "About 20 Soviet Jewish families, critical of the quality of Israel T.V., have purchased small rooftop satellite dishes that pick up Soviet T.V. in the southern town of Beersheba, the Ma'ariv newspaper reported yesterday.[5]"

British radio and television have a reputation for being among the best in the world. This is more cause for gloom than rejoicing. Most criticisms of BBC and ITV will apply *a fortiori* to other systems. British governments are continually trying, and often succeeding, to manipulate the news and current affairs material. But many foreign governments control radio and TV directly, and not only in 'Communist' countries.

Ministries Of Propaganda.

When people know this they can, and do, make allowances for bias. Their guard is up and they approach TV material with appropriate scepticism. Nobody expects objectivity from French state controlled TV or from the Soviet bloc, for example. This makes the apparent independence of TV in the United States and Britain doubly dangerous. News and comment have all the appearance of objectivity which increasing numbers of investigators are demonstrating to be fraudulent. In the United States critics like Robert Cirino[6] and Ralph Nader have catalogued lies of omission and commission in radio and TV, but it is like trying to measure the flow over Niagara with a bucket. Thought control in the West depends not on overt censorship but by swamping the public with the official view.

After all, unlike Russia, everybody is free to start a newspaper or buy a licence to run a TV station. This is not new. As Anatole France said:

> "The Law in its majesty forbids both millionaires and beggars to sleep under bridges, beg in the streets and steal bread."

Manufacturing Public Opinion.

Tendentiousness and lying in the newspapers and on ITV will not surprise. Only very rich people can own them so we should not be surprised to find that the view of rich people is expressed almost exclusively. But what of the BBC? A former Controller for the Corporation, Stuart Hood, has blown the gaff on how:

> "...the right bias is maintained in its staff. They use a series of filters - application forms, referees, school and university record, a civil-service-style appointment board, probationary periods, annual reports and interviews, sanctions such as witholding increments in pay, in-house training and security checks. Oxbridge 'high-flyers' are put on the fast route to the top. Those impatient of restraint are weeded out. They want organisation men. Few women make it."[7]

A former BBC producer for ten years, Chris Johnson, expressed his disillusionment in The New Internationalist magazine:

> "My career started in the North of England. I was told that listeners had had too much of depressing subjects like unemployment. We mustn't put off potential industrialists with too much gloom. Tell them about our glorious countryside. Find a blacksmith still shoeing horses, perhaps. Get in a couple of weeks walking the hills on the Corporation. We called it 'the last mole-catcher in Wensleydale' syndrome. The gentlest form of censorship. You hardly felt it had happened."[8]

Outside the Organisation, public watchdogs like Richard Hoggart, E.P. Thompson and Tam Dalyell have constantly monitored how the Government has tried to and succeeded in manipulating the medium. The Falklands War provided outrageous examples which recalled the Suez affair and the technique of Dr Goebbels. In the 17th century a war took place with the Spaniards over a Captain Jenkin's Ear. But history books will in future have to incorporate a war which was organised to win the 1983 election for Mrs. Thatcher!

The old adage for governments: 'Trouble at home, start a foreign adventure', was one thing. This was complete with televisually primed crowds to cheer the victors home in the passenger line QE2; they carefully avoided having cameras on the quayside to film the arrival of the corpses of several hundred soldiers who had paid to win the election with their lives.[9]

And how was it achieved? The investigators hooked out Brigadier Ronnie Stoneham skulking in Room 105 Broadcasting House. He was the censor, and nobody was supposed to know! Was there a censor over at ITV? Either that or they prostituted themselves voluntarily. Fortunately, Greg Philo and the Glasgow University Media Group, with their two books 'Bad News' and 'More Bad News' have recorded the lies hidden under the cloak of 'supporting our boys'. Patriotism is indeed, the last refuge of a scoundrel.

> "The Ministry of Defence has taken steps to suppress evidence of a secret agreement between the Government and the BBC on dealing with news in times of national crisis. Officials have asked for references to the agreement to be deleted from a study on the MoD's handling of the media during the Falklands War which is due to be published shortly.
>
> One of the authors of the study, Derrik Mercer, former editor of 'Channel Four News', has been shown an internal MoD memo written in April 1984 and marked 'Restricted'.
>
> It revealed that there are 'formal understandings with the BBC Board that in times of crisis it would act responsibly and consult fully with the Government.'
>
> The implication is that the BBC would co-operate with the Government in the way it handles news, not just in times of nuclear war, but also during periods of tension, perhaps leading up to war. The BBC has always maintained that it is independent from the Government and this is the first time the existence of such an agreement has been revealed.
>
> The Ministry is now insisting that reference to this agreement must be deleted from the 250,000 word draft report which was submitted to the MoD in July 1985.
>
> A BBC spokeswoman said she was unaware of these for-

mal understandings but thought they might refer to clause 19 of the BBC's licensing agreement, which says that when an emergency arises the Government has the right to take over both radio and television broadcasting stations."[10]

1984 Was A Long Time Ago.

The regimentation of society proceeds relentlessly in the East because it is part of the ethos, it is seen as not only necessary but a good thing. In the West, it is seen as not good but necessary. Either way we move to numbers, our liberties are encroached upon increasingly. One needs documents. One is required to fill in forms; failure to do so, or to do so correctly, can result in punishment. One is required to remember the postal number or code, the National Health number, Army number, telephone number, car registration number, passport number - the list is almost endless.

With the development of electronic recording, bureaucratic ambitions have grown. The prospect of every citizen's curriculum vitae from cradle to grave being held on a central computer grows closer every day. Big Brother or Big Sister and their acolytes will only have to press a button and the print-out will tell them more about us than we know ourselves.

The Policeman's Balls.

Authority, on the other hand, grows ever more secretive. It is a crime in many cases, simply to know what is going on. To communicate it earns a long term jail sentence. To do anything about it invites harassment from the uniformed police and the several secret police forces, and behind the police stand the Army, Navy and Air Force.

> "The Law should be used as just another weapon in the Government's arsenal, and in this case it becomes little more than a propaganda cover for the disposal of unwanted members of the public. For this to happen efficiently, the activities of the legal service have to be tied into the war effort in as discreet a way as possible," wrote Brigadier Kitson.[11]

Similar sentiments were expressed some years ago by the founder of the S.A.S., Colonel David Stirling. His plans for a private strike-breaking army GB75 were unexceptional. His mistake was to talk about it and he was drummed out of the Brownies for blowing the gaff. But if anyone believed that such attitudes were limited to Right Wing loonies like Stirling and Kitson they were disabused by the way the police and the legal process were manipulated during the Miners' Strike of 1984/5. And the marvellous opportunity for the Miners' president, Arthur Scargill, to twit the Government with using the tactics of the Russian puppet, General Jaruzelski, in Poland had to be foregone. Scargill did not object to Jaruzelski doing to the Polish miners what Thatcher was doing to his members.

None of the Parties is clean. All of the leaders are in a position to reply *tu quoque* to all charges of doubtful conduct, and regularly do so. Meanwhile those organs which should be informing us just what is going on - the Press, Radio and Television, crowd the scene with trivia; soft porn, Royal soap opera, entertainment which is 99% hype and 1% product (like many other commodities) and mindless hours of space fillers. When they deign to deal with the world that threatens us all, it is with tendentiousness when not with downright lying. The Press is in the hands of half a dozen millionaires ranging from convicted swindlers to people simply without scruples. A Press Council sits to monitor their villanies but this is simply ignored or its findings reported in small print on page 17. Radio and Television are monitored by concerned groups, notable among them the Glasgow University researchers. One might feel that Commercial Television would be more subject to control by lobbies, big business, and similar rascals to those who control the Press. But this has not turned out to be the case. Current Affairs and News on Commercial T.V. is of a far superior order of objectivity and investigation than the BBC which is under tremendous government pressure behind the scenes.

> "It is a reflection on the workings of the club (i.e. the Establishment) and the way its rules can be flouted on occasion that when, as Director General, Trethowan felt that the BBC was threatened by a Labour White Paper to the contents of which he was privy, he 'saw a number of friends in Fleet Street' before it was published, thus ensuring that it was met by a 'barrage of hostility'. People outside the club who do that sort of thing are likely to run into trouble".[12]

The Oligarchy Calls The Shots.

It goes without saying that for 'Labour White Paper' one can substitute 'Tory White Paper' or 'Liberal White Paper' or even 'Communist White Paper'. The 'Club' can be seen as a number of Euler's circles, i.e. various groups with a common area of overlap: a few tens of thousands of people, mainly in the South East, who, through money and influence, control the country regardless of the Party in power (any strong challengers are simply co-opted, sent to the House of Lords etc.),the Private School system, and Oxbridge. Most of the great national universities on the Continent have a roll of honour for achievements in science and art by their graduates. Cambridge made a late start with Newton and Darwin after mathematics had been introduced to the curriculum. Oxford seems to have produced no-one whose name might be recognised by a foreigner, after seven centuries with an almost total monopoly of higher education in England. The limp-wrist syndrome and disapproval of anyone showing concern about ideas, suffices for the 'club'. As the French journalist Rene D'Abernat has written:

> "What is remarkable is that the men responsible for the discoveries of the Industrial Revolution seem all to have been autodidacts and owed nothing to the great centres of learning, in contrast with Europe where the great names are located in the Universities."[13]

Or from Harold Goad, himself a Harrow and Oxford historian:

> "Take the hundred or so best known names in any Italian anthology of verse or prose, and the most cursory examination of their biographies will show that the vast majority were men of good family, educated in the classical church schools, seminaries, and universities, sheltered in life as regards their actual means of living, with leisure to polish and revise their works. Here is no Shakespeare from the village school, tramping to town to join a troup of actors and consorting with Kit Marlowe, the cobbler's son, Thomas Kyd, the scrivener, and Ben Johnson, the bricklayer; here is no Defoe, a butcher's child, or Gay, a mercer's apprentice; no Bunyan, a village cobbler; no Chatterton, a sexton's son, starving in a garret, no Keats from the livery stable and the country surgery; no Burns

> from the plough; no Ettrick shepherd; no James Thomson, a sailor's orphan,; no Dickens from the blacking factory; no Blake, Clare or Crabbe. The roll of English literature is filled with the names of men who, but for their literary fame, could never have set foot in good society."[14]

In the face of the overwhelming *trahison des clercs* it is a wonder that the truth has ever got out. Thanks to the mavericks, the good men and true, who refused to parrot the conventional wisdom, we can discover what has been going on since the Tudors took over. Behind the pantomime of kings and queens, of prime ministers and lord high admirals, of the psychopaths and buffoons who have been set in power over us, we can still trace the activities of the 99% of the people who never asked more than to be allowed to live and raise their kids in a modest sufficiency. Thanks to men like William Langland, John Ball, Thomas More, William Cobbett, Thorold Rogers - the roll-call is not very long but is increasing exponentially - we know where to look, and what to look for, in our search for what has gone wrong. And if it is pointed out that the whistle blowers are almost all out of the top drawer, the rest of us who have spent all our energies in the struggle to keep eating regularly can only say with Ecclesiasticus:

> "The wisdom of a learned man cometh by opportunity of leisure and he that hath little business shall become wise".[15]

New Opiates.

So much for news coverage, but what about entertainment? Those hours of panel games and quiz shows, soap opera, both royal and commoner? Television demonstrates more than any other producer of commodities, that Market criteria ensures that the worst wins. The costs of operating are so high that the widest audience must be found, and if it means getting down to the level of cretins (and it does) then so be it. Christopher Booker in the Daily Telegraph expressed the chagrin of all civilised people at the way television processes everything down to a uniform level of triteness:

> "Not only do millions of viewers now spend a great deal of their lives hooked into a dream-like stream of flickering images which ultimately have no more serious purpose than to entertain. The real catastrophe of television

> is the way it has sucked more and more of the real world into itself, so that everything in the end - from politics to education, from wars to hi-jackings, from terrorist atrocities to funerals - becomes part of one long, trivialised, sentimentalised stream of entertainment."[16]

And Professor Neil Postman of New York University draws parallels between what he sees as a cultural cataclysm which has fallen on the United States in the past thirty years through television, and the nightmare world of Aldous Huxley's 'Brave New World'. TV, he believes, is the soma of the novel; the drug by which everybody was kept in a state of zombie-like, if not happy, compliance. Quite clearly, it is not a thing that governments are going to complain about.[17]

Meanwhile a generation of children is growing up which cannot spell, punctuate, or in some cases, even read and write. The situation is not quite as bad here as reported in the United States where as much as a third of the adult population is claimed to be functionally illiterate, but it cannot give comfort to any government. Many adults here, on the other hand, cannot distinguish between the real world and the characters in soap opera, so that they send flowers to the studio when one of them dies, and a ward of Guy's hospital, London was filled with would-be suicides in imitation of one portrayed on TV.

> "The bleak scenario is that a cultural Gresham's Law will apply, whatever structure emerges in broadcasting television and new means of paying for it; that bad TV will drive out good TV, that all television will ape the pop promo, that style will finally triumph over content."

Struggles of the Theatre.

First the cinema, and now, finally, television has turned the theatre into a minor art form. The medium of Shakespeare and Chekhov, of Moliere and Miller has been shunted into a side turning. The professional theatre never existed much outside the capital cities; earlier societies enjoyed seeing live shows in their towns and villages but all that ceased with the development of the megapolis. The centripetal forces that grew along with the great cities sucked the cultural energy from the smaller populations. The clowning, the Miracle Plays, of the Middle Ages, the drama of ancient Greece, were proof that a gigantic population is not necessary to sustain live theatre; ancient Athens would rate as a very modest town today. The decay of villages, the loss of schools, the pub, the post office, are merely a continuation of the process. The trip up from commuterland to see a show, to the 'theatre of reassurance', is all that remains for many.

The theatre has had to adjust to this. After all, it's getting bums on seats that matters. That and the baneful influence of cinema and TV goes a long way to explain the difficulties of serious theatre, the sort of serious theatre the educated middle class of London enjoyed before the First World War. They were hopelessly spoiled: Shaw, Oscar Wilde, Ibsen, Chekhov, Strindberg. Even during the '20's and '30's, O'Casey and O'Neill found a place among the growing tide of drawing room pieces with their ever-opening and closing doors. And in the '50's the kitchen sink school of playwrights Osborne, Wesker, Delaney, offered an alternative to the RahDah accented drawing room comedies of Coward and Rattigan. They were followed by realist playwrights from the North, the West Indies, and the working class South East, to broaden still further the range of accents one could hear on the stage. A far cry from the theatre and cinema of pre-war and the forties when it would have been almost impossible to find an actor able to play a truck driver or bricklayer convincingly. When such characters could not be avoided they were introduced as tramp comics, Eliza Dolittles of both sexes, who came on and hopped and skipped about and made people laugh. The new drama featured them as people having the same pain and the same pleasures as the middle class.

Crisis in the Arts.

Meanwhile, unemployment among actors and musicians is higher than in any other occupation. Symphony orchestra musicians keep eating regularly by ghosting on record sessions. They frequently find themselves double-booked and so a conductor often has to conduct a concert with a lot of musicians in front of him who were not there at rehearsals. Jazz musicians similarly earn the bare necessities through backing pop-musicians in the latters' brief moments of glory.

Is there too much music for our distraction? Not exactly. Too much muzac, too much hyped-up rubbish coming from electronic machines. Are there too many plays? Well, no. But the overheads seem to have got out of control. Even if the actors were paid nothing at all, a lot of productions would still be uneconomic. Perhaps the theatres are standing on sites where banks would be more cost effective. Among other things, theatres have to pay VAT, banks don't.

As for graphic and plastic art, there is probably no other age in human history which found such little use for painting and sculpture than this one. Never have buildings and public places had so little decoration. But never have rich people paid so much money for works of art, not to brighten, beautify, or provide focus for our surroundings, but to place in a gallery somewhere far away for special people; experts, aesthetes, critics, to consider and report to us. But they have their problems. Up to half of the great works of art in the world's museums and galleries are forgeries. The great counterfeiters: Van Meegeren, de Hory, Tom Keating, Dossena, and hundreds of others have flooded the art world with copies and original works that cannot be told apart from the real thing by the experts themselves. This is embarrassing for two lots of people. One is the art experts who have never detected forgeries in the past until the forger, usually out of vanity, explains which is his own work and which the genuine.

It is also embarassing for the economists. Text books of economics explain to the students that a good is anything that satisfies a human need, and a commodity is a good that is produced for sale or reward. In addition to being limited in supply, otherwise people would not need to pay for it, the commodity must be reproducible. Now a work of art is unique, one of a kind, therefore it cannot be reproducible. But the forgers have been reproducing them for as long as artists have been creating. And never as much as the present where continuing inflation is producing enormous quantities of money in the coffers of the rich which is seeking boltholes: Ming vases, antique maps, books to be stored not read, antique furniture, sculpture, paintings. All of these and more are fair game for the forger. Means of detection are being up-dated all the time, but free-enterprise being what it is, our counterfeiter is always several jumps ahead. You want a Leonardo, a MichelAngelo? I can get it for you wholesale.

This is important to our argument. Production for need and not for the Market implies an ability to meet that need. These lovely little people with their fake Rouaults and Rodins, their Hokusais and their Hockneys are the artillery we can use to knock down the Chinese Walls of capitalism.

1. *New Internationalist : April 1985.*

2. *Benjamin Fontaine quoted by Derek Malcolm, Guardian, 1/12/86.*

3. Derek Malcolm : Guardian, 1/12/86

4. Reprinted in the Guardian, 31/06/86.

5. Reuter 13/03/86.

6. Robert Cirino : Don't Blame the People (Univ. Press Los Angeles)

7. Stuart Hood : Review of Split Screen by Ian Trethowan.

8. New Internationalist, April 1985.

9. "The BBC's assistant director general, Alan Protheroe has refused to allow confidential minutes of news and current affairs executive meetings, held during the Falklands conflict to be used in the programme, called War and Peace News.
The programme makers, the Glasgow Media Group, claim that the minutes, which were leaked by a 'mole' in the corporation, demonstrate that the coverage of the war was shaped to support government policy ...
The relevant minutes refer to meetings held between April and June 1982 and they demonstrate:

A. The BBC banned interviews with bereaved relatives.

B. Reporting was shaped to suit the 'emotional sensibilities' of the public.

C. Sticking to the BBC's normal detached reporting style was felt to be "an unnecessary irritation".

D. The weight of BBC coverage was concerned with government statements of policy.

One of them, dated June 1, 1982, quotes Protheroe citing a 'firm ruling' from the board of governors that there should be no interviews with the relatives of men killed in the war 'under any circumstances'." Sunday Times : 22/09/85.

10. Observer : 18/05/86.

11. Brigadier Kitson : Low Intensity Operations.

12. Stuart Hood : ibid.

13. Rene d'Abernat : Messieurs les Anglais.

14. Harold Goad : Language in History (Penguin).

15. Apocrypha, Ecclesiasticus, XXXVIII 24.

16. Daily Telegraph 17/3/86.

17. Neil Postman : Amusing Ourselves to Death (Methuen 1987).

Chapter 9.

Medicine.

The Disease Industry.

The National Health Service is, after the Red Army, the biggest employer in Europe, and is responsible for almost all orthodox medical treatment in Britain. There are over one million people who look to it to provide paid employment: doctors, nurses, dentists, opthalmologists, ambulance men, administrators etc. Many, nurses in particular, are very badly paid. There was a canard in circulation some years ago that nurses were obliged to ghost as prostitutes in order to make ends meet. Either way, they were abused as are most people in the Market economy who allow a social conscience to influence their career.

Established doctors are better off, but all have suffered a big fall in income in the last half century. The newly qualified ones are forced to survive on salaries which a street sweeper would reject. Press and television reports disclose that some unscrupulous dentists are making fortunes by drilling lots of holes in perfectly healthy teeth and filling them, but should one expect otherwise when they are paid, like factory workers, on a piece-work basis?

Manufacturing Disease.

The whole medical profession finds itself under pressure from several directions. Like so many Dutch boys with their fingers plugging leaks in the dike, new holes, new diseases are being created by the system all the time. Like the teaching profession, medicine is being asked to deal with problems that are economic and political in origin and to which it frequently has no answer. The smoking habit is filling hospital beds with men and, increasingly, women, dying from lung cancer. Many experts argue that tobacco is as addictive as heroin but the Government cannot move against the tobacco industry because the taxes on the product raise so much money, and no acceptable alternative sources of revenue exist. The asbestos industry, now almost closed down, is adding to the burden with its crop of lung cancer cases sown decades ago; the employers knew very well it would happen, but chose not to act. Likewise the coal industry with its contribution of emphysema, bronchitis and silicosis victims.

The nuclear industry, both military and civil, is adding its quotient of cancers. After three decades of official lying and prevarication officialdom has finally admitted responsibilty for the cancers produced by atom tests in Australia in the nineteen fifties, and for leukemia in children caused by emissions from Sellafield and Dounreay in the late nineteen eighties The lead, cadmium, mercury and nitrates in our water, soil and air are contributing their bit to sickness now and in the future.

The Disease Industry lives in symbiotic relationship with these and all the other externalities of the Market economy. If our world were, however inconceivably, cleaned up, then nine tenths of those given employment would need to find something else to do. Let me concentrate on one part of the body; it can be read as a paradigm for the rest.

If a tax of, say, £10 a pound were placed on sugar, most of the 17,000 dentists together with at least as many technicians, manufacturers and salesmen, would rapidly work themselves out of a job. Dental decay would simply disappear as a disease. This has been known for more than a century. The implication of heavy sugar consumption in heart and other diseases is also strongly suspected.

Dental caries is unknown among primitive peoples. It was unknown among our ancestors until defective diets were adopted. An American dentist, Weston A. Price, dissatisfied with what he was doing, gave up dental practice in the 1930's and travelled the world, examining and photographing the dentition of primitive peoples from the Arctic to the Tropics. He also investigated the teeth of people who had been exposed to 'civilised' foods and compared them with those of people of the same group who had not been so influenced.

The book he published[1] records a masterpiece of scientific research. With it he demonstrates overwhelmingly by means of samples and controls that dental caries is a man-made disease, is preventable, and that the whole science of dentistry is an irrelevance at best and a dangerous meddling at worst. Recent research reveals a modest capacity for decayed teeth to regenerate.

The implications of Weston Price's work also disturb much of our smug and complacent world far away from dentistry. His attention to the degeneration of the dental arch, leading to the bird, or rodent shaped mouth so common among civilised peoples throws our racial stereotypes: 'grinning picanninies', 'grinning natives', back in our faces. Birds can't grin.

When the 'canine eminences' occupy their proper place the mouth is squared off, so to speak. We see the twelve upper and lower incisors on their almost flat plane; posterior teeth are nearly hidden behind the canines. The result is a grin that is a real grin, something that many of us are incapable of producing.

Another syndrome, one which affects the poor more than the rich, is mouth breathing. Whether this is caused by the collapse of the dental arch, from tooth extractions or mere degeneration, or by overcrowded housing, the consequence is what dentists call a Class III maloclusion, or jutting lower jaw. It is maintained by some that the tendency of evolution is the other way, that is, towards the Class I or 'chinless wonder' profile. This was the term used a decade or two ago to characterise the idle rich, showing that even class differences show up in dentition. I recall seeing Italian Communist Party posters showing the two profiles perfectly as 'us' and 'them' - a gorilla and a fop.

This reverses the condition of rich and poor historically as far as teeth go. The rich were able to afford junk food as soon as it appeared, when it was still costly ; white bread, sugar, tea, coffee, confectionery. Queen Elizabeth I had lost all of her teeth before she was thirty: the skeleton of King Gustavus Vasa in Uppsala Cathedral, Sweden, who died in 1560 aged 64 shows terrible mouth condition. "The diet of the well-to-do included a preponderance of sugary cakes and marzipan sweetmeats; and even meat pies would be topped with a mixture that included a mess of sugar and rosewater."[2]

Sugar Addiction.

Why does the government not move to curb the consumption of sugar which causes such suffering and disfigurement to the victims and such enormous expense too the State?

> "The multi-million pound British sugar industry has been condemned by the British Dental Association and the Health Education Council for allegedly publishing 'grossly misleading material' in a campaign which is turning into a far from sweet battle for the stomachs and teeth of the nation.
>
> The Sugar Bureau is claiming in leaflets and videos issued this month, which are aimed particularly at school-children, that people are just as likely to get rotten teeth from bread, savoury snacks and cream crackers as from sticky sweets and sugar in tea. The key to improving teeth standards, it says, is better oral hygiene.
>
> That claim is fiercely contested in a counter campaign by the dentists' association which has spent more than 15 years arguing that sugar is the prime cause of decay. The dentists fear that their years of work could be seriously undermined. This week the association will urge all district dental officers to visit schools to warn children about the dangers of a sweet tooth.
>
> And a spokesman for the Health Education Council said: "We have formally written to the Sugar Bureau asking them to withdraw the material which we regard as grossly misleading and educationally unsound."

The British have the sweetest tooth in the world and there is much at stake with the industry worth about £800m a year, just £100m more than the health service spends annually on dental services.

Tom Dowell of the dentists' association dismissed the Bureau's campaign on minimising dental decay as a 'load of rubbish', adding that the overwhelming body of evidence drew a direct link between amounts of sugar consumed and the incidence of tooth decay.

But the bureau is determined to redress what it sees as a biased attitude towards sugar. It spent more than a year culling research data from around the world to support its argument. Its spokesman, Graham Somerville, said:

> "Our message to the public is that sugar is a good food and can be used sensibly in a balanced diet." He said that they were trying to stress that not one of the 57 factors that cause tooth decay should be picked out as the sole 'villain of the piece.' Sugar caused tooth decay, he said, but only when it came into contact with bacteria already in the mouth. Decay could equally be caused by starch in carbohydrate foods such as bread.
> 'Sugar has been picked upon as the cause of a number of health problems, I think, because we like it and enjoy the taste. It's become something of a popular whipping boy.'

Dr John Brown of the Health Education Council, however, argues that far from adding to the debate the Sugar Bureau evidence will merely complicate it by causing people to believe there is confusion rather than widespread agreement about the role of sugar in causing tooth decay."[3]

Governments are only too ready to be deceived. The sugar industry is a massive contributor to the funds of the Conservative Party, and Labour, when in power, refuses to move against an industry which provides work for thousands of its supporters. Dentists are not such a big or generous constituency.

Start Them Young.

Consumers are locked into the heavy use of this maleficent product. Baked beans, canned soups, breakfast cereals, ketchup, soft drinks, chocolates, sweets; the whole junk- food sector depends heavily upon sugar to make its products palatable. And to make sure that the addiction is a heavy one the industry likes to start them young:

"The manufacturers of rusks and drinks, mindful of the increasing awareness about health and nutrition among mothers, have been fiddling with their recipes and re- writing the information that accompanies their products.

"Farley's 'Original' Rusk used to contain 38% sugar (sucrose), which is sweeter than treacle tart. About 2 years ago, the sugar content was reduced to 31%, equivalent to a custard cream biscuit or a sponge cake, and the company also launched a new 'low sugar' rusk. Secure in the knowledge that they are being cared for by these well-meaning manufacturers, parents watch as their babies suck and teeth on rusks mashed in milk.

"After all, the Osterusk packet says 'less sugar, so less chance of your baby developing a sweet tooth. No added salt, less strain on baby's developing kidneys'. Or : 'The first spoonful: every mother wants her baby's first solid food to be safe gently and nourishing. This is why Farley's Low Sugar Rusks are an ideal food for your baby. The first crunch: Farley's Low Sugar Rusks dissolve quickly in the mouth so you can be sure they are completely safe.'

"But what does 'low sugar' mean? The Liga 'Low Sugar' Rusk claims 'the lowest sugar rusks you can buy - only 12.5% sugar (sucrose)', at the top of its nutrition information panel for knowledgeable mums. It's an improvement on the Farley's Original at 31%. But the ingredients list includes: glucose syrup (5% glucose) and sugar (12.5% sucrose).

"Glucose is also a sugar. Together with fructose it makes up the sucrose molecule. So the total quantity of sucrose and glucose in these Liga rusks is not 12.5% but 17.5%, which begins to sound less good. It is sweeter than a doughnut.

"Mr. John Wells, senior nutritionist at Cow & Gate, came up with some unimpressive high-tech jargon about glucose syrup being a 'hydrolysate of starch, a mixture which can't be classified as sugar' and pronounced that 'total sugars isn't a reliable index of cariogenicity', meaning that glucose doesn't make holes in teeth at exactly the same rate as sucrose. 'Anyway', he said with some satisfaction, 'sugar is legally sucrose, according to the Food Labelling Regulations 1984, page 37', so 'low sugar' labels are legal.

"The Ministry of Agriculture, Fisheries and Food agreed, and pointed to another bit of the regulations which say that if a manufacturer labels a food as low in any ingredient, provided he tells you the quantity involved, a 'low sugar' announcement is legal. In other words, the manufacturer sets his own level and boasts accordingly.

"Neither Mr. Wells nor the ministry mentioned that the 1984 Food Act Part 1, Section 6, says that if a manufacturer sells a food with a label 'which is calculated to mislead as to its nature, or its substance, or its quality', he is guilty of an offence. And Section 6 specifically includes nutritional or dietary value. So wake up trading standards officers and bite into a 'low sugar' rusk. In my view these labels are likely to mislead, and are therefore illegal."[4]

The effect of all the rotten teeth which result from sugar consumption is to create new industries and new problems. The toothpaste industry is enormously profitable and equally unproductive. You can no more protect your teeth from caries by brushing them with a paste of chalk, gum and flavouring, than you can keep meningitis at bay by washing your head regularly. This is not an argument against brushing your teeth. But it should be seen for what it is: a cosmetic activity, and no less pleasant for being so. One of the little bits of good news about the development of the modern world is the huge reduction in human stink. Queen Elizabeth I was regarded as a cleanliness freak because she insisted upon taking a bath at least once every three months.

Mercury Poisoning?

A more potentially frightening matter arises from efforts to deal with teeth after they have gone rotten. For nearly two centuries dentists have been drilling out cavities and filling them up with an amalgam, which is a mixture of metals, principally silver and mercury. Now mercury is one of the most poisonous materials known to man. When a very dilute form of the salts of mercury was allowed by a factory in Japan to discharge into the Bay of Minimata, thousands of people where either killed or horribly maimed. Similar disasters have occurred with mercury in Iraq, Guatemala, Ghana and the U.S.A. The expression : 'Mad as a hatter' arose through the effect of mercury on people who used it in the hat-making industry in 18th century England.

A debate raged through the last century between those who argued that the use of mercury amalgam in the mouth was dangerous and those who were in favour of its use.

> "In the early 1900's more and more dentists were using amalgam, and why not? The material had good long term qualifications, was easy to manipulate and insert, there were no alternatives, and apparently there were no ill- effects. Main-line dentistry forgot the issue and the battle was relegated to lesser arenas where the debate continued to froth."[5]

> "Recent research, however, has caused the debate to revive again and each new finding has increased misgivings about mercury amalgam. Conditions claimed to be caused by it include: "...bleeding gums, increased salivation, sour metallic taste, facial paralysis, irregular heartbeat, depression, strong pains in the left part of the chest, retinal bleeding, dim vision, uncontrollable eye movement, irritability, vertigo, headaches, joint pains, pains in lower back, etc, etc, etc."[6]

How many people with these symptoms will end up consulting and puzzling their doctor? How many maladies are themselves the result of efforts to deal with other maladies - on a piecemeal basis? Ivan Illich, citing medical sources, claims that 50% of illnesses are caused by medical intervention of this kind, iatrogenic disease, he calls it, i.e. illness caused by doctors. His book: 'Limits to Medicine, Medical Nemesis: The Expropriation of Health',[7] is a polemic against the entire practice of medicine. He is only one of many critics ranging right across the spectrum from Chicago School economists like Milton Friedman to people like Rene Dubos, who like Illich belongs to the 'alternative' camp and raises the fundamental issue of production for need and not for sale.

Illich appears to be urging the acceptance of pain and death with resignation, and argues that earlier societies did so. "Patience, forbearance, courage, resignation, self-control, perseverance, and meekness, each express a diffent colouring of the responses with which pain sensations were accepted."[7]

Now I don't believe that people in the past who had a stomach ache or found themselves sitting on a nail would be any more inclined to take up those attitudes than they are today. They would then and they will now, look for a remedy or jump up from where they are sitting.

Likewise, the acceptance of death, however inevitable. We join with Dylan Thomas and 'rage, rage, against the dying of the light', in the same way that Ovid's old man - *senex avidus vitae* - clung to life 2000 years ago.

Treating Symptoms, Not Causes.

But the theme which unites the mass of critics of the profession of medicine, the majority themselves doctors, is the preoccupation with treatment rather than prevention, with symptoms and not causes. The reason according to many is the way doctors are paid. In the 19th century Samuel Butler in his satire Erewhon had described a Utopia where doctors were paid not for how many sick people they had on their books, but how many healthy people. The theme was taken up some decades later by Bernard Shaw in the preface to his play 'The Doctor's Dilemma':"It is useless to tell him (the patient) that what he or his sick child needs is not medicine, but more leisure, better clothes, better food, a better drained and ventilated house. It is kinder to give him a bottle of something almost as cheap as water, and tell him to come again with another eighteen pence if that doesn't cure him."

That despondent piece was written nearly a century ago. The slight difference now is that the social ills have been added to by new fears: radioactive leaks, pollution, stress, the Bomb, the Nuclear Winter, and are affecting the rich as well as the poor, if not in the same measure. Poverty sharpens the pangs of most illnesses, but none of us can die more than once. As for the 'bottle of something almost as cheap as water', it will be over the pharmaceutical industry's dead body.

Fraudulent Claims.

The growth and power of what used to be called the 'manufacturers of patent medicines' during the past forty years has turned most doctors into pill peddlers. Most of the time they do not have the leisure to study the composition of what they dole out[8] - they do not have to pay for it anyway, neither does the patient, directly. Even if they had the time, few are qualified chemists. Instead they have to rely on the manufacturers' publicity material, most of it tendentious, much of it lying to a criminal degree. Headlines such as 'Drug Firm for Trial at Old Bailey' (Roussel/Hoechst) 'Drug Firms Challenged over Illegal Adverts' (Upjohn) appear in the serious newspapers regularly.

> "No doctor is uninfluenced by the slick advertising techniques used by the drug industry, according to Professor Michael Rawlings, of the department of pharmacological science at Newcastle University. In a severe rebuke to both doctors and the pharmaceutical industry, he says techniques adopted by the industry are costly, subtle, and sophisticated. The saddest aspect is the total lack of awareness by doctors of the way in which they are manipulated to prescribe drugs. Professor Rawlings finds the doctors' 'capacity for self-deception quite extraordinary'. He says that, although industry has discovered many life-saving drugs, only about a third of the 20 or so new medecines introduced each year are novel developments with significant advantages over previous remedies. The remainder are 'me toos' with pharmacological properties, therapeutic actions, and adverse effects similar to those already marketed.
>
> Professor Rawlings suggests that most doctors believe they are immune to 'the £180m a year' spent on promotion. General practitioners, who prescribe between 80 and 90% of National Health Service drugs, are singled out. The professor says many companies categorize general practitioners as 'conservatives' or 'risk takers'.
>
> Although it is not allowed under the code of conduct of the Association of the British Pharmaceutical Industry, doctors may be offered hospitality which is devoid of pro-

> motional content: for example, meals at a local restaurant or a day's fishing.
>
> The treatment of consultants is similar to that given to general practitioners, 'only laid on with a trowel'. The reason, according to Professor Rawlings, is not because they prescribe drugs in significant amounts, but because they are opinion formers 'whose endorsement of a product influences its use among local GPs'."[9]

The ruthlessness of the patent medicine industry knows no bounds. Doubtful features of their products are suppressed to the point of criminal irresponsibility. Enormous numbers of children and adults all over the world have been killed or maimed by products like Thalidomide (Distillers), Butazolodin (Ciba-Geigy), Opren (Ely Lilly), Junior Aspirin - the list would fill a telephone directory. Doctor Joe Collier, a clinical pharmacologist at St George's Hospital Medical School in London, said that 11 out of 28 full page advertisements in the British Medical Journal in the issue of 17th November 1984 were in breach of the Medicines Act 1968, i.e. they told lies.

> "The Swiss chemicals combine, Ciba-Geigy, admitted yesterday that it had falsified safety data on 46 antibiotics and other drugs submitted to the Japanese health authorities. The catalogue of faked data, which was uncovered after a tip-off to the Japanese Health and Welfare Ministry, is believed to represent one of the widest admissions of irregularities in drug testing ever made by a pharmaceuticals company. This is not the first time that Ciba-Geigy has been in trouble with the Japanese health authorities. In 1978 the company made payments, without admitting liability, of more than $150 million to Japanese victims of the disease, SMON, which a Tokyo court ruled had been caused by Ciba-Geigy's anti-diarrhoea drug, Clioquinol."[10]

Weight of Advertising.

The drug industry spends 9% of its turnover on promoting its products, which is about three times as much as other industries. The quantity of advertising material sent to doctors is enormous. One practitioner, in an effort to divert the unwanted material, kept returning it marked 'Doctor in Prison', but to no avail. Every device that the advertising industry can think of is used to persuade the doctor to prescribe the product. Lavish and expensive brochures, bogus research and fake scholarly work, bribes of every kind: holidays abroad disguised as conventions or symposia, study groups etc. electrocardiograph machines, 'leather writing cases and clutches of Brazilian amethysts.'

Of course some doctors do not need to be offered bribes by drug companies, they ask for them:

> "Doctors are demanding and often receiving bribes and lavish hospitality from drug companies, the Royal College of Physicians says in a report released yesterday. The President of the College, Sir Raymond Hoffenberg added: 'Doctors should ask themselves, would I be willing to have the gifts, benefits, air-fares, hospitality or subsidies made public knowledge?"[11]

The overwhelming conclusion one can draw from all this is that bad products need a hard sell. A great many patent medicines are either useless or a copy under a fancy name of one for which some benefit could be claimed. And a number are dangerous and possibly lethal. How many is almost impossible to discover. The evidence is buried, in both senses.

> "A leading epidemologist who has carried out extensive work on radiation hazards yesterday criticised the way Whitehall used the Official Secrets Act to put pressure on doctors to keep quiet about issues affecting public health. Professor Geoffrey Rose of the London School of Hygiene and Tropical Medicine, who was a member of the Black enquiry into incidences of leukemia around Sellafield, said that a doctor's first responsibility was to the health of the public.
>
> There could be a conflict of interests between a duty to be open on matters of public health and the possibility of a prosecution under the Official Secrets Act. A doctor's professional responsibilities must not be confused with the priorities of politicians who have different objectives."[12]

And so much for the Hippocratic Oath too, we all say.

The baneful influence of the Market directed sector of the Disease Industry has elicited outraged reactions from surprising sources. The private health insurance company Bupa 'launched a bitter attack on commercial, for-profit, private hospital operators, many of them owned by United States or Arab interests. Without naming names, Mr. Bob Graham chief executive of Bupa, said that the rising cost of medical care, driven up by a desire for a return on investment, was now the biggest threat to the private sector'.[13]

Private hospitals in the U.K. are losing £6 million a year, according to experts quoted by the Daily Telegraph,[14] by pricing themselves out of business. Most of them are American owned and quite clearly used to the profits gained from farming among the sick in the United States, where health care costs the economy double (12% of the GNP) what it costs in Britain despite leaving the American poor without any medical care whatever.

The gamesmanship practised by the drug companies provoked the rage of Margaret Thatcher too. She condemned as 'disgraceful' the pharmaceutical companies' campaign against Government plans to substitute generic drugs for more expensive brand-name medicines.[15] They claimed that their loss of profits would stop progress. They 'launched a £250,000 television campaign to extol the benefits of drug research. The advertisements claim that just as new antibiotics have made tuberculosis hospitals redundant, so yet-to-be-invented anti-cancer drugs could empty the beds in cancer wards.'

> "The industry blames its ills on the Thatcher Government, its main customer. The government is seeking ways to curb the cost of drugs prescribed under the National Health Service - a bill which will probably amount to £1.5 billion in 1986-7, a 12% increase on the previous year."[16]

As for research, the industry's real interest lies in finding a product which can be produced cheaply and patented. It is then handed over to the merchandising section to be hyped, packaged, and sold for a handsome reward to people who won't come back and complain, so it must not be complicated and provoke adverse reactions, allergies etc. This is, quite clearly, not the only way to deal with disease:

> "There are two ways to fight a mosquito-borne disease. One is to develop a vaccine or drug: the other is to try to break the life cycle of the disease by dealing with the mosquito. Most of the money spent on research into malaria, yellow fever and the like goes on the medical approach. Yet the other way seems more promising. It was, after all, the draining of mosquito-infested swamps, not drugs that rid Europe of malaria."[17]

So said the Economist magazine. My neighbour, Doctor Bob Gosling, whose experience of medicine runs from ship's doctor through general practice to Director of the Tavistock Clinic, says that the great advances in public health during the past century owe more to improvements like clean water, sewage and better housing than all the work of the medical profession. *Ipse dixit.*

> "The mere fear of contagious diseases which do not spare even 'respectability' brought into existence from 1847 to 1864 no less than 10 Acts of Parliament on sanitation."[18]

The merits of even those drugs with a reasonable claim to effectiveness has to be qualified. Tuberculosis was already losing a lot of its malignancy before Streptomycin was developed. The same is true of many other medical products. The epidemics of the 18th and 19th centuries; typhoid, typhus, cholera and the like disappeared without medical intervention. They were replaced by scurvy, rickets and other deficiency diseases, which are probably still with us in sub-clinical form.

The modern epidemic waves: heart disease, cancer, bronchitis, and the like are so obviously linked to the environment that treating them with medicines is like giving aspirin to the man sitting on the nail. The problem could be dealt with differently.

Meanwhile the medical profession soldiers on, the vast majority of its members desperately anxious to heal people, and aware, more than any of us that much of the time they are just spitting against the wind.

Across the Atlantic the growth of litigation in cases where doctors are accused of negligence and enormous sums in compensation are awarded, has led to a spiralling of insurance costs to protect the physicians, and a vast new field of work for the lawyers. A New York anaesthetist, Bob Potash assures me that the 40,000 dollars a year premium he has to pay for protection is not at all out of the way. Another case of symbiosis in the Market economy. This development has so far held off here. People who are maimed by drugs or incompetence in Britain get short shrift from the courts.

1. Weston A. Price: Nutrition and Physical Degeneration (Price Pottinger Nutrition Foundation Inc.)

2. John Woodforde : The Strange Story of False Teeth (Routledge : 1968).

3. Sunday Times 16/02/86.

4. Daily Telegraph 8/10/86.

5. Sam Ziff : The Toxic Time Bomb (Thorsons) foreword by Jack Levenson, President, British Dental Society for Clinical Nutrition.

6. ibid.

7. Pelican Books 1981.

8. "The fundamental causes of ill-health are beyond the control of doctors and their drugs. Yet recognising this would mean questioning the validity of expensive medical care. It is not in the interests of the medical profession to be examining or confronting the social roots of illness." Dexter Tiranti in New Internationalist, November 1986.

9. Times 18/09/84.

10. Daily Telegraph 3/10/86

11. ibid.

12. Guardian 9/6/86

13. Times 6/12/85.

14. Daily Telegraph 8/10/86.

15. Daily Telegraph 6/03/85.

16. Economist 17/05/86.

17. Economist 6/09/86.

18. Marx : Capital p.658. Both Queen Victoria and Prime Minister Gladstone caught typhoid and her husband Prince Albert died from it. This is one of the earliest examples of the externalities of the bourgeois system hitting the ruling elite and concentrating their minds. Previously, those who could, retreated to their estates and pulled up the drawbridge, as in Boccaccio's 'Decameron', and many continued to do so. But it is no good pulling up the drawbridge when the moat is polluted and acid rain and radioactive fallout is falling in the keep.

Chapter 10.

The Education Industry.

> "All intellectual improvement arises from leisure; all leisure arises from one working for another."

Samuel Johnson.

Over the whole of the modern world education, like money, crime, medical care, 'Defence', pollution, is out of control. Costs are out of control, children are out of control; as I write teachers are out of control - they are on strike. And the controllers, the local authorities, are out of control too. They are battling with central government. As with medicine, education is being asked to deal with problems which are social, political and economic. This it cannot do, but the effort is exhausting teachers and exhausting the patience of Government.

Schoolchildren are running wild because mothers have become the bread-winners or are trying to help out with the budget. They get home exhausted, having bought a packet of junk food on the way home from the factory or office. This adds to the chaos through overstimulation of the children by the additives in the food, too much television, and too little sleep.

> "Britain is the only country in Europe with a lower unemployment rate for women than for men and of the one million new jobs created in the economy since 1983 the majority have been filled by women, says Small Firms Minister, David Trippier."[1]

Employment of teachers fell by 43,000 in the first two years of the Thatcher Administration 1980-82. This was the fall- out from a wholesale closing of University Departments and village schools, with consequent bussing of children to schools several miles away. It still failed to curb the growth in costs.

It left 600,000 teachers and lecturers engaged in a struggle where few believe much progress is being made. University departments are denied resources unless they are for war preparation or from patent-medicine companies with the consequent strings attached. Schools are denied money for sufficient text books. The Press reports that local authorities in the North of England are experimenting with exercise and text books sponsored by commercial companies. The idea of ketchup and cornflake promotion being endorsed by the school system must disturb the most fanatical of the free-marketeers. We may yet see the revisions: Jack and the Heinz Beanstalk, The Coca-Colonisation of the Americans, The Three Little Dewhurst Pigs, Little Red Dulux Riding Hood.

Smacking Bottoms and Other Pleasures.

The newspapers which, without exception, support the Market economy, make repeated calls for a return to the discipline and order of earlier generations. Politicians of the Right demand the return of corporal punishment, by which they mean beating children with sticks or straps. This embarrasses their colleagues because research has shown that this gives sexual pleasure to some men and women. It is also against the European Convention on Human Rights. On the other hand, what does one do with children who have been forced into school with all the sanctions of state power and who do not show enthusiasm or appreciation when they get there. Why are the rulers of Britain and all the other developed countries anxious to get the children into school anyway? They are not so anxious to see them clothed or fed or housed.

After all, Education is for free. Food is not, neither is clothing or housing. Why are governments keen to educate children, who may be homeless, badly fed, and badly clothed?

It was not always so. At the beginning of the 19th century a number of English politicians were not afraid to voice their opposition to education of the children of the People. It would give them ideas above their station; it would stimulate demand for change, even revolution; it would invite discontent. To be true, this was a point of view more strongly held among the British ruling class than abroad.

Anti-Education.

There, it was felt much more, along with Victor Hugo that one should 'Teach the ignorant all you can. Society is culpable in not providing instruction for all.' And Continental Europe set about building schools in all the towns and villages during the age of the Enlightened Despots - in the 18th century of Frederick the Great, Joseph the Second of Austria and even in the Russia of Catherine the Great. In Britain it was different: "It has been estimated that in England and Wales before the Reformation, for a population of two and a quarter million there were about 400 grammar schools, a striking contrast to the position revealed by the schools enquiry Commission in 1864 when it was calculated that there were only 830 secondary schools of all types for a population of 19 millions."[2]

In 1983 only just over half of British 17-year-olds were still being educated whereas the proportion in Japan was almost double, with Germany and the United States not far behind. For every Briton at university there are, per head of population, two French youths, four Americans and eight Russians. The consequences of all this started to appear a long time ago. The British ascendancy ended about 1870 when Germany and the U.S. overtook Britain not only in production but above all in ideas and innovations. The American Century ended around 1970 when Japan started to overhaul the U.S., although the sheer size of the American economy has managed to mask the symptoms of arteriosclerosis up to now.

The knowledge that things are not altogether right has provoked some soul-searching in Britain. The distinguished historian Corelli Barnett holds the public schools, Oxford and Cambridge, and the grammar schools, who only ape the public schools, responsible for the decay in Britain. He told the Headmasters' Conference (Heads of private and 'public' schools):

> "For more than a century your schools have done much to bring Britain down as a trading nation ... The anti- industrial culture of the Victorian Public School and grammar school, and their close allies, Oxford and Cambridge, are responsible for Britain slipping behind in world trade."[3]

Some years before, the Editor of the New Statesman, Paul Johnson, had advocated dispossessing the public schools and Oxford and Cambridge altogether, but he subsequently changed his mind and concluded that the working class was responsible for all of Britain's problems.

One has to go back to the Greeks, on whom the public schools and Oxbridge modelled themselves, to make any sense of the system:

> "Gentlemen should learn what is useful to them, but not vulgarising; for instance they should not be taught any skill that deforms the body, or that would enable them to earn money. They should practice athletics in moderation but not to the point of acquiring professional skill. The education in English public schools remained until recently, almost exactly what he (Erasmus) would have wished; a thorough grounding in Greek and Latin, involving not only translation but verse and prose composition. Science, although intellectually dominant since the 17th century was thought unworthy the attention of a gentleman or a divine; Plato should be studied but not the subject Plato thought worth studying."[4]

It is not surprising then, that the products of the public schools and Oxbridge have never had much enthusiasm for either facts or ideas. "An Englishman not only has no ideas, he hates an idea when he meets one."[5]

As for facts, their discovery owes nearly everything to people outside the formal educational system and very little to those inside it. Samuel Smiles' mawkish 'Self Help'[6] is a catalogue of great names in British history, almost all of them auto- didacts; inventors, artists, writers, who achieved success despite a ruling class who were and are coarse and uneducated compared with their Continental equivalents.

The achievements of women writers during the past two centuries: Mary Woolstonecraft, Mary Shelley, Jane Austen, the Bronte sisters, George Eliot, are again staggering when one considers the social pressures on them to conform to enormously restricted intellectual, social and physical environments.

Writers, both here and abroad, have frequently referred to the anti-education, anti-intellectual attitude of the British ruling class. 'Too clever by half' is the stock response to any idea which threatens to disturb the complacency of the gentlemen in their club chairs. The key words are compromise, and muddling through; it is important to avoid arriving at conclusions; they might be unpleasant, they might even threaten the status quo; one must avoid dogmatism at all costs, and if possible, opinions themselves. And not only in Britain:

> "'Objectivity' has come to be simply the academic uniform of moral cowardice; one who is objective never takes a stand. And in the fashionable 'realism' of technological determinism, one is shed of the embarassment of moral and intellectual standards and of any need to define what is excellent or desirable. Education is relieved of its concern for truth in order to prepare students to live in a 'changing world!' As soon as students begin to be dictated by a changing world (changing of course to a tune called by the governmental-military-industrial complex) then one is justified in teaching virtually anything in any way - for, after all, one never knows what a changing world is going to become. The way is thus opened to run a university as a business, the main purpose of which is to sell diplomas, after a complicated but undemanding four year ritual - and thereby give employment to professors."[7]

Education Sold Like Soap.

That was Wendell Berry writing of the United States. In Britain the idea of running education like a supermarket has its enthusiasts too. Various politicians on the free-market Right led by Sir Keith Joseph have argued for schools to offer their services for sale, the purchases to be effected by means of vouchers which will be distributed free to poor parents. Thus the successful schools will attract a lot of business, can pay their teachers more money, although the teachers will have more faces in front of them, and will have to do more marking, etc. Enthusiasts of this approach point out that this is how the private fee-paying schools have always operated. These schools, called 'public' schools by a remarkable piece of Orwellian Doublethink, were originally founded, - Winchester, by William of Wykeham; Eton by Henry VIII, for example - for the education of 'poor and needy scholars' but they soon filled up with fat and wealthy cuckoos, and the original purpose was lost. They are now the preserve of the very rich, and the enormously valuable foundations (what are Eton and Harrow, Rugby and Charterhouse worth simply as real-estate?) are added to tax- concessions to help the poor little rich boys get on in the world. To them that hath shall be given.

Opponents of these voucher schemes point out that where they have been tried abroad they have only benefitted those who were already able to look after themselves.

> "Unfortunately, the schemes have brought fewer emptyings of awful schools than reformers hoped and teachers feared. Poor and ignorant parents are not always brilliant at deciding whether and whither to send their children under a strange new system, and the new schools suddenly touting for custom may prefer to attract preppy middle-class recruits anyway."[8]

Now why is the Economist so concerned about the education of the children of poor and ignorant parents? It does not concern itself with their food, or clothing or housing problems, or simply says they are insoluble anyway. So why education?

> "The boy going to the worst schools was three times more likely to be delinquent by age 18 than if he went to the best schools ... Ten year old children in Brixton are twice as likely to have emotional, behavioural and reading problems. They therefore become twice as likely to blow us up."[9]

So that's what it's all about. Apart from the confirmation of symbiosis between crime and social conditions, which might be fiercely denied elsewhere, the moral for its inhabitants is to keep Brixton burning, don't be in a hurry to conform, and you might screw a decent standard of living out of the System as well as a better education.

Underlining Class Divisions.

One cannot begin to understand the education system and the forces contending over it without reference to the class division in society. It exists in all countries but its character in Britain is starker than in any other developed country, for historical reasons I do not propose to go into here. The ruling elite in Britain chooses to be educated in its own schools, separate from the rest of the population, where its offspring acquire a special accent, a lot of chutzpah, a contempt for the ordinary people ('pardons', 'oicks'), a surface gloss, and no regional attachment. Thus an uppercrust Scot has an accent indistinguishable from a ditto Yorkshireman, Londoner or Irishman. They are incapable, respectively, of rendering Robert Burns, Ilkla Moor B'aht at, My Old Man said Follow the Van, or an Irish folk song.

This incomprehensible to a Frenchman, Italian, Spaniard or German, however elevated their status. The German politician from Bavaria, Franz Joseph Strauss, never misses an opportunity to remind people where he comes from; a wealthy Dutchman is delighted to drop into his Frisian or Maastricht dialect to greet a friend, an Italian aristocrat to greet a 'Paisano'. And across the Atlantic a wealthy and powerful Texan would regard an attempt to affect a Boston accent as bordering on treason.

All of this comes from the education systems in the respective countries, which, whatever their differences, are host to the local populations, rich or poor. In Britain the offspring of the rich and powerful are packed off to boarding school at around 8 years of age, thence to public school and, if they are not hopeless duffers, to Oxbridge. Before World War II there were no entry qualifications to the older universities provided you were the right type, or the son of your father. There were five grades of degree from Alpha Plus to Epsilon semi-moron, and if you didn't present yourself for examination at all you could get an Aegrotat degree, which meant you were ill on the day of the examination.

Not that any of this mattered much anyway. It was bad form to show too much enthusiasm for academic matters, or for anything really. One had to be cool, above all. But these people had and still have the power of deciding the form and content of the education to be provided for the vast mass of the population who did not and do not go away to school. The result is that the tremendous ferment of discussion and ideas which has exercised governments abroad for two centuries and more, simply have not been felt in Britain. The great names of educational theorists are overwhelmingly foreign: Rousseau, Montessori, Pestalozzi, Froebel, Herbart, Rudolph Steiner, John Dewey, Homer Lane. One might advance the names of Matthew Arnold and John Stuart Mill, without much confidence that they would be recognised by a foreign educationalist.

Alarm bells are set ringing from time to time by people like Corelli Barnett, aforementioned, and by captains from the Confederation of British Industry. Even the Economist, striving with might and main to keep resource allocation in the hands of the Free Market, ends up with the most amazingly complicated schemes to frustrate the effects of the Market from funelling all the resources into Advertising, War preparation, Crime, Unemployment, and manufactured rubbish.

Docile Plebs.

At the back of these preoccupations lies not education, but Vocational Training, coupled with a desire to reduce the mayhem in the streets, crime, vandalism, and other misconduct that increases constantly. The definition of John Dewey: "The education process has no end beyond itself; it is its own end." or the dream of the Education Minister, R.A. Butler: "The Government's purpose in putting forward the reforms described in this paper is to secure for children a happier childhood." are forgotten. Instead we have programmes to produce docile machine-minders and paper- bashers for the Brave New World which looks suspiciously like the Old World of 19th century England; and England free of troublesome things like trade unions, where workers, having been robbed of the land will have no choice but to accept any offer of wages and conditions that their oppressors might make them.

Teachers' salaries and status, like those of all professional employees, have been falling, relatively, for at least a century. The result has been to radicalise teachers, like the other professional groups: doctors, lawyers, architects.

Governments howl that the teachers no longer behave like the members of an honoured profession, but band themselves into trade unions like coal miners and sheet-metal workers. Yet it was those same governments which insisted on treating teachers as commodities in the first place, buying as cheaply as possible and when the low prices for teachers' labour had driven 100,000 women teachers out of the market, talked of importing teachers from Germany where there was a better supply, as a consequence of better wages and conditions.

> "Sir, - I would like to tell you and your readers why, for the first time in my life, I went on strike in January 15 in support of the Association of University Teachers. The Government's continuing financial squeeze on education is having a serious effect on research as well. I spend about half my working time typing letters, because our secretarial services are so stretched; this is done during time which I would formerly have spent in mathematical activities. The universities cannot go on receiving less and less money for more and more work. Older colleagues retire as soon as possible, and bright young students can rarely be encouraged to deepen their knowledge through studying for a higher degree. Yours sincerely, (Prof.) W.K. Hayman, University of York.[10]

To a free-marketeer this seems a perfect solution; free, rootless, labour, swilling about the world like all the other commodities: copper, pyrites, palm-oil. But when the consequences of this febrile motility appear, the instigators start screaming from the rooftops. The same people who were in favour of importing Sicilian labour to work in the Bedfordshire brick-fields in the 1950's, of London Transport recruiting conductors and drivers from the West Indies, of factories in Southall importing Pakistanis and Indians; were the first to talk of raising the drawbridge, of calling out the troops to deal with race riots, and of shipping back all who could be persuaded to go, with an offer they could not refuse.

Meanwhile, the hapless proles, their boroughs swamped by people who did not share their laughs, their mores, their cuisine, their music, were invaded by counsellors to help them 'understand' the cruel and wicked things that had been done to them. The extent to which they have not lashed out with more Paki-bashing, inner-city riots, and holocausts - I use that much abused word in its true meaning - is a measure of how some social-cement has still survived the disintegrating force of the Market economy. But there are still people who will not allow an ugly fact to upset a beautiful theory:-

> "If a producer of anything sold on markets is between three and five times more harmful to his customers than a competing rival, he quickly goes bust as customers switch to his rivals. This is how production is kept innovative in computers, and non-poisonous even in tinned spinach. Britain has not allowed the same self-cleansing process of consumer sovereignty in education for disadvantaged kids; it has instead left education under upper-middle-class producer sovereignty, with all of history's usual results. Most first delinquencies, drug-takings, nasty sexism or racism (including some racist acts by blacks against whites, but more by whites against Asians) are committed in gangs; and the awful truth is that in the worst British schools the passport to friendship and group membership for a new entrant is to indulge in them. Same thing in America."[11]

Let us ignore the equating of education with the marketing of personal computers, a half million of which now lie neglected like hula-hoops or yo-yos in attics, after the wretched parents who, conned into buying them by the salesmen's hype, realised their uselessness as educational aids. As for tinned spinach, perhaps we shall need the same battery of consumer protection acts that is still inadequate to save us from junk food. Can we look forward to more controls and policing to protect us from junk education?

The racist gangs referred to by the Economist are, of course, a simple Pavlovian reflex of people who find themselves confronted with large numbers of aliens; people whose lifestyle they do not share or even understand. When people feel threatened they band together. To complain about this is like complaining that water won't flow uphill.

Most of the problems that beset education today can be laid at the door of the Market economy. The new illiteracy and innumeracy has more to do with the debasing effect of Market culture: advertising, the gutter-press, television - or rather its content, than anything else. The barbarism of children who see greed as the greatest good, and altruism as simply wet, are true disciples of Adam Smith; those whose cultural Everest is last week's computer-composed pop song, even the middle class with their wall-to-wall Mozart, can hardly blame the teachers for their tastes.

Meanwhile governments which succeed each other; Free- Marketeers from Interventionists, wrestle with rising costs and rising chaos. And that appears to be the good news. The bad news is that applicants for primary school teacher training were 12.2% down at the end of 1986, and for secondary school training no less than 22.2% down.[12]

The New Barbarism.

As for higher education, Philip Brockbank of the Shakespeare Institute, University of Birmingham writes:

> "In recent years we in the west have been using our remarkable new technologies to create unemployment in order more efficiently to compete with one another. Whatever the effect on the economy, the side-effect on what remains of our civilisation, including the study of Shakespeare, has been damaging; over the past decade, as a consequence of the erosion of our Arts Faculties, half our leading Shakespeare scholars have left this country."[13]

The Classics departments have closed down in many universities. Archeology, Medieval History, Music, Fine Arts, are under the shadow of the axe. Room is being made for Computer and Business studies, merchandising and selling, packaging and promoting, information technology, - information about what we dare not ask.

Huge quantities of facts are being spewed out by the electronic wizardry; facts that no-one will read. The inflation of information has long passed saturation point and with the inflation has come the inevitable loss in value of the product. Most of it is of surpassing banality.

> "As the piles of reports and computer printouts drown public policy in a blizzard of incomprehensible often deliberately mystified data, citizens have learned that it is not just a matter of 'garbage in, garbage out' but also (as pollsters have always known) 'ask a silly question and you get a silly answer'."[14]

Riots in France.

The situation in other European countries appears to be better, if only by a margin. In France the riots of 1968 induced the Government to offer free university education to all who passed the baccalaureat (like A levels, but with a wider spread) but it did little to build the extra accommodation. A subsequent government under Jaques Chirac tried to 'reform' the situation in 1986, 'reform' meaning withdrawing the rights of many students by introducing selection. New tests were to be introduced to exclude students for whom there was insufficient space or funds or teaching staff. One might have thought that another solution might be simply to provide the extra facilities.

At all events the students reacted in typical French fashion by taking to the streets and the new government reacted in typical fashion by calling out the particularly brutal mobile police force, the CRS. One student was killed and many injured; the TV cameras exposed a conspiracy by the police to use agents provocateurs giving them a pretext for brutality, and the government withdrew the proposed measures.

Another measure introduced after the 1968 riots was called Formation Permanente. The idea was that everybody in work was to be regarded as preparing for the next job up the line. One has to temper one's respect for the freer social mixing in France, - freer than in Britain, that is, with the feeling that we have heard it before. If only we could forget the 'us' and 'them'; if only management and labour could get to understand each other, etc. etc.

At the same time there is an idea contained in the scheme which goes back to the Greeks and before, and that is that education should be part of life, a constant enrichment, and not just a training to fit one into a slot in a factory or an office.

1. Guardian 17/11/76.

2. W.O. Lester Smith : Education (Pelican 1966).

3. Daily Telegraph 24/09/86.

4. Bertrand Russell : History of Western Philosophy p. 204 (Allen & Unwin 1967).

5. W.O. Lester Smith : Education p.32.

6. Samuel Smiles : Self Help (Penguin Business Library 1986)

7. Wendell Berry : The Unsettling of America (Sierra Club Books 1977).

8. Economist : 20/09/86.

9. ibid

10. Guardian 10/01/86.

11. Economist 20/10/86.

12. Guardian 11/11/86.

13. ibid.

14. Hazel Henderson: Politics of the Solar Age, (Doubleday N.Y.)

Chapter 11.

The Unemployment Industry.

Both the extreme Left and the extreme Right have long been in agreement over the fact that unemployment is an essential feature of laissez-faire capitalism.

False Claims.

Totalitarian governments - Stalin's Russia, Hitler's Germany, Mussolini's Italy, Franco's Spain, always claimed, as do their Eastern European successors, to have eliminated unemployment, but they did not. They simply absorbed it in the bureaucracy and military. Germany closed its labour exchanges the day it mobilised its armed forces in 1933, for example. And in Russia, the first secretary of the Soviet capital spelt out a pattern of private corruption, public complacency, and bureaucratic inefficiency, stretching back over the 20 years that Mr Grishin ran the city.

His successor, Boris Yeltsin, began his speech to the Moscow party conference by saying: "Maybe some of you will find my assessments too tough. But sooner or later this had to be said."[1]

He said that health care provision in Moscow was so bad that it could barely cope with two thirds of the city's population, that bribery and gifts to doctors to ensure service had become the norm, that 20% of the city's capital investment in health facilities was simply disappearing. To which we could add: it sounds as bad as the United States.

More False Claims.

However, for 40 years from the publication in 1936 of Keynes' 'General Theory', reformists claimed to be able to deal with unemployment. By increasing taxes and creating credit, money could be found to put the workless back to work, and the 'spin-off' or trickle-down would stimulate the rest of the economy back into activity. Pump-priming, fine-tuning, little more than fine words, and deficit financing - economists' gibberish for governments forging money, it all sounds very quaint now. Time has dealt cruelly with much of it; for example the following written by an admirer of Keynes just before the current depression arrived: "Whatever the qualifications, the basic fact is that with the acceptance of the 'General Theory', the days of uncontrollable mass unemployment in advanced industrial countries are over. Other economic problems may threaten, this one, at least, has passed into history."[2]

Unemployed Part of the Structure.

Karl Marx argued that the 'industrial reserve army' was an integral part of capitalist production. In periods of expansion the unemployed could be hired and in depression they could be fired. Without such unemployed, production would be bound and gagged at a depressed level and businessmen unable to take advantage of a rising market.

> "The course characteristic of modern industry ... depends on the constant formation, the greater or less absorption and the reformation of the industrial reserve army or surplus population... This peculiar course of modern industry which occurs in no earlier period of human history, was also impossible in the childhood of capitalist production."[3]

Marx goes on to quote conservative economists in support of his argument: First, H. Merevale, Professor of Political Economy at Oxford:

> "...suppose the nation were to rouse itself to the effort of getting rid by emigration of some hundreds of thousands of superfluous arms, what would be the consequence? That at the first returning demand for labour, there would be a deficiency. However rapid reproduction may be, it takes, at all events, the space of a generation to replace the loss of adult labour. Now the profits of our manufacturers depend mainly on the power of making use of the prosperous moment when demand is brisk ... they must have hands ready by them, they must be able to increase the activity of their operations when required, and to slacken it again, according to the state of the market ..."

And the Reverend Malthus, enemy of lasciviousness and philoprogenesis in the poor (Marx cruelly and uncharitably says that this was because he had to take a vow of celibacy to become a Fellow of Cambridge University: '*Socios collegiorum maritos esse non permittimus*' etc.) balks at the idea of an economy without a surplus population of workers: "Prudential habits with regard to marriage, carried to a considerable extent among the labouring class of a country mainly depending upon manufactures and commerce, might injure it ..."

More recent writers have speculated upon other possible advantages to be gained from a pool of unemployed. A.W. Phillips in 1958 pondered upon a possible link between full- employment and inflation. 'The Phillips Curve' was seized upon by the Monetarists led by Milton Friedman who argued the necessity for a 'Natural Level' of unemployment. The unemployed themselves were, quite clearly, not going to be consulted about the possible benefits. The key argument was that unemployment keeps wages down and reminds workers of their place. Unfortunately for the Monetarists this was a beautiful theory overturned by ugly facts. On numerous occasions inflation continued, wages rose faster than inflation and 3.5 or 4.5 million were unemployed, these last figures depending on whether you believed lies, bloody great lies, or statistics.

Of course the innocent fool will wonder how it can pay to keep people in enforced idleness when so much needs to be done: houses falling down, sewers collapsing, roads potholed, roofs leaking, not to mention trees to plant and barrages to be built across the Severn, The Wash, The Solway Firth, The Mersey, Morecambe Bay, all of which could provide fuel-free electricity from now until the end of time. The fool does not understand that the Market is a delicate mechanism which we interfere with at our peril.

New Sources of Unemployment.

Bill Jordan of the University of Exeter,[4] citing Ricardo, says that what he calls the relative automation of the past which replaced men with machines was balanced by expanding output, which absorbed the men put-off. He argues that Britain, as front runner, is now encountering absolute automation, where there is no expanding output to absorb suplus labour - hence permanent, mass unemployment.

Giles Merritt provides evidence for this view: "For example, Belgian industry which exports rather more than half its output has since 1970 improved its productivity by a Japanese-style 90% plus. It has maintained its share of vital export markets in Western Germany and Holland, but has also jumped to the head of the EEC's league table for unemployment. Instead of a constant number of workers producing an increasing volume of goods, the reverse has happened. It has remained competitive because a decreasing number of workers have been producing a roughly constant volume of goods."[5]

Since Merritt wrote Britain has overtaken Belgium, and has the highest percentage of unemployed in its history, currently 14.2%.

Unemployment Provides Employment!

There is a familiar ring about this argument. At least it shows a concern for the millions of wretched workers and their families struggling to make ends meet on poor-relief handouts while fighting back the debt-collectors. But we cannot predict the future simply by projecting present trends. J.K. Galbraith says that "financial genius is a rising stock market and a short memory". This remark can apply to macroeconomic predictions too. Unemployment has waxed and waned since the people of Britain were robbed of the Common Land at the beginnings of the Market Economy - at least 500 years. Unemployment tends particularly to affect the productive sector of the economy. The non-productives - war expenditure, crime, merchandising, financial juggling, were never busier. It is true that huge changes are taking place in the paper-bashing business;

shorthand typists are a dying breed, warehouses are becoming lonely, computerised places, but there seems to be little mass unemployment among office staff. The tremendous inflation in paperwork may have something to do with it.

And unemployment itself is economic activity of a sort. It is no argument to say that there is no product. There is no product in banking and insurance and betting; and in the war industry and crime the product is a negative one when it results in injury to persons or damage to property. Whether this is caused by soldiers or criminals does not make much difference from an economic point of view.

Unemployment provides direct employment for the 102,000 clerks and managers and snoopers who service the industry. A sizeable part of the building industry is engaged in constructing the offices to house them, and their gas, electricity, water, sewage and telephone consumption must provide work for many more.

Then there are the activities generated by governmental efforts to deal with or conceal various aspects of unemployment: "Some of the early measures were admittedly naive and crude, but the whole effort of the Commission became diverted, if not subverted, towards the camouflage of rising unemployment under successive Labour administrations. The 'body-count' mentality of temporary measures to absorb as many unemployed as possible resulted in an alphabet soup of programmes over the second half of the 1970s: Temporary Employment Subsidy (TES) - Temporary Short-Time Working Compensation Scheme (TSTWCS) Small Firms' Employment Subsidy (SFES) - Recruitment Subsidy for School Leavers (RSSL) - Youth Employment Subsidy (YES) - Adult Employment Subsidy (AES) - Job Creation Programme (JCP) - Special Temporary Employment Programme (STEP) - Work Experience Programme (WEP) - Community Industry (CI) - TSA courses for young people (TSAYP) - Youth Opportunities Programme (YOP) - Training places in industry (TI) - Job Introduction Scheme for disabled (JIS) - Job Release Scheme (JRS)."[6]

How many tens of thousands are employed in this area of the unemployment industry is difficult to say. The Thatcher Government closed some parts of it down while opening up new enterprises of its own.

Unemployment Is A Low Cost Industry.

The unemployed themselves make much less demand on the productive part of the economy than those employed in banks, law courts, office blocks, barracks, or prisons. At most they spend a few hours queuing in the Social Security Office to obtain their ration of money, clothes, furniture, or other supplements; even less time in the Post Office cashing their unemployment pay cheques.

The other non-productives demand much more of the productive part of the economy: marble halls, thick carpets, heating, lighting - accommodation altogether superior to that enjoyed by those engaged in manufacturing ; mountains of paper, costly computers and word processors, not to mention the enormously expensive demands of the War Industry for tanks, aeroplanes, submarines and their installations.

The capacity of the non-productive sector of the economy to absorb the unemployed should never be underestimated. Parkinson's Law as enunciated by Northcote Parkinson[7] was a right wing complaint against the bureaucracy of state control. But the maxim "work expands so as to fill the time available for its completion", applies to any large organisation, as Parkinson, a former university don, would know. There are few organisations more feather-bedded than the older universities. But the movement towards non- productives is not merely a bureaucratic problem.

The tensions and contradictions and complexity of the Market Economy is throwing up new demands all the time, and sucking-in labour in the attempt to deal with them. War preparations are continuing, crime continues to grow, tension between government and various sectors of the governed increases. Police numbers are being increased and they are more heavily equipped, and secret police forces multiply : MI5, MI6, MI99, Special Branch, the S.A.S. and endless numbers of specially selected groups to deal with ever growing problems.

It all recalls the Spain of General Franco and his "57 Varieties" of secret police we used to laugh at and feel superior about.

That is the problem. We lose perspective so quickly. Who could have anticipated the Banana Republic atmosphere we live in today? But every cloud has a silver lining. Those secret police jobs, the private security company jobs, store detectives, t.v. snoopers, new jails being built, all join with the rest of the war-making and money-shuffling to keep people busily if not usefully employed.

Despite the Money Economy's capacity to create these millions of squirrel wheels, however, they are not sufficient to absorb the surplus labour spewed out in times of economic spasm - invariably caused by the eccentric flywheel of the capitalist system. And despite their pretensions, economists have greater difficulty getting it right than they would have in picking the winner of the Grand National. Giles Merritt was writing in 1981: "At the bottom, and reassuring end of the scale are the claims of the Liverpool group of economists (led by Patrick Minford KS) who have used a monetarist econometric model to predict that UK unemployment will drop to 1.7 million in 1984 once the economy emerges leaner and fitter from the recession."[8]

Perhaps Old Moore's Almanack would have been a better guide. Anyway, unemployment was more than one hundred per cent higher than the Liverpool boys predicted. Professor Minford! Put the dunce's hat on and stand in the corner - not just for getting it wrong, but for presumption.

Meanwhile the inter-relatedness of the parts of the bourgeois system, the symbiosis between unemployment and the medical industry, for example, becomes more apparent. Professor John Catford, Director of Health Education at the University of Wales, said[9] that the health gap between those in work and the unemployed is widening according to the largest British survey of class health differences.

Doctor Richard Smith, assistant editor of the British Medical Journal said[10] at the launch of his book : Unemployment and Health - A Disaster And A Challenge, that unemployment has probably caused 20,000 deaths in the last decade and may claim a further 40,000 deaths by the end of the century if action is not taken."The deaths will come from suicide, cancer, accidents, poisoning and violence, brought about by the poverty, stress, stigma, changes in lifestyle and damage to mental health caused by being jobless."

An American expert is even more disposed to say it like it is. Thomas Cottle, of the Harvard Medical School says:[11] "I'm now convinced that unemployment is the killer disease in this country, responsible for wife beating, infertility, and even tooth decay."

In the meantime the Government in Britain was busying itself abolishing as many of the unemployed, on paper, at least, as it indecently could. The techniques of creating non- persons varied from encouraging some, with an offer of five pounds per week on top of the unemployment pay, to call themselves 'self employed'. These entrepreneurs, launched by a government dedicated to laissez faire, included snake- charmers, sword-swallowers, and smelters of guaranteed genuine 24 carat gold bricks.

> "Is the Government deliberately under-counting the unemployed? Britain's figures are now based on the narrowest, and the most frequently adjusted, definition of unemployment in the European Community... ...in eight years the Government has made 19 changes in the way that it counts the jobless. All but one have reduced the official total. Other EEC countries with comparable systems include thousands of people who are banished from Britain's monthly count... ...it appears that, alone in Europe, the British Government has grasped that useful public relation points can be gained from a more rigorously selective approach to counting the unemployed."[12]

1. Guardian 29/01/86.

2. Michael Stewart, Keynes and after (Penguin 1973).

3. Marx : Capital vol. 1. p.633.

4. Bill Jordan, Automatic Poverty (Routledge 1982)

5. Giles Merritt : World Out of Work (Collins 1982).

6. Adrian Sinfield : What Unemployment Means (1984)

7. C. Northcote Parkinson : Parkinsons Law, or the Pursuit of Progress (John Murray 1961)

8. Giles Merritt : World Out of Work p.34.Nothing, if not a tryer, is our Professor Minford though. He was back, in the Daily Telegraph (22/01/87) this time after seven years of government endorsed by him and his friends. It was still jam tomorrow but not today : "Manufacturing has diminished, absolutely as well as relatively, since 1979; it now accounts for only 25 per cent of our output and employment. But other industries and especially services have grown to replace it and add further to economic growth.

Among them the City takes pride of place, with banking and financial services generally now contributing no less than 14 per cent of our national output and 10 per cent of employment." Bank charges and stockbrokers fees and insurance premiums 14 per cent of wealth production? Are we supposed to eat them or wear them?

9. Guardian 20/02/87.

10. Independent 17/09/87.

11. US News and World Report 23/06/80, quoted by Giles Merritt ibid.

12. The Independent 18/09/87.

Chapter 12.

The Money Industry.

> "If you sincerely want to be rich, don't horse around with lamp globes or steel; work directly with money itself."

Bernie Cornfeld.

Money is the biggest employer in the non-productive sector of the economy in times of boom. In times of slump, for example the 1980's, it yields first place to the Unemployment Industry. Currently the number employed is in excess of 2 million but how much in excess is almost impossible to calculate. The most remarkable feature of this industry is that it continues to grow, whatever the economic climate. The numbers employed in banking, insurance, and finance, alone have doubled in the past 20 years, from just over 1 million to well over 2 millions. And it is not just a question of numbers.

A Good Business To Be In.

The rewards for employment in the Money Industry, whether it is selling life insurance, being upwardly mobile in the banking system, or getting on the inside track of building society management, outstrip those of any other.

The work of the Money Industry is to provide a link between owners of money or goods or services so that they can be bought or sold or hired or rented. The following list, by no means exhaustive, gives some idea of the range of employment in the industry:

Accountants
Advertising Agencies
Auctioneers
Auditors
Banking
Bailiffs
Bookkeepers
Bookmakers
Building Societies
Buyers
Capitalists
Cashiers
Casinos
Charities
Christmas Club
Consumer Protection
Credit Card Agencies
Credit Worthiness Investigators
Debt Collectors
Economists
Estate Agents
Excise Officers
Financial Advisors
Finance Houses
Friendly Societies
Football Pools
Fundraisers
Grant Awarding Trusts
Health Finance Schemes
Hire Purchase Firms
Holding Companies
Income Tax Officers
Inspectors of Weights & Measures
Insurance Brokers
Insurance Companies
Investment Consultants
Licensing Officers
Loan Companies
Luncheon Voucher Schemes
Management Consultants
Market Analysts
Mints
Money Lenders
Mortgage Brokers
National Health Insurance
Patents Offices Copyright Enforcement
Pension Funds
Post Offices
Public Relations Officers
Raffles
Ratefixers for Piecework
Rates Offices
Receivers
Rent Collectors
Salesmen & Women
Security Firms
Social Security Offices
Stock Exchanges
Stock Brokers & Jobbers

Superannuation Schemes
Tax Consultants
Ticket Sellers, Collectors & Inspectors
Totes
Trade Unions
Treasurers
Underwriters
Unemployment Benefit Offices
Unit Trusts
Valuers
Wages Clerks
Work Study Engineers[1]

It will be noted that nearly all of these occupations are new and did not exist a century ago.

Earlier Times Managed Without Money.

During the 5 million or so years of human existence, all save the last few centuries were managed without a Money Industry. True enough, classical antiquity had its money and its money changers, the *aes circumforaneum* of Rome, the tax collector of ancient Egypt, but these things impinged very little upon the lives of most people. The Roman poet Horace advises his friend Varus not to be a miser, burying his silver coins in the ground, but to let them shine with moderate use. The advice would have puzzled the average yeoman; his contact with money would have been only when he wanted to convert a small surplus from his farming activities into salt, metal for tools, items to bring variety into his diet etc. This remained true for nearly another 2,000 years even for today's developed countries, and still remains true where there is a sizeable peasant population.

The world of Homer and Hesiod, of Beowulf, Taliesin and Aneurin, of the Eddas and Sagas, of the Desborough Mirror and the Sutton Hoo ship burial, managed without a money industry and almost without money itself. Where the beginnings of a Money Industry appear, whether in classical antiquity, or Raquel and Vidas financing the campaigns of El Cid, or the Merchant of Venice lending to Antonio, it is merely the emergent ruling class who are concerned, not the people at large.

The same is true of Medieval England. The Norman invasion of 1066 and the building boom which followed - fortresses to secure the conquest and cathedrals to provide ideological backup - increased the number of people working for wages by some tens of thousands. They were still a drop in the ocean of peasants outside the money economy, which is not to say that they weren't a measure by which living standards of the others could be compared.[2]

Forced Into The Money Economy.

The position would have remained largely the same for a long time, but for the Enclosure Acts. By their being robbed and driven from the land the peasants were brought into the money economy, both as wage earners and customers. The first Enclosure Act, the Statute of Merton, was as early as the 13th century, but it was only in the 15th century that enclosures began to have a serious effect and provoked a literature of protest, including Sir Thomas More's Utopia. Numerous laws to limit enclosures failed to stop the plunder.

A century later there were enough dispossessed peasants affected by Henry VIII debauching the currency to create a race of 'the poor': "In England the natural increase in the supply (of money) was augmented in the reigns of Henry VIII and Edward VI by a deliberate debasement of the currency in order to raise revenue for the Crown. Earlier monarchs had reduced the weight of the coins while maintaining the fineness of the metal; beginning in 1542 however, Henry began reducing the silver content of the metal from the 'ancient and right' 925 parts per 1,000; this process was continued until, in the reign of Edward VI coins were struck from alloy containing only 250 parts per 1,000 of silver, and the base money remained in circulation until Elizabeth's re-coinage of 1560-16."[3]

Four centuries later "the British Government ... went on printing money to help meet the extra costs (of oil)" Patrick Hutber 'Decline and Fall of the Middle Class'. *Plus ca change*! With paper money the game of official counterfeiting becomes easier. Instead of rows of men snipping round coins with shears, or heating them until beads of metal form and then brushing the beads off, the printers are simply told to let the presses run.

According to Victor Morgan "the bank note originated with the London goldsmiths who began to perform several banking functions in the 17th century". After that the progress was swift. The Bank of England was founded in 1694 with virtually the sole right to issue banknotes - backed, of course, by gold. But, human nature being what it is, the Bank suffered a 'run' in 1797 and Parliament ordered the Bank to suspend handing over gold against the notes it had issued.

A Growth Industry.

Since then things have not looked back for the banking business. You only have to go into a bank to feel that it is a good business to be in. All those marble halls, mahogany panelling, thick carpets. Much better than metal spinning or weaving - the rewards and the growth prove it: "Banks in Common Market countries boosted their payrolls by around 70% during the last 20 years and now employ almost 5 million people."[4]

And despite huge investment in labour-saving technology the banks continue to take on additional labour; "If the American banks were to provide the same range of customer services as they do now, without any of the office technology that since World War II has made these improvements possible, then they would need to employ every single adult woman in the United States."[5]

According to Social Trends, the Money Industry in Britain increased its labour force by 52% in the 4 years to 1983. The great majority of these toilers where no better paid than in the rest of the economy. But for those with connections, the situation is different. The fact that a barely literate young man in the City with the right presence and enough chutzpah can earn ten times the salary of a works manager in Bootle or Birmingham or any other place where wealth, not money, is made, is causing a certain disenchantment and is working against the Oneness of the Nation.

> "More top-flight engineering students are now looking to the City for high pay and rapid promotion rather than the long slog to acquire membership of an engineering institute."[6]

The steady grumbling of the productive sector shows who is doing well: "What irritates the hell out of me," said Sir John Harvey Jones, late chairman of Imperial Chemical Industries, ".. is that at home, I'm surrounded by stockbrokers who contribute damn little to the game, add nothing to the gaiety of nations, yet make so much money that they look down on me as a poor down-at-heel tramp."[7]

Booming Banks.

In January 1986 the Chairman of Barclays Bank, Sir Timothy Bevan, was embarrassed by the inflation in earnings in the City of London and pleaded for restraint. He told the annual Overseas Bankers Club banquet that the City was "subject to a lot of political and social opprobrium for paying what is perceived generally as too much."[8]

The Observer was more graphic :

> "Get-rich-quick opportunities are galvanising the Square Mile much as the 49ers once set San Francisco alight. And the booze flows with similar abandon. A Bank of England man listed among the essential qualities for success the ability to operate when tanked up.
> Salary stories are mind boggling; some dealers in their twenties have had their salaries more than trebled between lunch and gin-and-tonic time, from £30,000 perhaps to £100,000. Foreign institutions are said to be pumping £1 billion into their head-hunting adventures."[9]

The whole business was in anticipation of the de-regulation of the Stock Exchange on October 27th 1986, abandoning fixed minimum commissions and allowing its members both to represent investing clients and gamble themselves. This running with the hare and hunting with the hounds at the same time had been forbidden for nearly a century - to protect the investors.

Patriotism Is For The Mugs.

From the position where no outsider could own a stockbroking company, after March 1st 1986 every City stockbroker, bar one, was owned by outsider institutions, most of them foreign. A City lawyer speaking to newspaper columnist Robert Chesshyre said: "The amount of nonsense talked about dealing skill is incredible. On a scale of A - D, the average dealer is B minus. Their value lies in their short term scarcity. No one in the City has asked whether it is patriotic to sell out to foreign interests, Stockbrokers who rah-rah-rahed about the Falklands don't care who buys them up. They've just cashed in, there's no contest between pockets and principles."[10]

As will be clear from the above, the banks have been joined at the pig trough by increasing numbers of other entrepreneurs in the money shuffling business. Variations on the theme of credit are endless. "At the end of 1984 the British public owed £22 billion in consumer credit, which does not, of course, include mortgages."[11] It all recalls Tennesse Ernie Ford singing: "I owe my soul to the Company Store."

Borrow Now, Pay Later.

The A.T.V. Midlands television company sent one of their reporters out into Birmingham and in the space of an afternoon he negotiated £10,000 of credit on the strength of a name and address, without having to give any details of status.

The environmental consequences of all this are to be seen in every town and city centre. All those bakers and butchers' shops have fled, the tea shops and cafes have given way to the temples of loan-sharks - banks, building societies, finance companies - and the latest - share dealing companies.

The rents that the money merchants are able to pay cannot be matched by anybody save shops owned by a cartel or enjoy near monopoly status, like the shops of the British Shoe Corporation. Others, like the tailor shops of 50 years ago, are having to fight for their very lives.

A condition of survival for many of them lies in offering credit, often through the medium of junk mail. Few members of the public, it seems, are able to resist:

> "Debt now lies below the surface of British life, like some great geological flaw, a San Andreas Fault which may, at any time shift and lead to earthquake and disaster. It has already happened to an awful lot of people. All over the country Citizens Advice Bureaux are swamped with requests for advice on debt. Since the start of the year the number of people who are falling behind with mortgage payments has doubled. Small businessmen go to the wall when, having given credit, they are not paid and cannot therefore meet their own bills. Husbands and wives live separated by the secret wall of money owed."[12]

Sending The Bailiffs In.

A new and expanding branch of the Money Industry lies in snatching back houses from defaulters on mortgage. Until recently it was only hire purchase companies which engaged 'heavies' to repossess cars from H.P. defaulters. Now, firms of bailiffs are discovering a lucrative line in prizing people out of their houses and throwing them into the street - people who, perhaps through business failure or unemployment are not able to keep up mortgage payments. The victims then, as often as not become a charge on the rates and have to be housed in 'bed and breakfast' accommodation at enormous expense.

The availability of so much credit to buy houses has had the inevitable consequence of driving house prices up. Roy Cox of the Building Societies Association says: "We have been deliberately wanting to satisfy mortgage demand for some time. Some people cannot believe we are serious". A wry sense of humour has our Mr. Cox. After a Dien Bien Phu bombardment of press and television publicity to sell mortgages in the '70's and '80's, a £5,000 house in 1970 was costing £29,648 by 1984.[13]

Small wonder that by the middle '80's there were more people working for house financing than there were building houses! At the same time the efforts of the Thatcher Government to limit spending both privately and nationally were completely out of control. The government which had come to power on a programme of tax cuts and financial rectitude had through its Chancellor Nigel Lawson raised taxes from 33% of the Gross Domestic Product to 39% of the Gross Domestic Product and had abandoned all talk of limiting the Public Sector Borrowing Rate.

Money Out Of Control.

The old yardsticks for measuring money in circulation: M.1, M.2., M.3, were proving as unreliable as anyone but an economist could have told them. And worse was yet to come. With the enormous revolution in speed of money transaction around the world caused by electronic technology, the multi national companies could juggle with their prices and tuck their profits into tax havens as never before. The trick was not new. In the 1970's the investigative journalists on the Sunday Times dragged into view the quaint goings on of the Vestey family, polo-playing friends of the Royal Family, living in baronial style in the lush Cotswolds. Vesteys own vast expanses of Scotland, England, Uruguay, Argentina, millions of cattle, factories, canning plants. The Vestey- owned Dewhurst chain of butchers' shops paid £10 tax on £2 million profit in the year in question! And a poor man can pay a third and more of his entire earnings in income tax in this sceptred isle.

Meanwhile, money traders and commodity brokers are switching intergalactic sums of money into and out of countries like Britain,[14] so that any talk of controlling the economy is just rubbish. The American journal Business Week provides a clue to the increased activity and employment in banking: "Instead of local banks dealing in a single currency in a national market place - as banking used to be - there is now a vast integrated global money and capital system that can send billions of Eurodollars, Euromarks and other stateless currencies hurtling round the world 24 hours a day. Huge amounts of these Eurocurrencies have leaked across national boundaries and out of government hands despite increasingly tough exchange controls that are specifically aimed at slowing the movement of capital from country to country. The money has moved instead into the Euromarkets, where there are no controls and where anyone can trade or invest in it."[15]

Winner Takes All.

The greatest centre of this new gambling industry was London which recovered the position it had lost to Wall Street after World War I. The sole merit of London was that its regulations were less strict than New York's; the bloodhounds of the Securities and Exchange Commission had no equivalent in London. There, things were organised like a gentlemen's club. Rascals were expelled quietly and the mess swept under the carpet. With the 'Big Bang' of October 1986, when virtually all regulations were finally swept away, the players were left by the Thatcher government to shoot it out among themselves: Self Regulation, i.e. no laws.

After a slow start in the late '60's and early '70's, the American banks decided to join the European game, since there was no prospect of one at home. An official in the Paris branch of the Citibank of New York (then biggest bank in the world) one David Edwards, from Wichita Falls, Texas, reported to head office that tax and foreign-exchange- control laws were being broken, officials being bribed etc. He was sacked, found it impossible to get another banking job in New York and went back to Texas. The Securities and Exchange Commission bloodhounds had been replaced by chihuahuas: "Fedder's position (John Fedder, lawyer and

Enforcement Chief of the S.E.C.) was that Citibank's European transgressions were no business of the S.E.C.

'I do not subscribe to the theory that a company that violates tax and exchange control laws is a bad corporation and that disclosure of illegal conduct should be forced as a prophylactic measure.'[16]

This was a thoroughly British view of things. The gossip that the National Westminster Bank went bankrupt in 1974 and was only saved by being bailed out by the Bank of England was only gossip, after all. And the sleazy affair of the Johnson Matthey Bank in 1985/6 was discreetly dealt with by the Thatcher government. The British public was not burdened with facts it did not need to know. There was no freedom of information law. And the Labour Party had never been in favour of such a law.

Making Money, Not Things.

But all this drift from making things to making money, the slide from metal bashing to paper chasing has been producing a rising chorus of protest from both ends of the political spectrum and a warning of the consequences. In 1976 the Oxford researchers, Bacon and Eltis, published their warning entitled 'Britain's Economic Problem: Too Few Producers'. The Federation of British Industry, having cheered the coming to power of a monetarist government in 1979, after the drift and dither of the Callaghan, Foot and Wilson governments, lost its bottle in the 1980's. The Thatcher government behaved as if economics was simply about buying and selling, the view of a grocer's daughter. But the problem was not only Britain's.

> "The world economy has contracted a quintessentially British disease. In Britain the real economy is dying, but the City is flourishing as never before. The City's ancient pubs and private restaurants are jammed with hearty spirits and rowdy laughter. But beyond the square-mile City, depression and bitterness dominate the landscape. Increasingly the same is true of the world at large."[17]

The words are not those of a Trotskyist or Anarchist but those of Michael Moffitt, Investment adviser at Shearson / American Express in New York and an associate fellow at the Institute for Policy Studies in Washington, D.C.

Still less a voice of the extreme Left (or the extreme Right, for that matter) is that of Michael Heseltine who as Minister for Defence, resigned from the Thatcher Cabinet rather than see the Westland Helicopter Company treated like any other item on the grocer's stall: "Associated with the decline of our industrial base is the problem of the drift of resources and power from the old manufacturing centres of the Midlands and the North to an ever growing and seemingly remote concentration in the City of London. You cannot spend any time talking to the managers of British Industry without realising the huge gap in perception about industrial policy; where the wealth is made - in the factories and in the work places - and where it is increasingly owned, in the City of London."

1. *World Socialist, No.3 (Pub. 52, Clapham High Street, London SW4).*

2. *The peasant could become an artisan by moving to a town and becoming an apprentice. The towndweller would find it difficult to move to the country and acquire rights on the land. The rewards of peasant life must have been judged at least the equal of that enjoyed by the town worker, otherwise there would have been a flight from the land, evidence for which is lacking. At the very time when building workers real wages were at their highest - the 15th century - protests at enclosures and laws attempting to curb them were most numerous.*

3. *E. Victor Morgan : The History of Money (Penguin 1965).*

4. *European Commission 1980 quoted by Giles Merritt, op. cit.*

5. *Ray Marshall, former US Secretary of Labour,(Giles Merritt op. cit).*

6. *Guardian 30/01/86.*

7. *Daily Telegraph 29/12/83.*

8. *Guardian 4/01/86.*

9. *Observer 9/02/86.*

10. *ibid.*

11. *Gillian Reynolds, Daily Telegraph 10/02/86.*

12. *ibid.*

13. *Observer 9/02/86.*

14. *Quite clearly, the situation is not new, merely the scale and speed of it all. Writing of William Cobbett, Raymond Williams says: "What Cobbet had identified was a form of ruling class, and an attendant form of state power which was centred on income from*

money, in any of its possible kinds and on the use of this income for its own social purposes in power and display and consumption: a class and a State which saw production as a means to these ends rather than to the sustained prosperity of its own lands and people. If these different ends coincided so much the better, but if they came into conflict there would be no doubt which would be chosen. This is the English class and the English State which would under-invest in its own land, its own people, industries, but send capital flying to any spot in the world which would yield a higher money income, to continue to finance its ever more conspicuous consumption." - Cobbett, by Raymond Williams, p.67.

15. Michael Moffitt : The World's Money, (Michael Joseph 1984).

16. ibid.

17. ibid.

Chapter 13.

The Crime Industry.

The Law is Ruthless with the Felon
Who steals the grey goose from the Common
But lets the greater Thief go Loose
Who steals the Common from the Goose.

Anon.

For many men's malt we mice would eat
but had ye rout of rats your way
you would rend men's clothes.

William Langland: Vision of Piers the Plowman.

(Note: Mice = the peasants, Rats = the burgesses.)

Like most non-producing industries the crime industry is strongly bullish, it grows continually, particularly in times of depression. At present the numbers[1] engaged are as follows (I have rounded the numbers up or down to the next digit since what we are recording is a process, not a fixed state) :

Police, including cadets, specials,
civilian employees, etc...250,000

Security firms, private police forces,
store-detectives, security guards, etc ... 600,000

Prison Service ... 30,000

Judges and Magistrates ... 35,000

Barristers ...5,000

Solicitors ... 40,000

This yields a total of a little less than a million on the side of law enforcement. On the other side and living in symbiotic relationship with them are the law-breakers. Any urge to censure their chosen way of life should be tempered by the thought that they give gainful employment to the above. We have only to think of the frightening consequences of a rush of conscience among the villains; a go-slow, or worse, perish the thought, a strike. The near- million toilers above suddenly thrown on to the labour market might cause the most hard-nosed monetarist to blanch.

Prisoners, on remand, parolees ...50,000

Criminals at large ... ?

This last figure is information we are unlikely to obtain since, after acquisition, confidentiality is their main concern. The 1986 edition of Social Trends showed that 30.6% of a sample of men born in 1953 had a conviction (for an indictable offence such as theft) by the time they were 27 years old. Notifiable (was 'indictable') offences doubled between 1973 and 1983.

With regard to the earlier figure for store detectives, security guards etc., this is an estimate based on conversations I had with people in the security industry. Mr. Charles Rice at 'Group 4' headquarters in Broadway, Worcestershire, said that apart from the security companies like his own he had no figures for the 'in-house' part of the industry, but offered "at least 200,000" off the top of his head, and referred me to the British Security Association. The lady on the telephone at the B.S.A. offered the figure of 45,000, but this clearly excluded the 'in-house' part of the industry.

According to Stuart Henry[2] private security companies total manpower is well over 100,000 and in 1975 Securicor, one of the big four companies, had 300 branches, 18,000 staff, 3,000 armoured vehicles, over 1,000 ferocious guard dogs, a network of shortwave radio masts and 35 specially constructed security depots.

Public Police and Private Police.

It was Mr. Rabbitts of the International Professional Security Association in Paignton, Devon, who offered me a clue as to the approximate total. He said the general assumption in the profession was that for every policeman there were 3 security workers. This would yield a total of three-quarters of a million. Diffidence obliged me to reduce this estimate to 600,000. To those who still find this number excessive, I would point out that every shop assistant is a security worker for some of the time. After all, the job of the assistant is not just to see that you get what you want, but to make sure you don't get it without paying for it. And there are three million employed in the 'distributive' trades!

Returning to the question of criminals-at-large, we can be sure that unsolved crimes greatly outnumber those detected; equally that the number of criminals on the loose greatly exceeds those in jail. Most crimes are trivial in nature: 62% of cases of vandalism, 60% of thefts from motor vehicles, 63% of burglaries, 51% of thefts from the person were not reported to the police because nothing was taken and no damage caused. (In cases of assault, 30% were not reported because the victims 'dealt with the matter themselves' - too bad for the assailants).

But if the great majority of crimes are trivial, the minority are very big indeed. And I am not thinking of crimes against the person like rape or wounding or murder. Despite the shock-horror obsession of the tabloid press, such crimes are extremely rare and occupy little time of the police and none at all of the security industry. It is of crimes against property that I speak.

Most Crime Against Property.

I telephoned the Gloucestershire Police Headquarters and spoke to a senior officer. I asked him to give me a figure, off the cuff, of the proportion of crime which was against private property. He replied: "99%, and you can add a few more nines after the decimal point."

The bigness I spoke of was in financial terms, not in degree of moral turpitude; people's attitude to that can be surprisingly flexible.

Big Villains and Little Villains.

When it comes to crime, the rich are much better at it than the poor. If they are found out they can hire more and better lawyers - the Law, after all is a commodity like everything else - and they belong to the same social class as the judges, so they are going to get a more sympathetic hearing.

Professor Robert Lecachman of New York University puts it succinctly: "The lesson to the small fry is, when you steal, steal big."[3]

The concern in Britain was voiced like this: "We in this country are extremely concerned about what appears to be an explosion in white collar crime, brought about partly because sentences for bank robberies are very high while sentences for white collar crimes are ridiculously low."[4] These words were spoken by John Wood, when as Principal Assistant Director of Public Prosecutions, he addressed the American Bar Association at their annual conference in London in 1985.

The sentences for white collar crime are not only low, of course. There are, as often as not, no sentences at all, no trial, just a deal behind the curtain.

> "Customs officers have been instructed to avoid instituting prosecutions wherever possible in favour of doing cash deals with suspects accused of huge frauds particularly on VAT." [5]

Max Hastings pleaded in the Sunday Times on October 6th 1985: "How is it possible for a Tory government plausibly to demand ruthless penalties for muggers and soccer hooligans, if large scale crime in the upper reaches of society is daily going unpunished, indeed richly rewarded."

On the Left, as well might be expected, the denunciations rang out. Gerald Kaufman in a Parliamentary debate claimed that in the City of London alone crime (fraud) was running at £3 billion per annum. And Michael Meacher, Chief Opposition Spokesman for Health and Social Security, contrasted the treatment reserved by the Thatcher Government for poor delinquents as opposed to the rich:

> "All supplementary benefit fraud - of which single-payment fraud is a negligible proportion - has been estimated at less than £50 million a year by the Commons Public Accounts Committee, while tax fraud has recently been estimated by the Treasury Select Committee as costing more than £4,000 million a year. But it isn't the money so much as the further deliberate degrading of people made poor through no fault of their own, which is so despicable. The American health and welfare system puts a premium on the discriminatory mortification of its poorest applicants; Mrs. Thatcher should learn that the people of Britain no more want such ostentatious humiliation for its poorest citizens than they do for the miners."

Or :-

> "The burglars of Brixton, the Bronx or other such 'disadvantaged' areas do not theorise about their way of life and it consequences. If they get caught they risk imprisonment. Common criminals expect to 'do time'. White collar criminals, by contrast, do not. Stealing millions by computer transfer of bank balances or an insider manipulation, rarely, even when detected, leads to jail. Many were surprised when Mr. Paul Thayer, the former chairman of LTV who became America's deputy defence secretary, was sent to prison for insider trading. They should not have been. Jail is arguably often a poor punishment. But if that is what the criminal poor get when convicted, it is what the criminal rich should get too. The tarnished reputation of Lloyds of London will not be polished clean by condoning the public prosecutor's aversion to prosecution."[6]

Crime And The Swiss.

It goes without saying that corporate and white collar crime is not restricted to Britain and the U.S. In purely monetary terms they are probably eclipsed by Switzerland, which like all criminals, treats confidentiality as its second most important concern. Switzerland's economy operates like that of a criminal pawnbroker. It acts as a 'fence' for laundering the swag of all the criminals in the world, be they smart financial operators from the Bourse, Wall Street, or the City, or political operators like 'Emperor' Bokassa, Marcos of the Phillipines, and banana republic dictators preparing a luxurious retirement.

As a consequence Switzerland is awash with capital on which it does not have to pay interest - in many cases the depositors have to pay to leave their money there! (They don't take it away. People might ask where they got it.) The Swiss don't ask questions, like any good fence. This leaves them free to use the capital almost entirely, leaving only a tiny sum for reserves. There is no likelihood of a 'run on' their banks, the number of which is staggering - some 4,000 in all.

Once laundered, the money is available for all sorts of worthy causes. Switzerland, otherwise a country of peasant cultivators, has ten times the foreign holdings of the United States, on a per capita basis. On top of an agriculture which is medieval - I recall seeing a man mow a field with a scythe not far from Lausanne some ten years ago - is grafted an economy of industrial giants, from Nestle through Alusuisse, Sulzer, Brown-Boveri, to some of the biggest patent medicine firms in the world: Ciba-Geigy, Hoffman-La Roche, and Sandoz. It helps to have lots of cheap capital like Switzerland has, if you sincerely want to be rich. As for scruples, the answer is always: if we don't do it, somebody else will.

Jean Ziegler, Professor at Geneva University and Member of (the Federal) Parliament, writes of a meeting in Berne with the Councillor for Finance of the Swiss Federation, approximately our Chancellor of the Exchequer.[7] He raised the question of the flight of capital from the poorest countries in the world, stolen by the oligarchies in power and deposited in Swiss banks. The Councillor, Nello Celio, replied that the problem of capital in flight, the life blood of poor peoples, preoccupied him deeply. He added that this operation, in particular, was the cause of poverty, of hunger, of the death of so many people living precariously around the edge of the industrial world.

Ziegler asked if Celio accepted his proposal to block the flight of this capital. The Councillor replied that if he followed his convictions and accepted the proposal, the same money would simply go to Monaco or the Bahamas. The proposal (a parliamentary motion) was voted down. Ziegler in his disenchantment quotes Voltaire: "If you see a Swiss banker jump out of a window, jump after him. There's sure to be money in it!" And more sourly quotes Chateaubriand: "Neutral in the great revolutions of the states which surround them, the Swiss grow rich on the misfortunes of others and build banks out of human calamities."

It is not only the tight lipped Swiss who are attractive to criminals round the world, there are other places which welcome monies of dubious provenance with no questions asked; various West Indian Islands and small countries with few resources have put out their signboards with varying degrees of success. But the Swiss have a joker in their hand: Calvinism. The thin-lipped, unsmiling, Uriah Heep manner is reassuring to depositors. The buccaneering attitude toward international finance is fine but it must stop there. Once the money is deposited an upright, even sanctimonious front is *de rigeur*.

Crime Abroad.

Within each country of the modern world a perusal of the national press will demonstrate that the incidence of corporate crime is world wide. The creation of the European Common Market has added a local variation in cross-frontier crime.

> "The official auditors to the Common Market have uncovered evidence of wholesale fraud in the trade of farm produce. Exporters are claiming millions of pounds in subsidies for food which in many cases does not exist. As much as £600 million a year could be involved."[8]

And on the other side of the world, upper class crime is flourishing too. According to Peter Grabosky, Senior Criminologist at the Australian Institute of Criminology, Canberra:

> "It has long been apparent in the Western World that the severity with which courts deal with 'street' criminals far exceeds the penalties imposed on white-collar offenders. In September, for instance, Queensland company director Ian Beames was sentenced to two years jail for his part in

> a 'bottom of the harbour' tax scheme intended to defraud the Australian Government of $16.5 million in taxes. Beames claimed to have received only $182,000 of a supposed fee of $640,000. The maximum jail term Beames could have received is only three years. Commenting on the crime, senior law lecturer Ari Friebers said: 'A person can break into a house and steal perhaps $100 and be liable to a 14 year penalty but a person who takes $5 million can only get a maximum of five years.'"[9]

The pettiness of the individual sums and indeed the total involved in poor people's crimes are overshadowed by the huge resources devoted to tracking them down. London Transport spent £55 million on automatic barriers and other devices to save £6.5 million in fare avoidance. The Government has 30 Specialist Claims Control Units comprised of 175 staff each, chasing welfare chisellers.

Dog Does Not Eat Dog.

On the other hand the Fraud Investigation Group of the Director of Public Prosecutions has a qualified but under-paid staff of 21 to police rich men's crime running into billions (Economist).

There has not been a single prosecution in the last few years against any of the public villains in the insurance market where 'names' have been swindled of £500 millions.

Ian Hay Davison, the chief executive of Lloyd's wrote to the Prime Minister Margaret Thatcher, and to Nigel Lawson, Norman Tebbitt and John Gummer, Chancellor of the Exchequer, Industry Minister, and Chairman of the Conservative Party respectively, protesting against the failure to prosecute insurance swindlers. Davison was an outsider brought in to clean out the Augean Stable at Lloyd's.

He got little satisfaction from Thatcher and Co. According to reporter Tony Levene of the Sunday Times, the Government was "aware that many fugitive underwriters have threatened to turn Queens Evidence if they are brought back to a British court, and implicate senior Lloyd's people who have so far avoided any hint of scandal."

Levene wrote too soon. Shortly after he found that Peter Miller, Chairman of Lloyd's had taken part in 'baby' syndicates (i.e. where greater risks where shrugged off on to other 'names' and greater profits on to his portion) and, in cahoots with his predecessor at Lloyd's, Sir Peter Green, to have been secret buyers of land in the Caribbean. He understandably refused to comment when invited to by the Sunday Times.

There was clearly not room enough in Lloyd's for both Peter Miller and the whistle-blowing Ian Hay Davison and the latter was forced to resign in 1985 to the great relief of the old gang.

Outside the City rich men have equal difficulty in keeping their hands off other people's property. The annual report of the Inland Revenue makes interesting reading. Fewer than 2% of companies were investigated, but of those 90% made false returns. The amount recovered rose from £265.6 million in 1982 to £352 millions in 1983.

Paytriotism.

The Defence (pronounced W-A-R) industry here and abroad has always provided rich pickings for those companies whose patriotism doesn't stand in the way of a fast buck or a fast quid. Even during World War II companies were being caught out in 'costs plus' frauds.

Surprise, surprise, they are still at it. The Ferranti company was obliged to return several millions to the Defence Ministry in 1965 and 20 years later in March 1985 the Observer reported a scam run by the £175 million aerospace division of the Dowty Corporation, but a few miles from this spot in my native Gloucestershire. Dowty were using men paid for by the Defence Ministry to do defence work, for other commercial schemes, getting paid twice over, so to speak. A patriotic commercial assistant, Mr. Burgess Cooper, protested at the taxpayer being ripped-off thus and threatened to expose the fraud. He was sacked for 'threatening to reveal confidential company information'. But how much does not get revealed?[10]

Across the Atlantic U.S. administrations had cause to suspend or bar more than 400 defence contractors in 1984 alone. These included the biggest names: General Dynamics, General Electric, Pratt and Whitney. Charges included everything from coffee machines at $7,000 each, hammers for a mere $500,to an overcharge of $7.5 million in connection with the Sergeant York anti aircraft gun, which was finally scrapped.

American Swindlers Sentenced.

But if crime tends to be more colourful in the United States, there is less of the old pals act, less solidarity among the oligarchy. "E.F. Hutton, one of the biggest stockbrokers in the United States, has been found guilty of defrauding small banks of $10 billion (£8 billion). Investigators have also tracked down several other investment houses which were operating the same illegal overdraft scheme. Two banks, Shawmut and the Bank of Boston, received heavy fines last month for laundering $1.3 billion allegedly passed on to them from crime syndicates in stacks of $20 notes. General Electric has pleaded guilty to defrauding the US Air Force by filing 108 false invoices. The conservative pundit, William Safire, a former speech writer for Richard Nixon, has criticised prosecutors in the E.F. Hutton case for failing to file charges against any member of the Hutton management. 'Faceless companies don't filch money from banks; people in those companies do' Safire said."[11]

The difference between Britain and the U.S. does lie in the readiness of American Law to send upper class swindlers to jail. In 1962 a judge in Philadelphia sent a group of executives from General Electric, Westinghouse and Alliss Chalmers to jail for conspiring to rig prices. This would be unthinkable in Britain.

Equally unthinkable would be the four year sentence meted out in 1985 to Defence Secretary Weinberger's deputy, Paul Thayer, for insider trading, mentioned earlier, or the similar prosecution of Thomas Read, former deputy national security adviser to President Reagan himself.

But the most dramatically successful prosecution of a white collar criminal must be the case of Jake Butcher, who owned one of the largest banking chains in Tennessee. Butcher, who had raised funds for Jimmy Carter's presidential campaign, became a target of the Justice Department after his banking empire collapsed. He pleaded guilty to defrauding his own bank of $13 million, and was sentenced to 20 years imprisonment.

A Nod And A Wink.

Much more the flavour of Britain was the report in the Times of March 3rd 1986:

> "Reporting of fraud to police 'unnecessary' - Requiring auditors to report any fraud or financial irregularity they

discover in their client companies to the police or other third party would constitute unnecessary interference by the state in business affairs, according to a survey of senior businessmen.

Two out of three directors and top executives surveyed by the Chartered Association of Certified Accountants thought that auditors should be required to report fraud only to their client companies who would then undertake any necessary action on their own account."[12]

Fraudulent Prospectives.

The judges are not totally out of sympathy with this view. As Michael Clarke puts it in his book, 'Fallen Idols': "When five men, including officers of the London and County Securities were tried in 1980 for fraud over the inflation of the balance sheet by £4 million with worthless cheques, a remarkable recognition was given by the judge of one of the main themes of this book. Mr. Justice Talbot dismissed the charges against two of the defendants for lack of evidence of criminal intent. In the case of a third there was evidence that a jury could consider, but in the case of the final two, to quote from the Times report (4th October 1980): 'What concerned the jury was the accepted practice in 1973 of window dressing by companies. At that time no-one thought the practice dishonest, if not done overwhelmingly. In the climate of that time it would be quite unsafe to try to pin-point the degree of criminality in the minds of the two defendants.'"[13]

Thirteen years later the jury would have equal cause for concern. The Times again on March 3rd 1986: "The Stock Exchange is banning the photographs from new issue prospectuses except on the front page. Many recent new issues, particularly in the advertising and publicity industries, have been characterized by documents that look more like promotional brochures than representations of the companies' financial position."

If We Don't Do It Somebody Else Will.

But the Stock Exchange is in a cleft stick. Crime prevention is bad for business and could easily drive it away. At the very moment the City authorities were agonising, the Belgian Government was trying to deal with a similar problem: "The famous diamond town of Antwerp is reeling from the shock of the biggest tax fraud investigation in Belgian history. And some dealers hint darkly that if the government persists in its investigation the industry will move to other centres, such as Tel Aviv.

Tax authorities are investigating Kirschen Roger, a currency dealing and stockbroking company which handles overseas investments for many of the city's diamond dealers. The inquiry involves undeclared income overseas and non- payment of investment taxes and value added tax to the government of more than $20 million."[14]

No country is free of the problem and the situation is made worse by the new communication technology. If the going gets rough the rascals can simply move camp:

> "My word is my bond: that's still the theory. But in practice all too often my nominee holding is my escape. The City, about to be released by Government edict to the full winds of international competition, is awash with scandals which can only get worse as surveillance slithers away from national control. The latest embarrassment is the Stock Exchange's admission that 50 out of 284 full scale investigations into insider dealing since the practice was made a criminal offence in 1980 have been frustrated by the use of offshore companies. Swiss banks used to be the most popular conduit, but less stringent enforcement of secrecy has shifted offshore business to the Caribbean and Liberia. The City explains it as a fact of life: without a blind eye you lose business in international markets. (It is not just the Stock Exchange and Westland. The whole Eurobond market thrives on anonymity which breeds institutionalised tax avoidance.)"[15]

The wage and salary earner is spared this temptation. The deduction of tax at source, P.A.Y.E., eliminates the possibility of tax evasion crime. No cars, entertaining, other expenses are allowed against it, so that employees are shielded from the Sin of making false claims.

The bad news here is that a useful expansion of employment is foregone. If those on salaries and wages were left to fill in their own tax returns, the mere possibility of fraudulent claims could make for an expansion of the Inland Revenue, Police, Prison Service, Probation Officers, and After Prison Care.

It would, nevertheless, still be straining after a gnat when there is a camel to go for. The opportunity for a vast expansion of employment in crime investigation and detection of the corporate sector is even more attractive. The number of potential criminals is not great - a mere 2,000 people pull all the strings in the City,[16] for example. But quality, quality of crimes and of their perpetrators calls for a quality approach. The Edgar Wallace, Agatha Christie type of policeman with his "Nah then, Wot's goin' on 'ere?" approach simply will not do.

The Eton and Oxbridge criminal needs a Lord Peter Wimsey type of policeman, with an appropriate six figure salary. The other poor devil would merely be intimidated.

What the situation calls for is a complete Hooray Henry police force - our up-market investigators cannot work in isolation and experience shows they cannot communicate with C and D category policemen. This will undoubtedly be costly, but not to the Government.

Strict cost/benefit controls can ensure that monies recovered will more than balance expenditure - there is so much to go for. Which is more than can be said of most efforts to chase poor crooks.

1. *Social Trends 1987.*

2. *Stuart Henry : The Hidden Economy (Martin Robertson, Oxford 1978).*

3. *Robert Lecachman: Economists at Bay, p.141.*

4. *Guardian 30/01/86*

5. *Sunday Times : 15/04/84. In June 1988 the press carried the admission of the Inland Revenue that it did not bother with prosecution in the case of VAT frauds of less than £75,000.*

6. *Guardian 30/03/85.*

7. *Jean Ziegler: Une Suisse au-dessus de tout soupcon, p.103 (Editions du Seuil, Paris, 1976)*

8. *Sunday Times : 6/10/85.*

9. *New Internationalist, December 1985.*

10. Dowty were reported in the local press in the summer of 1987 as having paid back some half a million pounds to the Ministry. No action against any guilty party was reported.

11. Sunday Times : 16/06/85.

12. Times : 3/03/86.

13. Michael Clarke: Fallen Idols (Junction Books Ltd 1981).

14. Today 9/03/86.

15. ibid.

16. Becket's Directory of the City of London, reviewed by the Economist 30/11/85: "names, titles, telephone numbers and even secretaries of almost 2,000 City greats and near- greats. But it is the 600 pages of biographical details on almost 1,100 people (only seven of them women) that makes the most interesting reading. Business in this great financial centre, it seems, is still conducted between people who come from similar places and who do similar things. Half of those who admitted to being educated at a British university went to Oxford or Cambridge, and more than three-quarters went to private schools."

Chapter 14.

The War Industry.

Dedicated by the licentious soldiery to the greatest of them all; The Good Soldier Schweik.

Eyes right, arseholes tight,
Tadgers to the front;
We are the boys that make no noise
And we're always after cunt.
We're the soldiers of the night,
We would rather fuck than fight,
We are the Foreskin Fusiliers.
(Soldiers' song, World War II.)

Preparation for World War III occupies the energies of about one million people in Britain. They are made up as follows:

Service personnel ..	325,900
Ministry of Defence civilians ..	232,500
Defence expenditure jobs - directly	240,000
Ditto - indirectly	190,000
. . . .Total	988,000[1]

This is approximately 4% of the labour force. In money terms, the Defence allocation is roughly 20% of the entire budget or 10% of the Gross National Product. This proportion is greater than that spent by any other major power except the U.S. The composition of the civilian population working on war material is noteworthy. More than half the highly skilled scientists, more than half the Research and Development budget goes on military work. While the country is awash with Japanese, German, French and Italian hi-tech goods: cameras, cars, videos, medical and industrial equipment, major British hi-tech companies devote their resources to military equipment.

"The General Electric Company is a good example of the way in which resources are directed away from civil business. In its military production branches 32% of employees are qualified scientists and engineers but only 2% of employees in its consumer products divisions are so qualified."[2]

Another factor in the cost to all countries of the War Industry lies in concealed losses. Nuclear power stations and processing plants are going to sterilise areas for many thousands of years after they are de-commissioned. Add to those costs not merely the regularly occuring catastrophes: Windscale, Siberia, Three Mile Island, Chernobyl - we can add another one every few years - but the continuing unreported radioactive leaks from the nuclear installations which, the experts assure us, are much more significant public hazards.

More Fraudulent Balance Sheets.

What would be a realistic actuarial figure for these on- costs to be added to the nuclear industry balance sheet? The answer is, of course, that it has nothing to do with the case. Nuclear power stations in Britain and everywhere else were built for the war material - plutonium - they provide. The electricity is a by-product, and a grotesquely expensive one if the balance sheet is not fraudulent.

If a fraction of the gigantic sums spent on nuclear power stations had been spent on energy conservation, if the taxes had been handed back to the people to spend on insulation and stopping up draughts, the demand for electricity would be enormously reduced.

But all of these questions, dear War or cheap War beg the question, why War at all? For the medieval kings and aristocracy, war was a matter of desireable pieces of territory, treasure, treaties, dynastic claims. The common people were not invited to participate. Still more, they were discouraged from acquiring those skills and weapons which allowed the aristocracy, like the Chicago gangsters, to carry on their protection racket.

War for the ruling class in the Middle Ages was looked upon variously as a gentlemanly sport, a matter of honour or chivalry or as a large scale jousting tournament. There was enough violent death to give a little frisson to the combatants but no more, and often less: "Machiavelli mentions, as an example, the battle of Zagonara (1424) a defeat renowned throughout all Italy for which there died only Lodovico degli Obizzi, with two of his men-at-arms, who, fallen from horseback were smothered in the mire."[3]

Henry V of England broke the rules during the 100 Years War by hiring Welsh archers at Chester and Carmarthen. They were certainly not from the top drawer, but being foreigners and almost certainly unable to speak English could not drag the tone of the proceedings down in the same way as Anglo- Saxon oafs.

Not Playing The Game.

The casualties they caused with their seven foot longbows and four-feet-long-half-inch thick arrows among Henry's French cousins and their horses was clearly not the way the game was played. It was nevertheless a hint of things to come. Clausewitz says: "Although we know very little about the tactics in the battles between the Swiss and the Austrians, the Burgundians and the French, (in the War of the Spanish Succession) still we find in them unmistakable evidence that they were the first in which the superiority of a good infantry over the best cavalry was displayed."[4] And his editor, Anatol Rapoport, says that it is strange that Clausewitz does not mention the battles of Crecy and Agincourt.

If the lesson was not lost on the Continentals it still did not radically alter the way the English played the game for centuries. Prince Rupert's cavalry was still charging the Parliamentary pikemen in the Civil War during the 17th century and being punished for it. Two centuries later still Lord Cardigan with his Charge of the Light Brigade in the Crimean War (1854) was still trying to prove that sticks and stones can break your bones but cannons never hurt you - if you are a gentleman.

Officers and Gentlemen.

This event typifies the amateurish character of the British army, or rather of its officer caste. The Industrial Revolution had come (and gone), Britain ruled a fifth of the world, its manufacturing power was never greater, yet its army and navy was under the command of a gaggle of aristocratic buffoons. At the beginning of the century Napoleon had said "If I had had an English army I would have conquered the Universe." One of his best generals, Maximilian Sebastien Foy had qualified this with: "In the British Army will not be found either the strong sympathy between the leaders and the soldiers and the paternal care of the captains, the simple manner of the subalterns, nor the affectionate fellow-feeling which constituted the strength of the revolutionary armies of France."

Matters had not changed much a century later when Hindenberg said that the British Army consisted of lions led by donkeys. As for the Senior Service: "Ten years before the outbreak of the First World War the gunnery of the Royal Navy, in its own estimation the finest as well as the largest fleet in the world, was not much better than that of the dilapidated Russian ships that Roshdeshventsky sailed round the world to destruction at Tsushima. This was the result of the long Victorian peace and of the near monopoly of the navy's officer corps by the aristocracy and gentry. For the navy was no longer a deadly functional instrument of policy, it was an exclusive yacht club."[5]

Corelli Barnett goes on to say that the Navy was a service that regarded guns as objects that made ships dirty when fired. It was a luxury that Britain's ruling class had been able to afford prior to 1914. Since the Battle of Waterloo ('a damn close-run thing', according to the Duke of Wellington) the British Army had not been called upon to face anything nastier than unarmed or half-armed tribesmen; Fuzzy-wuzzies, Zulus, Afghans and the like, and even these caused problems from time to time.

Continental Europeans were playing in a different game. Armed nation-states had replaced the small professional armies of the 17th and 18th centuries, endlessly scrapping over religious and dynastic issues:- Frederick the Great, Catherine the Great, Louis XV, Gustavus Adolphus of Sweden - surely the last king to come anywhere near a battlefield, let alone be killed on one.

Changing The Rules.

All of this was swept away by the French Revolution and its military expression : Napoleon. The old regimes had hesitated to arm the peasantry - the latter might have got other ideas about using their arms - but the upstart Frenchman with the Italian accent had no such hesitation. The nation-at-arms appeared and the arms included more cannon than anybody thought could be usefully employed. More than that, cannons on such a scale did not fit into the old way of hitting and running away to be able to fight another day. When Napoleon hit, the enemy stayed hit, and the names of the Paris Metro stations bear testimony as to where it happened: Austerlitz, Marengo, Wagram, Jena and so on.

> "Pitched battles were generally avoided in the pre- Napoleonic era. The object of the campaign frequently was to reach a situation (by proper manoeuvring) in which it could become clear that one's own side had a strategic or tactical advantage over the other. Because of a universal acceptance of strategic and tactical principles by the homogeneous military community, such situations were sufficiently clear to all concerned ... Capitulation was not a disgrace."[6]

But Napoleon raised the stakes: "The revolutionary French army was not of professionals nor of conscripts who had neither a stake nor an understanding of the war they fought, but of 'patriots', a new concept in European politics. These people believed they were fighting for something ... Many of them felt that they were carrying the Rights of Man on their bayonets across Europe."[7]

The military lessons were not lost on Continental Europe : The military academies, Potsdam, St Cyr, Moscow, Vienna, adjusted their syllabuses. Sandhurst continued and continues to produce chocolate soldiers complete with bearskins and busbys and brass helmets with plumes - suitable escorts for debs. It is also regarded as a suitable training for a captain of British banking if not British industry.

Wars in Ruritania.

The political lessons were more difficult to absorb. Italy and Germany were, until 1870, divided into countless comic-opera monarchies and dukedoms, Spain was also divided into several de-facto regions, and by choosing to continue doing things in the old way, had introduced a new concept into strategy: the guerilla, or little war, which is still very much with us: "The siege of Zaragoza is among the most heroic acts in the annals of Europe."[8]

Russia, a vast backward country, also introduced a new concept; that of the aggressive retreat, or 'scorched earth' strategy. If Napoleon's army was weakened by his Spanish expedition, the it was destroyed by the invasion of Russia. The army that finally confronted Wellington and Blucher's forces at Waterloo was made up of prematurely old men who had survived twenty years of campaigning, padded out with boys of fifteen and sixteen.

It is, perhaps, a sobering thought for those who interpret the Materialist Conception of History too literally, to consider that Britain, which ended absolutism and entered the age of Capital fully a century before France, did not conscript a citizen army until 1915, fully a century after France.

World War I was the last war where the massive slaughter was almost exclusively of soldiers. The twenty million dead were almost all military.

Total War.

World War II introduced the massive slaughter of civilians as well. Dresden, London, Cologne, Coventry, Hiroshima, Nagasaki, were as dangerous to be in as the frontline. Moscow, Leningrad, Stalingrad, were the frontline. Total War, which had been stipulated by the philosopher of war, von Clausewitz, drawing upon the lessons of Napoleon, had been eagerly taken up by Adolf Hitler. All that remained was Total Elimination. The end of World War II provided the beginning of World War III.

War, we are assured, like the Poor, has always been with us. And the one statement is as false as the other. The truth is much simpler. As Clausewitz says: "War is not merely a political act, but also a real political instrument, a continuation of political commerce, a carrying out of the same by other means."[9]

War has always been a squabble between pimps as to who shall control the whores. Appeal to the history of primitive man is a nonsense. To argue that the migrations, the *volkervanderungen*, of prehistory led to wars is to indulge in bourgeois fantasy - to think that all epochs are tarred with the same brush.

> "In ancient times, the cirumstances connected with War, as well as the method of carrying it on, were different ... The farther we go back, the less useful becomes military history, as it gets so much more meagre and barren of detail. The most useless of all is that of the ancient world."[10]

War Comes Home To The Rich.

By the 20th century, however, the consequences of war were proving increasingly disconcerting to the ruling elites. In the early part of the 1914 War, life went on much as before for the wealthy. But as the brave young subalterns who had gone out with wooden heads, started to come home in wooden boxes, doubts crept in. One in five officers was killed, one out of eight other ranks. The ordinary people, needless to say, were worse off than ever. Most things, food in particular, were in short supply, but those with money were scarcely affected. Still, money is not much good to a dead son or husband, even if he is a Hooray Henry.[11]

The slaughter of officers in the 1939-45 War was different. The exclusive preserve of aristocrats and gentlemen was invaded by petit bourgeois types and grammar-school educated proles - particularly in the Air Force, where the slaughter was greatest. Still, the effects of war were coming a little too near home. With the Nuclear Age, the bluster served as much as anything to cover self doubt. Nuclear fall-out threatens to make everybody radioactive; the Nuclear Winter will make everybody cold.

But as far as the 99% of the population who have to be at the factory gate at eight, or the office door at nine on a Monday morning, are concerned, the issue has always been a different one. How much blood, their own and that of their nearest and dearest, should they be prepared to shed to defend that right to be at the office or factory. What should they be prepared to sacrifice to prevent an invader cutting their wages or lengthening their hours? Most governments oppose any efforts of people to preserve, let alone improve, their circumstances. Has anyone ever heard of a government which supported a strike for more money or better conditions?

Advancing The Wrong Way.

Disenchantment with the war has always posed several problems for the ruling classes. Bright uniforms were worn by common soldiers in the 18th and 19th centuries as much to identify those who got second thoughts about fighting, as for any other reason. In some parts of Europe they over-lapped the Sumptuary Laws, obliging the peasantry to wear dull colours and plain weaves so as not to get ideas above their station.

Those with second thoughts were treated brutally, worst of all in Britain. The branding of deserters with red hot irons marking a 'D' on the forehead was not abolished until 1870, and flogging not until 1881. And there was always the death penalty.

Sheep To The Slaughter.

Judge Anthony Babington12 traced 346 soldiers of the thousands of British soldiers murdered by the British Army during the First World War. The real total is unknowable, it is part of Official Secrets in the most secretive country in the world after Soviet Russia. The majority of the victims were children of 17 and 18, lured into the services by the primitive propaganda machine of 1914: military bands, posters of Kitchener 'I Want You', sold like Sunlight Soap, a shilling a head to the sergeant for every man recruited. My grandfather, a labourer with 8 children, and approaching middle age, was recruited in a pub, with half a dozen of his cronies, all drunk on the hospitality of the recruiting sergeant.

The British Navy was organised upon a different basis. It was the first line of defence of the country and just had to be more professional than the army. Its crews were drawn from the seafaring population of the long coastline and though less well equipped than other fleets - the French, in particular - made up for it frequently with better seamanship.

When given better ships they were capable of extraordinary things. The Scots fisherman John Paul Jones, who threw in his lot with the American colonists and is to the American Navy what Nelson is to the British, succeeded in humiliating the latter. Having rubbished the King's Navy along the American coast, he crossed the Atlantic and, equipped by the French, circled Britain, occupying towns, taking hostages, and generally frightening the wits out of the Lords of the Admiralty.[13]

Whose Navy?

The Navy shared a problem with the Army: the common people frequently did not see what the struggle with other governments had to do with them, and so, forced labour, first with press gangs, and later with conscription was the only answer. The origin of the Marines, royal or otherwise, was as (floating) concentration camp guards. They were always quartered amidships, armed to the teeth, because the officers in the stern were afraid of the men in the foc'sle. Dr Johnson as usual had little doubt: "No man will be a sailor who has contrivance enough to get himself into jail; for being in a ship is being in a jail, with the chance of being drowned."

Winston Churchill as late as the early 20th century dismissed the Navy as nothing but 'Rum, sodomy, and the lash'. Brutality and foul conditions: rats, fleas, lice, bringing typhus and dysentery and a gamut of other diseases produced endless mutinies - as with the Army. Information about these was always suppressed - it still is - but was occasionally on such a scale that concealment was impossible.

Mutinies At Sea.

Such mutinies as those at Spithead and the Nore (1798)[14] involved the whole fleet, where men were induced to give up their arms upon the promise of improved conditions and no reprisals. The Officers were as treacherous as they were cowardly. The spokesmen were singled out, 30 of them were hanged, hundreds transported, and flogging went on as merrily as ever and conditions were not improved.

130 years later the Navy had to admit to having another mutiny on its hands, this time in the Northern Fleet at Invergordon and Scapa Flow. Because of the Wall Street Crash and the world slump which followed, the British Government had gone on a cost cutting expedition ; for the unemployed it was the Geddes Axe and the Means Test, for the sailors it was the halving of wages. But the mutiny was suppressed, the ringleaders went to penal servitude, wages were cut, and the sailors settled down to wait for an opportunity to die in World War II.

Mutinies On Land.

Peter Tatchell wrote:

> My own limited researches over the last decade have uncovered more than 40 mutinies, strikes, mass demonstrations, and riots by soldiers and sailors in the latter stages of the 1914-18 war and the two years thereafter. Some of these military rebellions were far more spectacular than the events at Etaples and most of them were much more

> successful in that the chiefs-of-staff were often forced to make major concessions to the mutineers.
>
> In January 1919, for example, 4000 soldiers demanding improved camp conditions and speedier demobilisation called a general strike and seized control of the army headquarters in Calais. Within 3 days, 20,000 troops joined the uprising and elected delegates to soldiers' committees which took over the administration of all army camps in the Calais district. When General Byng arrived with troops to put down the mutiny, his men were reluctant to act against the rebels, and many ended up joining them. Powerless to crush the mutineers, the army brass was forced to concede the soldiers' demands for improved food, new barracks, increased leave.
>
> About the same time there were also mutinies at 19 army camps in Britain. One of the biggest was at Folkestone where 10,000 troops went on strike. After marching through the town centre, they voted to form a soldiers' union to agitate against poor food, excessive officer privileges, and orders that they return to France. Field Marshall Sir Henry Wilson later recalled in his autobiography that unrest in the ranks was so intense and widespread that an unofficial cabinet meeting was held to discuss the situation. Churchill warned the prime minister that military discipline was disappearing fast, and General Haig said the British army in France was on the verge of total collapse."[15]

The situation was little different during the Second World War, particularly towards the end. News leaked through of mutinies in India, Palestine, Egypt and the Western Desert. This time no-one was shot, but Anthony Babington has managed to trace four who were hanged for lack of enthusiasm, one in London and three in the Pacific. There were 36 military executions for murder during the same war; one can only hope that it was for killing their officers. In any event they must have been a tiny fraction of the total number of officers who had the backs of their heads blown in by the men behind. But these executions only came out in a parliamentary written reply 25 years after the end of the War. By this time the 'fragging' of officers by their men in the Vietnam War had become a serious problem.

Working Ones' Ticket.

For 90 out of every 100 servicemen, the most important thing in life was to 'work one's ticket', to get out. 85,000 managed it as conscientious objectors. Many more tried it but had their plea of conscience rejected:

"What would you do if the ememy came and killed your father and your brothers and raped your mother and your sisters?"

"I would call a policeman."

Or less optimistic:

"I would suffer!"

Many more tried a different tack by malingering: feigning madness, homosexuality, flat feet, gastric ulcers, or any other ills that the flesh is heir to.

What Was The War About?

There was some confusion for a long time over what the War was about. It was certainly not about Czechoslovakia which was the first country to be attacked by Hitler's army. The Prime Minister himself assured everybody that it was 'a small country, far away' and therefore, presumably, of no consequence. But when Poland was attacked it was different, and war was declared on Germany. The Press and radio wound themselves up to a frenzy of denunciation of Germany and praise of pre-war Poland.

Much of the press had difficulties at first. The Daily Mail and its stable companions of the Rothermere Press had been staunchly pro-Hitler ; the Daily Express could not believe that Britain could ally itself with Bolshevism to fight Germany and proclaimed 'There Will Be No War', right up until the day war broke out. Then, with the Molotov- Ribbentrop Pact, where Hitler's Germany and Stalin's Russia got together to divide Poland between them, the Express denounced Russia for infidelity. The Times and Telegraph were relieved that Hitler had a short way with the unions, but were uncomfortable with some of his measures.

The newspapers merely reflected the divisions in the British ruling class. There was a small group led by Churchill, Eden, and Hore-Belisha, who were selected by Nazi propaganda for most of the abuse; they were plainly anti-dictator, although Churchill himself had said at the end of the '20's: "If I were an Italian I should be proud to serve under Signor Mussolini."

Hore-Belisha, as a Jew, could hardly be sympathetic to the Nazi movement, although his co- religionists issued an appeal in support of Hitler during the Reich's Presidential election in August 1934:

> "We members of the Association of National German Jews, founded in 1921, have always, both in war and peace, placed the welfare of the German people and the German Fatherland, with which we feel ourselves indissolubly bound, above our own welfare. That is why, despite the fact that it brought hardships in its train, we welcomed the national rising in 1933, because we regarded it as the only way to repair the damage caused in fourteen years of misfortune by un-German elements."[16]

The majority of those on the Right were and still are anti- semitic. But one has only to peruse the publications of the 'Right Book Club' of the Thirties to feel the difference from the post-war ethos. As a consequence, the propaganda machine waited until almost the end of the War to tell us that, indeed, the treatment of the Jews and the effort to free them had been the real *casus belli*. Only cynics would commit the indiscretion of saying that if that were the case, then the effort was an utter failure.

> "Your review of the book 'Breaking the Silence' raises a distant memory. During the war I was the editor of a British weekly in Stockholm. One morning in 1942 I received an anonymous letter containing a cutting from a Swiss newspaper. With the help of a dictionary I got enough out of it to realise that I had in my hand 'the scoop of the century'.
> I called the press attache of the Swiss legation and told him about the article. He excused himself and there was a long silence on the line. When he returned he told me that the paper was a small provincial and socialist publication and he could not vouch for its editorial accuracy. Whereupon he hung up. The article dealt in some detail with the Nazi concentration camps in Eastern Europe and the wholesale extermination of Jews. Since I did not trust my telephone I brought the cutting to the press attache of the British legation, in civil life a professor of northern languages at Cambridge. He knew more German than I and his reaction was the same as mine. He kept the article and that was the last time I saw or heard of it. When I later asked him about it he shrugged his shoulders and shook his head. He brought out a bottle of whisky and when we

> had finished our drinks and I was about to depart he looked at me and uttered 'sorry'."[17]

Still, the propaganda campaign on behalf of the Jews made it impossible to continue the overt anti-semitism of the Thirties. The laws against it merely formalised its social unacceptability. And the change in public feeling (or the transfer to other groups: Pakistanis, blacks) caused the disappearance of Jewish cultural paranoia. The tiny minority who retained it emigrated to Israel, to create cultural paranoia in the Palestinians - and a new theatre of War.

So ended five centuries of Wars beginning with the Reformation, where religion was the pretext. Religion was a dead issue. Rabbis and priests bemoaned the breakup of their communities and parishes, the Protestant sects were selling off their empty chapels and churches. Henceforward the only place where religion was a pretext for War was in the Third World, particularly the Middle East.

What Will The Next War Be About?

In the Developed World, there is as much confusion about what the cause of the Third World War will be attributed to as there was about World War II. The memory of pro-Russian propaganda has faded, but is still difficult for the machine to convert the Soviet system into a bogeyman to frighten West Europeans with. It would have been a lot easier in the 1940's with Stalin's butchery still fresh on the record. Still the Industrial-Military Complex has a momentum of its own, perceived in the early 1950's by President Eisenhower, and preparations for War continue, frequently updated because of new discoveries. Vast underground bunkers have been built at a cost of zillions to house those who will be selected to survive: "The British Medical Association is to spell out who will be allowed to live, and who should be left to die after a nuclear war. An expert group similar to that which embarrassed the Government with its assessment of the medical effects of a nuclear attack, is now being set up and is due to complete its report next year.

Those picked to survive would include market gardeners, mechanics, and nurses, Dr John Dawson, head of the BMA's science division, told a weekend conference.

Anyone unable to contribute to the survival and regeneration of the community would be denied treatment. That, he said, would probably include doctors because they tended to know little about first aid and were helpless without their equipment.

Britain's one million diabetics, and all those needing constant supplies of drugs to survive, would be left to die. The report would not be for or against civil defence, it would be a careful examination of the facts, Dr Dawson told the European symposium of International Physicians for the Prevention of Nuclear War, meeting in Madrid.

'To duck the issue is to con the public' he said. 'There is a cosy assumption put out by the Government that treatment will be all right, we'll muddle through somehow, and Vera Lynn will be singing again.'

The Government had no plans for selecting which of the millions of casualties of an attack should be treated, Dr Dawson said later, so the BMA would do it for them. 'We say there should be an open public discussion on the selection of casualties for treatment so we are setting up a working party to study it,' he added.

With no health service, desperate shortages of blood, dressings, and drugs all resources would have to be concentrated on those who could contribute to the survival and possible regeneration of the community. He said that the rest 'should not be treated if they are injured, because to do so would be to waste resources.'

The BMA's first report forced the Home Office to rethink its calculations of the numbers who would be killed in an attack. Civil defence plans are being revised to take account of data which suggests that a full scale attack would kill 26 million people - half the population of the UK - and not 16 million as the Home Office had previously assumed."[18]

For those of us who are not mechanics, nurses and market gardeners, and therefore condemned to the knackers yard, we can be assured and relieved that preparations are in hand to deal with us in a manner showing respect for the dead:

"The most economical method of disposing of the dead in nuclear war, would be by mass burial, Mr. Alan Bullett, Kent's deputy surveyor, told the Cremation Society conference at Harrogate yesterday. We should be planning them now.

A mass grave of 'manageable proportions' would be up to 50 metres long, 4 metres wide, and 2.5 metres deep to accommodate five layers of 200 bodies - 1000 bodies in all. One mechanical digger could dig a grave in

25 hours using 25 gallons of fuel.

Sites would have to be near the explosion because the mass movement of bodies would be both a health risk and 'terribly damaging' to the morale of survivors. Quarries or mine workings could be used but mass burials risked polluting water supplies. In Kent for example 90% of all water was pumped up from underground aquifers. Burial sites should be close to those urban centres carrying lesser risk of water pollution or in areas where graves could be protected by impervious linings.

Cremation would have to be considered after burial, but the problem would lie in finding the right type of fuel in sufficient quantities to burn the heavy pyres of bodies.

Mr Bullett drew some guidance from Ministry of Agriculture advice on the burning of animal carcases after an outbreak of foot and mouth disease. The greater the number of cattle to be burned the more the fire would be fuelled by their own fat. If a pyre of 150 cows could be made, the fuel needed would be 100 bales of straw, 7.1 tons of kindling wood, 105 railway sleepers, 3.8 tons of old tyres and a supply of napalm-type chemical to help ignition.

This would be a reasonable method of disposing of the dead in a conventional war when the structure of the country was still intact. But in a nuclear war fuel was likely to be used only for the transport of food and medical supplies. Crematoriums could be used as radiation sickness took its toll. A member of the audience said that bodies needed a hard base for loading into a crematorium. If coffins were not available a sheet of corrugated iron would do.

Mr Bullett gave some idea of the likely death toll by quoting Home Office estimates. A ground burst of one megaton in a city with a population of 520,000 evenly spread would mean that about 16,500 bodies would not be recovered at the centre of the explosion. Deaths occurring up to 3.3 miles from the burst would leave 200,000 bodies for disposal, with more to come from radiation sickness.

The Government has given local authorities the task of disposal. The Home Office, in an emergency circular of 1976, devoted 3 paragraphs to the subject.

Mr Bullett commented:

> 'My descriptions of the disposal of the dead will have given a picture of ruthless pragmatism, and you may wonder whether any civilised procedure, such as your society epitomises, or even religion, would come into it.
> It is therefore noteworthy that even in the desperate days after the Dresden raid (where 137,000 people were killed) and when terrible tasks were performed, respect for the dead was always evident.'"[19]

But the prediction of Nuclear Winter, which will spare no- one, has put a new joker into the pack, worth more than the whole suit of trumps. Even before this calculation the country's senior soldier, Field Marshall Lord Carver, and the number one scientist, Sir Solly Zuckerman, had dismissed the idea of nuclear war as not only unwinnable for unfightable. They were joined in their conclusions by 5000 senior scientists worldwide in late 1986.

1. Annual Digest of Statistics 1987 (HMSO).

2. Sunday Times 5/10/86.

3. Anatol Rapaport: Introduction to Clausewitz On War (Penguin 1968).

4. ibid.

5. Corelli Barnett : The Swordbearers p.109. (Eyre & Spottiswood 1963).

6. Clausewitz / Rapaport p.19.

7. ibid p.20.

8. Grant & Temperley : Europe in the 19th and 20th Centuries (Longmans 1945).

9. Clausewitz on War, p.119.

10. ibid p.237.

11. Pallida mors aequo pede pulsat pauperum tabernas regumque turres. Horace, Odes.

12. Judge Anthony Babington : For the Sake of Example, (Secker & Warburg 1983)

13. cf. John Paul Jones, A Sailor's Biography by Samuel Eliot Morison, Rear Admiral and Professor of History at Harvard (Faber 1959).

14. cf. Manwaring & Dobree : The Floating Republic, an Account of the Mutinies at Spithead and The Nore in 1797 (Penguin 1937).

15 . Letter to Guardian 19/09/86.

16. Hjalmar Schacht : Account Settled (Weidenfeld 1949).

17. Letter to the Economist 3/09/87 by Gosta E. Sandstrom.

18. Guardian 20/10/86.

19. Guardian 28/07/83.

Chapter 15.

Manufacturing Industry.

By 1987 manufacturing industry in Britain was employing some 5 million people, half the number of 20 years earlier.

"Industrial employment fell 1,986,000 or by 246,000 a year from 1966 to 1974 ... The structure of the British economy started to deteriorate slowly after 1966 and rapidly after 1970."

So wrote Robert Bacon and Walter Eltis in 1975 (Britain's Economic Problem: Too Few Producers). But these innocent enthusiasts for the Market economy had no idea what was in store for them - and us. Employment in industry went on falling steadily until 1979. Then the Thatcher government came to power and the situation rapidly got even worse, another 3 million jobs were lost in industry. Some found employment in the non-productive sector of the economy : finance, merchandising, private police forces - i.e. those sectors of the economy which were expanding, and the remainder joined the ranks of the unemployed, which totalled some 4.5 millions by the middle of 1987.

Rakes' Progress.

This should have produced economic and financial collapse. Poor relief was taking two fifths of all taxation, the budget had increased from 33% to 38% of the Gross National Product. The collapse was delayed however, by the coming on stream of North Sea Oil, which masked the situation by replacing imported oil and the need to earn foreign exchange to pay for it. It even provided a net surplus which together with the 'invisible earnings' of the gambling casino of the City, and foreign investments, created a euphoria among certain financial columnists and the Chancellor, Nigel Lawson, himself a former journalist, which provoked a snarling rebuke from industrial directors like Sir John Harvey-Jones lately of ICI and Lord Weinstock of GEC.

The future of Britain lay in 'service' industries said the Chancellor. We were living in the post-industrial age described by Herman Kahn, W.W. Rostow and Daniel Bell (and echoed by dozens more fatheads). Weinstock asked did they think that in the absence of industry we could all make a living by selling ice-creams to each other? There was no reply to that one, but Geoffrey Maynard of the Chase Manhattan Bank and the University of Reading wrote that the U.K.'s manufacturing deficit didn't matter because the gap was being filled by oil experts. And after that?

> "The widespread fear that the UK no longer has the manufacturing capacity to fill the gap left by oil is probably overdone. A much greater danger seems to lie in the difficulty of bringing about a necessary fall in the UK's efficiency real wages (that is real wages relative to productivity) as compared with our major competitors."[1]

At the time that was written in January 1986, the wages of British industrial workers were little higher in real terms than they had been 20 years earlier and were the lowest in the developed world. (See graph fig.3). Because of the lack of investment, British industry was also the least automated, and the number of hours worked was the highest in Europe. But Professor Maynard was simply one of many arguing that way, academics, bankers, financial columnists, politicians. One thing that linked them all was their ignorance of industry. As engineers might say, they wouldn't know whether their arses were punched or bored, wouldn't know swarf from suds, wouldn't know a podger from a putlog.

> "The average production worker in America cost his boss $13.10 an hour to employ last year. This was more than in any other industrial country - partly because of the dollar's strength. The same worker cost $10.10 an hour in West Germany and $8 in Japan. The cheapest worker in all the 13 countries shown in the chart was in Spain, at $5.50 an hour. These figures include such indirect costs as social security and pension provisions as well as wages. In West Germany, Italy, France and Austria these additional charges were equivalent to more than 80% of the basic wage. In America, Canada and Britain they added only about 40% to wage costs."[2]

De-skilled Britain.

The attitude betrayed was one responsible for much of what was and is wrong with British industry. The idea that it could be allowed to die for 5 or 10 years and then resuscitated by mouth-to-mouth, or chest thumping techniques, is breath-taking, literally, if I may use that much abused adverb. The consequences of de-industrialisation are not overcome so easily, as the Thatcher government found out, and struggled to deal with.

"Britain is facing a desperate shortage of trained car mechanics, it was claimed yesterday." Kenneth Vincent, chairman of the Council of the Institute of the Motor Industry, said: 'We used to have 13,000 apprentice mechanics coming out of their training every year. Now it is only 400.' Mr. Vincent said that a few years ago many garages were reluctant to sign trainee mechanics for a 4 year apprenticeship, because if business turned down they could not dismiss them.

'As an industry, I think we were also uncertain as to which way training should go, but now we are reaping the wind. We need young flexible minds in today's market, since cars are becoming much more complicated and reliant on computers and engine management systems. We have to have closer liaison with technical colleges or we will be facing serious problems soon.'"[3]

In the midst of massive unemployment British industry nevertheless found itself short of skilled manpower in the mid 1980's. The old apprentice system had been allowed to die and it had not been replaced with the appropriate amount of further education: "Three out of four firms in America, Britain and Japan claim to have adult training programmes of their own. So companies in all three countries share the same committment to raising the qualities of their employees, right? If only it were true. Japanese firms do more than anyone else, followed by American corporations and a long, long way behind come British firms.

Overall, Britain plc. is reckoned to have spent two billion ($2.8 billion) on training in the last year. In America it is at least $40 billion, for a work-force only 4.3 times larger. The Japanese figure is even more difficult to gauge. But Mr. Konosukematsushita, founder of Matsushita Electronics, puts it at three or four times the American figure per employee."[4]

With regard to wages, foreign companies in Britain have historically paid 50% more, and made 100% higher returns on capital invested. Ford established themselves at Dagenham in the 1920's, General Motors at Luton in the 1930's and they were followed by a mass invasion from the United States into Europe in the post-war years, which led Jacques Servan-Schreiber to write his 'Le defi americain' (The American Challenge).[5] In the 1970's the Japanese electronic companies set up shop in South Wales, Nissan in Newcastle; the only complaints about British workers came from British companies.

Ill Fares The Factory.

Meanwhile the traditional centres of industrial wealth creation, the Midlands, home of metal-bashing; the North- East and the Clyde, home of heavy engineering and ship- building; Yorkshire and Lancashire, heavy engineering again and textiles, all of these and the other areas which have been the source of wealth began to ressemble the bombed cities of wartime Europe. Everywhere there were collapsed north-light roofs, weed-covered approach roads and factory entrances; a rust blight spread over Britain North and West of Watford.

The particular lack of feedback or of any self-correcting mechanism in the market-based economy encouraged things to go from bad to worse. The poor prospects in industry drove those with money to invest, to place it anywhere but in industry: in property, for example - real estate oscillated between prosperity and boom from the early '60's to the late '80's. The balance, after foreign exchange was freed by the Thatcher government in 1979, was shipped abroad, some £100 billions of it, and British industry was flattened still further.

As a consequence Britain's per capita Gross National Product was overtaken by countries like Japan, Italy and Spain, and was beginning to be bracketed with Greece, Portugal and Korea. Manufacturing output in 1986 was 3.9% lower than it had been in the first half of 1979, and 6% lower than it had been during the 3 day week in 1974![6] The rot had started a long time before that, however:

> "When the British people in the euphoria of victory put up the bunting in the streets on VE-Day in 1945, they took it for granted that Britain was, and would always remain, a first-class industrial power. They assumed that, once the short-term economic difficulties caused by the war were overcome, Britain would again be among the wealthiest countries in the Western World. After all, she alone of pre-war European great states had never been defeated or occupied, while - as everyone knew - her war production had displayed prodigies of inventiveness, output and team effort.
>
> Yet four decades later Britain finds herself the debilitated sufferer from 'the British Disease' - diminished to 14th in the GDP per head in the non-Communist world, with manufacturing output per head only a third of that of West Germany, and with the wreckage of great industries up for auction to foreigners. Alas, there is a simple answer to this apparent puzzle.
>
> Total war submits nations to a ruthless audit of skills, resources and failings. In the case of France, Germany and Japan in the Second World War this audit was manifested by the blunt fact of outright defeat. In the case of Britain the audit was hidden behind the brilliant facade of victory. It has remained buried ever since in secret wartime government files - files that have only just surrendered their secrets.
>
> From old Victorian heavy industries, like coal and shipbuilding to new high-technology sectors like machine-tools and aircraft, the bare productivity record reveals the

> wartime existence of 'the British Disease'.
>
> In the aircraft industry, peak British productivity was only four fifths of the German peak and less than half the American. It took 3 times the man-hours to build a Spitfire Mark VC as its rival the Messerschmitt 109G. In aero-engine output Rolls-Royce in 1944 managed only seven-tenths of the productivity achieved by Daimler-Benz, despite heavy bombing and the dispersal of plant. Urgent wartime field investigations into low productivity in various industries identified one common primary cause in a lack of able skilled management. There were too many ill-trained managers of poor personal calibre who could neither plan complex production flows nor give effective leadership to the workforce: true of shipbuilding; true of coal mining; true of aircraft and electronics production.
>
> This, then, was an industrial economy only fit to ride up passively on a swelling tide of world demand, and only so long as Britain's old trade rivals remained prostrated by defeat. What it needed was root-and-branch restructuring and modernisation; massive capital investment - exactly the programme which Western European countries carried out for themselves in the late 1940s and early 1950s. But Britain was never to embark on such a programme."[7]

I recall taking a motor tyre to be repaired in a provincial German town in the early fifties. The mechanic took the wheel and placed it on a vertical spindle and that was about all the physical effort he made. With a series of pneumatic contraptions he got the inner tube out, took it to be vulcanised, replaced it on the wheel and got the cover back on with no more exertion than one would use in washing dishes. I watched, fascinated, thinking of the way in the job was made a wrestling match with levers and lump hammers back home. If my memory serves me right, those devices did not become standard here until the 1960s. But, after all, if labour is cheap, why bother?

Of course there are those who argue that a manufacturing industry isn't necessary, or not very much, anyway: "Manufacturing has diminished, absolutely as well as relatively, since 1979; it now accounts for only 25%

of our output and employment. But other industries and especially services have grown to replace it and add further to economic growth. Among them the City takes pride of place, with banking and financial services generally now contributing no less than 14% of our national output and 10% of employment."[8]

Or from another cretin: "The notion that unites (critics) against the moneymen is a myth. It is the idea that financial markets are a zero-sum game: nobody gains except at somebody else's expense. Because one man's profit is allegedly another man's loss, society never gains ...

The attack misfires in two ways. First it implies that bankers and brokers produce nothing which is desirable in its own right, nothing as worthwhile as a car or a pair of shoes. Anybody who has bought an insurance policy or opened a bank account knows that is false."9

Only economists can write rubbish like that. The proprietor of a whelk stall or an ice cream kiosk who started entering his insurance premiums and bank charges on the credit side of his ledger or among his assets would not survive in business for five minutes. They'll be telling us next that that road accidents are added to the Gross National Product. But as Ralph Nader has pointed out, they are, they are!

The largest sector of manufacturing today is occupied by the motor industry; it took £25 billion out of a total £144 billion consumers expenditure in 1983 and can only have grown since.[10] In some families it can account for a third of total outgoings; it is difficult to run any kind of vehicle on less than £25 a week. Yet with the decay of public transport and the need to travel increasing distances to work, there is no alternative to car ownership for the majority of people. The fate of the British motor industry can be taken as a paradigm for the rest of manufacturing industry in these islands and has some relevance for the rest of the developed world.

Motor Manufacturing.

From its beginnings in France and Germany in the 1880s motor vehicle construction and use spread slowly to the other European countries and across the Atlantic. The importance of the French contribution as far as the Anglo-Saxon world is concerned is attested to by the vocabulary of motoring: carburettor, chauffeur, garage. France and Germany were still responsible for 58% of world production in 1906, but European production in its entirety was less than 50,000 vehicles. They were aimed at a luxury market, beautifully made, by highly skilled craftsmen, with which Europe was well endowed.

Then the First World War intervened and car manufacture yielded to the military. But the position across the Atlantic was very different. The United States population was scattered across an enormous land mass and poorly served with communications, at least by European standards. North America lacked the thousands of feeder lines linking smaller communities with the main rail networks and its roads were poor. It had a need of cheap mass transport; not expensive, exquisite, and exclusive horseless carriages. It also needed a simple design capable of being executed by operatives who were at best semi-skilled. The people who had emigrated and were available for work had not come from Turin and Milan but from Sicily and the Mezzogiorno, not from Hamburg and Cologne but from Poland and the Ukraine. After several false starts Henry Ford settled upon the Model T design which incorporated the best ideas of a number of other producers.

"From 1,700 vehicles in the company's first year (1903) production rose slowly to 10,000 in 1908, when the Model T was introduced, but then exploded to 300,000 in 1914, when the assemble line was fully installed. By 1923, when Model T sales peaked, Ford's U.S. production totalled 1.9 million. At that point, after the economic devastation of World War I had completely halted European production for 5 years and crippled the postwar economy, Ford was producing 44% of the world's output of automobiles from his American production base.

In that year other American producers, notably the rapidly growing General Motors, accounted for additional 2.1 million units, bringing the American share of world auto production in 1923 to 91%."[11]

This was achieved by a comparatively small labour force. The American car manufacturer was in reality an assembler of bought-in components. The British manufacturer attempted to make everything in-house at the beginning, and when he was driven to buy-in components before World War I William Morris, for example, was able to obtain engine units from Detroit at half the price he was quoted in Coventry. The situation was little different after the war when Morris found he could buy-in engines from Hotchkiss, a French subsidiary in England, cheaper than he could get them made in his own factory. From that time on the car industry assumed the form that it has kept until very recently.

Mass Production.

The assembly line was, and still is, the core of the business. Ford was credited with the application of the technique to car manufacture, but the system was widespread in 19th century processes. According to D.G. Rhys[12] Ford got the idea from the Chicago slaughterhouses, and it is not such a long distance from the nightmarish world of The Jungle, as Upton Sinclair portrayed the meat-packing business, to the mind-destroying slog on The Line at Ford, chez Renault, or at B.Ae/Rover.

Between the wars the motor industry went its different ways in the European countries, shielded from competition by tariffs and the idiosyncracies of local markets. France and Italy, with heavy duties on petroleum products, concentrated on high performance: overhead valves, 'oversquare' i.e. short-stroke wide-bore engines, calculated to produce the maximum effort from the minimum amount of fuel.

Britain, with a bizarre tax on cylinder bore diameters, ended up with cylinders like bicycle pumps. The engines were not competitive in export markets but the tax kept out the competition from home and empire markets. American home production developed in directions as odd as any. Having begun as small light vehicles before World War I, American cars became bigger and bigger, while European cars became smaller to meet the mass market and more crowded urban conditions. American cars settled down to an unchanging and primitive basic design: beam axles, cart springs, and enormous, inefficient side-valve engines - petrol was cheap in the U.S. The market was kept alive by endless variations on body-trim, wryly satirised by cartoonists like Steinberg in the New Yorker.

European Individualism.

The Italians were meanwhile producing some of the most beautiful and superbly engineered cars in the world - for the luxury market ; Maserati, Ferrari, Alfa-Romeo; and, with the French, completing the development of the motor car. Overhead-valve engines, independent four-wheel suspensions, yielding simultaneously power with economy, and a comfortable ride over rough surfaces while not rolling on corners; all of the basic elements of the modern car were available before the end of the 1920s.

American Amalgamation.

The industry had begun in all of the developed countries with a large number of small companies. In the United States the General Motors Company united many of these before World War I, and by the 1930s there were only three producers in the United States: General Motors, Ford and Chrysler, although G.M. marketed many of its models under the old names of Pontiac, Cadillac, Buick etc.

In Europe many small companies continued producing up to and even after World War II. Once production got going again however, names started to disappear; the companies were either wound-up or were absorbed by other producers. Simca, Panhard, Riley, Humber, Singer, Standard. In France Citroen, a brilliantly innovative company, was absorbed by Peugeot, whose engineering was not so good but whose book-keeping was better. In Britain a number of companies were gathered together under the heading of Rootes Brothers, which was brought up by Chrysler, which then sold it to Peugeot. In Italy the market is dominated by one producer Fiat (Finance-auto) which bought up Lancia and Ferrari.

Germany, which shared with France the original creative achievement of the motor car, suffered more than any country from the effects of two world wars on its motor industry. Nevertheless, the Volkswagen Beetle, which as the name indicates, began life as Hitler's 'People's Car' and was designed by the great engineer Porsche, in 1934, ended up as one of the motor industry's great successes in the post-war markets. It continued to be manufactured until the middle 1970s in Germany and is still being manufactured in Brazil in the late 1980s.

Americans Drop Their Guard.

The Beetle enjoyed great commercial success in the United States in the sixties and was the first foreign car to do so. American tariffs against foreign cars, which had been 45% before World War I, were reduced to less than 10% after 1950, such was the confidence felt by the American producers in the control of their own market. European manufacturers followed suit from 1968 with the creation of the Common Market: tariffs were eliminated altogether between European countries and reduced to just over 10% for non-European producers. At this point, enter the Japanese, centre stage, bowing.

Japan had developed a very sophisticated motor-cycle and fractional-horsepower industry in the 1950s and 1960s which swept all before it. All the light motor-cycle manufacturers in France, Germany and Britain went out of business. In Italy, an Argentinian of Italian extraction had become head of the principal manufacturer of motor scooters and motor cycles: Lambretta, Moto Guzzi. Having taken a good hard look at Japanese export and import tactics, he issued an ultimatum to the Italian government; either do something about Japanese imports or he would go back to Argentina. The Italian Government did something about Japanese imports and Italy is the only western country left with a motor cycle industry in the medium and light- weight divisions. In the heavy-weight class the United States has moved against the Japanese to protect the home producer, Harley-Davidson, having preached free trade to the rest of the world. In Germany the government has done much the same to protect BMW, whose beautiful twin cylinder models are so much favoured by the British police, and seem almost unchanged since the 1930s.

In the wake of the motor-cycle exports the Japanese started to follow-up with motor cars. Their first efforts met with limited success. "The initial Japanese efforts around 1960 to export a very basic product sold on the basis of very low price were not successful. These cars were not up to a minimum international standard and could not be sold merely on the basis of price."[13]

They Don't Break Down.

A few years later they were back in the export markets with cars that still lacked sophistication, but made under quality controls that started to win them a growing share of the market. Private and company buyers were pleasantly surprised that Japanese cars did not seem to have been made in conspiracy with the repair and spare-parts men. It says something for the Market-based economy that people can take over a market simply by producing something that works and doesn't break down every five minutes.

Italy immediately put up the barriers against the Japanese exporters, pointing out, rightly that the Japanese were ruthless with competition they did not like. Both Ford and General Motors had established Assembly Plants in Japan in the 1920s and were simply squeezed out in the 1930s by the 'Law Regarding Auto-mobile Manufacturing Enterprise' of 1936. France also severely limited Japanese car imports and so the main thrust was directed at the U.S. The petroleum crisis and jump in prices following the three- day war in the Middle East made the large American cars less attractive to many buyers and they switched to imported models, particularly Japanese, whose fault-free reputation was growing, and whose prices were extremely competitive.

By the 1980s Japan was exporting 2 million vehicles to the U.S., 1 million to Europe - mainly Britain, and 0.9 million to the rest of the world. The effect of the continually rising tide of imports devastated the American industry. In the late 1970s Chrysler was bankrupt and had to be bailed out by the Government. Ford and General Motors were bringing in smaller cars made in their (mainly) European subsidiaries to meet home demand and the Japanese challenge, and the Government finally persuaded the Japanese to set up assembly plants in the U.S.A. and promise to incorporate an increasing content of locally made compounds.

The effect of Japanese imports on the remains of the British car industry was almost terminal. The sole British manufacturer, whose name changed almost almost every year : BMC, British Leyland, Austin Rover, B.Ae./Rover was case for intensive care. The profits which had been made in the '50s and '60s had been blown; there had been no re-investment, wages were lower than on the continent, not to mention North America, and the plants were battle-fields. Of course, the workers were to blame; they did not work hard enough and they wanted too much money. Nevertheless, Ford at Dagenham was keeping its parent afloat at Detroit, so profitable was the business. And Peugeot which had taken over the old Rootes plant at Coventry was transferring work there from France.

Intensive Care For Britain.

Various company doctors and whizz-kids were brought in from time to time to administer to the sole British owned company. Austin-Rover limped on, second to Ford at Dagenham in number of cars manufactured. Then Nissan set up in business assembly in the North-East, and Honda proposed to start manufacturing in South Wales - it already had a joint production arrangement with Austin-Rover. Other European producers and American subsidiaries were disturbed at the oriental Trojan-horse being wheeled inside the E.E.C's tariff wall. They had cause to be :

"... the Japanese auto industry requires fewer hours of labour by factory workers, designers, technicians and managers at all levels of the production chain to make a vehicle of any given description than any other nation's auto industry. In addition, the Japanese auto industry on average has a very high level (perhaps the highest level) of manufacturing accuracy ... the notion that quality costs more has been reversed. Defect prevention turns out to cost less ... Instead of sending manufacturing orders from the top down and bringing information from the bottom up, the Japanese producers have learned that moving knowledge, skills and decision making down the system into the hands of the primary workforce makes the old supervision and information-gathering systems redundant."[14]

The authors of this report return frequently to the theme of the Japanese 'upside down' approach to work-organisation frequently, as if anticipating resistance to change among interested parties : middle management, foremen, chargehands: "The Japanese practice of group co-ordination, by contrast, clearly offers a competitive plus. Its aim is co-operation and mutual information flow between the parts rather than rigid top-down hierarchy."[15]

So much for the conventional wisdom that people need to be told how to do their job, or at any rate, cannot do it without supervision. One does not have to be told that Japanese firms are paternalistic and that social relations in the country are feudal. It does not affect the truth of the Japanese experience that people can co-operate in large scale industry to produce whatever they want, to standards much higher than the norm today, neither do they need top management, but merely coordinators, to maintain links with related activities elsewhere.

But what of the future of the motor car in a world organised to satisfy needs and not the Market? Enthusiasts for public transport, from express bus services to bring-back-the-trams and steam train freaks, can point out the savings that this or that system might bring. They miss the point that it is compulsion that we are trying to escape from. Only when we have freedom to travel by plane, train, car or bus can we decide how much or how little we want to budge. There can be no doubt that access to a car offers a house-to-house flexibility that no other form of transport can provide.

It does not necessarily mean my car, and your car, and her car, and his car, spending most of this time parked and blocking the street. In any case, the majority of cars in Britain are not owned by their drivers, even at present, but by the company that employs them. And often not even that. Companies are increasingly turning to leasing firms who offer cars, plus maintenance, servicing etc. more efficiently.

Cars For Free?

But what if all restraints, like inadequate income, are removed, can the world ever supply all the cars that will be demanded? J.C. Tanner of the British Transport and Road Research Laboratory, and staff of the Organisation for Economic Cooperation and Development have tried to estimate the level of car ownership at which various countries will reach saturation. In most countries 60-63% of the population are of the age and fitness to drive a car. The OECD estimate that saturation will occur at 700 per thousand of population in the U.S., 600 per thousand in France and Germany, and at 450-500 per thousand in Italy, Japan, Sweden and the U.K.

The figure for Britain is about twice the present level of 'ownership'. Leaving aside such considerations as road deaths, atmospheric pollution, world limits to the supply of fuel, there are simple physical barriers to unlimited car use. It is already impossible to get from Camden Town to Croydon and back at any time other than the early hours of the morning. Yet the distance is a mere 20 miles, or so. The Chinese will require 500 million cars to come up to the present American level of ownership. Clearly, car driving will lose its charm some time before that happens.

A lot of thoughts about motoring, both by users and producers, are not entirely about mobility. The industry is notoriously unstable and producers are much given to whistling in the graveyard: "Their fear for the future is that the consumer who has a fixed number of dollars to spend will choose to spend less on his automobile and more on items available in other areas, such as home entertainment systems or computers."[16]

Consequently a lot of projections from the trade representatives contain strong elements of wish fulfilment. The alternative is slump and unemployment. We should not be surprised if anticipated sales are optimistic

> "Product planners already note that nearly half of the value added to automobiles is for items not directly connected with getting from point A to point B."[17]
> "The purchasers of new cars commonly dispose of them for reasons that have more to do with fashion and convenience than necessity, and they can easily defer replacement when they feel financially pressed."[18]

But the auguries are not good. In Sweden, where incomes are among the highest in the world, 'the median age at which passenger cars are scrapped has risen from 9.4 in 1965 to 16.2 years in 1982.'[19]

1. *Financial Times 29/01/86.*

2. *Financial Times 19/07/86.*

3. *Independent 25/11/86.*

4. *Economist 20/12/86.*

5. *Jacques Servan-Schreber : Le Defi Americain (Denoel 1967).*

6. *Professor Wynne Godley, Observer 1/06/86.*

7. *Corelli Barnett : The Audit of War (Macmillan 1986).*

8. *Patrick Minford, Daily Telegraph 22/01/87.*

9. *Editorial in the Economist 20/12/86.*

10. *Annual Digest of Statistics 1985.*

11. *Massachussets Institute of Technology : The Future of the Automobile (Counterpoint 1985).*

12. *D.G. Rhys : The Motor Industry (Butterworths 1972).*

13. *M.I.T. : The Future of the Automobile, p.31.*

14. *ibid.*

15. *Economist 1/02/86.*

16. *M.I.T. The Future of the Automobile.*

17. *ibid. p.100.*

18. *ibid. p.111.*

19. *ibid p.112.*

Part III.

False Solutions and Real Ones.

> The friend of the present order of things condemns all political speculations in the gross. He will not even condescend to examine the grounds from which the perfectibility of society is inferred. Much less will he give himself the trouble in a fair and candid manner to attempt an exposition of their fallacy.

Robert Malthus: An Essay On The Principle Of Population.

Chapter 16.

The philosophers", wrote Karl Marx, "have interpreted the world. the problem is to change it."[1] But how? Any solutions incorporating Cloud Nine, or Shangri La; in fact, any of the Utopias which have been held out as the answer to all our ills, have been, and will continue to be given the short shrift they deserve. They not only suffer from a credibility gap but from the gap that has always separated reality from manic delusion, from a determination to see the world as they would like it to be and not as it is.

The real Utopians can be found at both ends of the political spectrum, Left and Right. At the one end we have the Free Marketeers; as fantastical as Alexandre Dumas' famous trio ever were, and at the other, the enthusiasts for some degree of State Control or Intervention. The thought that the economic system itself, whether 'free' or controlled is at the root of the problem, is never allowed to intrude. As a result, a lot of the polemics around the subject take on the air of conversations heard in the psychiatric ward, or of the old music hall exchange:

> "What have I got behind my back?"
>
> " A battleship!"
>
> "What colour?"

If only, say the Free Marketeers, there were no tariffs, no trade unions, no cartels or monopolies, no insider trading or other corporate crime, everything would be alright on the night and we'd all live happy ever after.

They conveniently forget that the jungle of regulations and red tape, of workers combination and cartels, of consumer protection and crime prevention, arose from attempts to deal with the failure of the Free Market to deliver the goods in the first place.

> "The road to the free market was opened and kept open by an enormous increase in continuous, centrally organised and controlled interventionism. To make Adam Smith's 'simple and natural liberty' compatible with the needs of a human society was a most complicated affair. Witness the complexity of the provisions in the innumerable enclosure laws; the amount of bureaucratic control involved in the administration of the New Poor Laws which for the first time since Queen Elizabeth's reign were effectively supervised by a central authority."[2]

The failure to deliver the goods is in more than the figurative sense. J.M. Keynes pointed out that the free market economy is perfectly able to settle down at an equilibrium where millions are forced to sit around while necessary work goes undone[3] and the unemployed are used as a pretext to raise the taxes of those in work. It happened in the late twenties and thirties and the Market only expanded with the promise of the Second World War. It happened in the nineteen seventies and eighties after the damage of that war, and the interruption of production, had left what those with money to invest saw as opportunities to make a profit.

Euphoria.

Then, as they got chicken, they started to store the money under the bed, lending it out at interest as the occasion arose, instead of launching out into new production. So the same amount of goods and services available were confronted with greater amounts of money, which being interpreted, means inflation. Nothing succeeds like success, but nothing fails like failure. The Market is a shit-or-bust economy, and its defenders' mental states reflect that bowel condition exactly.

In times of boom, e.g. the 1950s and 1960s, we are told we have reached Shangri La and we will never grow old but will stay young and beautiful for ever.

At the paranoid stage, in times of slump, e.g. the 1970s and 1980s, those who have not jumped out of sky-scrapers or taken an overdose warn us that Armageddon is on the way, that the sun will never shine again, and that it is all our fault, because like Oliver Twist, we asked for more.

But the Mantra that the gurus of the Free-Market faith chant to get the faithful really going is: Allocation of Resources. Leave the Market free to find its own level, like water, they say, and the holes of need will fill up. Small use pointing out that those economies keeping a very tight ship: tariffs, non-tariff-barriers, exports organised like military campaigns; - economies like Japan, Germany, France, are the ones doing better. Those where the money markets are most free: Britain and the US, are the ones doing least well. As even that organ of the Free-Market the Financial Times puts it:

> "Why is it then that the 'slaves' of West Germany, Sweden, and Holland have managed to overtake the living standards of Americans who are still comparatively free of taxes? Mr Friedman has an unexpected retort to this objection.
> Because taxes are heavier and governments bigger in Europe than in America or Japan, Europe has more room for improvement. It would, therefore, be entirely consistent with a laissez faire outlook if a newly liberated Europe started performing better than America and even Japan.

> To the true believer there is obviously nothing that market economics can fail to explain."[4]

Likewise in the less well-developed world. Those countries practising some sort of free-trade, usually because of colonial status, never take off. Their industries cannot form, let alone get off the ground because the developed countries can dump the ends of their production runs on them and stifle them at birth. Britain is the only country which did not build up its industries behind a tariff wall, and that was because it did not need to. There were no other industrial countries to protect itself against.

The True Faith.

But ugly little facts like these will never upset the beautiful theory of the Free-Marketeers because it is a quasi-religious matter like Mormonism or Theosophy. It is shot through with contradictions and is preached with the language of the huckster and the snake-oil salesman: Free- Market, Free-enterprise, Free-choice; the word 'free' is the most powerful in the armoury of the advertising industry and the trade manuals urge caution in its use because of the danger of overkill.

The reality that the word conceals: the freedom of the poor to go without, freedom to be unemployed, the freedom of the old to freeze to death, - even the alternative freedom of businessmen to die of cardiac arrest or to kill themselves with alcohol or cigarette abuse through stress; all of these unfortunate things arise because, however free the markets are, they are not free enough. They never could be, of course. Sin would always get in the way. But what we are dealing with here is the hopeless optimism of true believers. Listen to them:

> "Yes, the theoretical guarantee that free markets can achieve economic efficiency hinges on numerous assumptions which, as these briefs have shown, rarely hold in the real world. But the case for market- based, as opposed to centrally-planned, economies rests securely enough on comparisons of the two systems at work. So the role of economic theory is not to justify an approach to allocating resources which all but fools and liars can see works better than any feasible alternative. Its urgent
>
> task is to explore the tricky ways of making the market based economy work better still."[5]

Fidei Defensor.

So that's it. You settle on a conclusion and scratch around for some facts to back it up. Michael Harrington views the scene somewhat less simply, though whether this is because he is a 'fool' or a 'liar' is difficult to say: "The very existence of crisis management in Washington is eloquent testimony to the destructive impulses of the system when left to itself. Markets were organised by monopolies, oligopolies, cartels and multinationals, which permitted managerial planning and the elimination of price competition; technological innovation was institutionalised to create new needs and markets; and state intervened in the economy with counter-cyclical policies. Two of these tactics could be adopted by corporations on their own, but the third, and most crucial, that of state intervention, could not."[6]

Interventionists.

At the other end of the political spectrum are the mechanics, the spanner and screwdriver boys, tightening the economy up a bit here and slacking it off a bit there. They do not use the evangelical language of the Free-Marketeers, but they are no less religious. As the Free-Marketeers never tire of pointing out, the mere idea that a central authority could regulate the Market for the benefit of all, requires the belief that it could anticipate the decisions of millions of people to buy, or supply, or not to buy or supply, the myriad things that people do buy or supply. And that is a very big act of faith indeed.

> "The attempt of the Welfare Economists to discover ways to bring social and interpersonal costs and benefits into the market system, if necessary by legislation, reminds one of nothing so much as Ptolemy's construction of epicycles to correct the failure of predictions based on an earth-centred model of the solar system."[7]

It is conceivable that if there were no organised scarcity, no problem of substitution, no problem of alternatives being forced on people because of inadequate means, people's decisions could be anticipated in a year-on-year basis. But in the context of the Market, where in the event of a slump and unemployment, for example, a mass move into margarine from butter could provoke crisis in the dairy industry and boom in the palm oil plantations of the Third World, makes the whole idea of planning the

Market quite ludicrous.

People could not themselves predict what their decisions would be when presented with either/or situations so that even if the government were wired into the brain of each one of them, it would be to no avail. The consumption of unmetered water is predictable years ahead, almost to the last gallon, but the consumption of metered gas and electricity in people's houses swings up and down like a roller coaster on the waves of boom and slump.

The attempt to deal with the contradictions, either through direct state control, Russian style, or through tinkering, Western style, results in much the same sort of life for all concerned: there is no pretence of freedom in the East and freedom is a fraud in the West.

Yet neither type of economy is prepared to let people starve, go unclothed or without shelter. In the East, Big Brother doles out the ration; in the West there are 'safety nets': charities, food parcels, soup kitchens. If anybody really believed in the Market they would either be left to die, or all would enjoy some prosperity. What we have now is a half-life at enormous financial, social, environmental, physical and psychic costs. The squirrel cages spin ever faster but only economists believe we are going anywhere.

The Fraud of Politics.

People's growing disenchantment with the quack nostrums of political parties of both Right and Left is measurable in the opinion polls. As Jeremy Seabrook puts it:

> "It is against this vast, impious design that the muted and not always clearly directed protests of people break and scatter. This is what is meant when they write off all politicians, saying 'Let them get on with it', 'It's six of one and half a dozen of the other', or less elegantly 'They all piss in the same pot.' In this way politicians act as lightning conductors for the capitalist system, taking responsibility for its vicissitudes, the reward of landslide victories at its peaks, the disgrace of resounding defeat in its troughs. The pretence that they retain mastery over these uncontrollable and often perverse processes is now a major part of their function."[8]

The pie in the sky, the jam tomorrow but not today, held out in the Labour landslide of 1945 when Nationalisation would give Britain back to the British, was exposed for the scam it was when the Thatcher government of the eighties sold the industries 'owned' by the people back to people, or rather those who had the money to buy them: Amersham International, British Telecom, British Gas, British Airways, neatly underlining the fact that the British Governmen, Labour or Conservative, does not represent quite the same thing or group of interests as the British people as a whole.

Likewise the scam of a shareholding democracy or a property- owning democracy coming from the Conservatives in the eighties. Perhaps it wasn't a scam. Perhaps the idiots believed it, just like the Russian rulers believe that the Russian people, somehow, own their country; that they can be employer and employee at the same time: that a few hundred or even a few thousand pounds in former nationalised company stock would create new entries in 'Who Owns Britain'. The evidence is overwhelming that only the Free-market freaks, if anybody, believes the nonsense. But away from these political bucket-shop operators of Left and Right, things are happening of real significance.

Self Help.

Local authorities have a statutory duty to see that people are housed. Some deal with the homeless the hard way, paying outrageous 'bed and breakfast' charges out of the rates, or building more council houses, or freeing rent controls. Other authorities have discovered that helping people to help themselves, with materials from bricks to bathroom suites to roof insulation, and expert advice from building tradesmen, surveyors, and architects, is transforming some slum areas.

These moves are not coming necessarily or even principally from the Left. The Sunday Times, solidly on the Thatcher wing of the Conservative press was unambiguous in its support for free roof insulation:

> "It is time for a bold and imaginative initiative. If the nation managed to re-equip itself for North Sea Gas, with workmen going into every home, something similar could be done with an insulation scheme. At the present rate of progress, it will take about thirty years before our roofs are protected as well as Sweden's. Such a scheme is a quick job creator and, if there is any doubt about where

the money could come from, why are not the same questions asked about, say, Sizewell B (Power Station)? Energy conservation may be less glamorous than energy creation, but it is all part of the same equation for people who need warmth."[9]

And in the same newspaper, Brian Walden, Mrs Thatcher's favourite TV interviewer, went one further:

"The Government has an excellent record in selling council houses to their occupiers and, significantly that policy is now accepted by all political parties - or so they find it prudent to say. The next step is to give thought to making a gift of much of the remaining council property to those who live in it.Such a proposition will be resisted, both by some bureaucrats and by the Left, who love having millions of clients living under their grace and favour in council property."

The caution in the last paragraph echoed one on the other side of the Atlantic by Richard Carlson regarding possible objections to changes in the status quo:

"If a law to transform all western corporations into workers co- operatives were to become a serious possibility, its most ardent opponents might well be neither stockholders nor managers but many labor unions. Most managers could expect to retain their employment and stockholders to receive reasonable compensation for lost property. By contrast the jobs of labor union officials depend closely upon the present system of labor relations based upon collective bargaining and the socio-economic class division that this entails.

Similarly, suppose that in the year 2075, a proposal to sweep away the maze of overlapping welfare programmes, which sometimes work at cross-purposes, seriously threatens to pass the United States Congress. In its place would come a guaranteed annual income, with built-in work incentives, which puts a 'decent' income floor under every household ... A portion of the federal bureaucracy which handles existing programmes is threatened with a decline in demand for its services. We would expect it to fervently oppose the reform."[10]

While reserving comment on proposals for compensation for stockholders, other than invitations to help themselves to any goods they fancy, we know what he means. As for "guaranteed annual income", we can agree, as long as it is in the form of goods and services and not money, otherwise we shall be walking back into the madhouse. If money is left in the equation, we shall know that we have not escaped from the cuckoo's nest and that nurse will be coming back with the straight-jacket and tranquilisers.

Recovering Control.

People begin to recover control of a little area of their lives: their very own homes, 'defensible space' as the sociologists call it. The alternative to a slot in a high rise building where they are filed away by bureaucrats, and the only person they see is the rent collector, is a place designed by themselves to fit their own needs - the way a peasant or an early settler in the New World would have done it.

Recovering control of their own lives in the home becomes inseparable from recovering control of their own health and education. The doctors and medical auxiliaries are seen increasingly as allies in the struggle to regain health and less as god-like creatures who can produce well-being out of any life style, however irresponsible and rotten. Many still work on the assumption that the only fruitful approach is to tinker with symptoms. This is palpably untrue, but so is the unstated assumption of many fringe practitioners that all germs are saprophytic, i.e. that they feed only upon decaying tissue, and that if we lead healthy lives, no germs can hurt us.[11]

But none will deny that an improvement in diet, physical activity, and stress reduction would reduce enormously the number of visits to the doctor. Many people, particularly women, are working on this assumption. Smoking is finally on the decrease despite the reluctance of the Government to combat the advertising of the tobacco interests.[12]

Many are cutting down on excess drinking. And tens, hundreds, of thousands have taken to walking, jogging, squash, yoga, aerobics, swimming, and improving their diets.

As for education, enormous numbers are abandoning the assumption that it must be considered separately from life, a once and for all thing. The French Government, largely as a reaction to the riots of 1968 brought in a series of measures under the heading of *Formation Permanente*, or permanent education, in an attempt to deal with what it saw as a broken connection between people at large and the administration. This proposed that people at work should, all the time, be preparing and educating themselves to take on the job at the next level; in essence, that the ward orderly was preparing to become a brain sugeon, in due course.

We do not have to assume fraudulent motives in the people who thought up this idea. It is enough that the socio- economic structure would destroy any such aims, however noble. The children of the comfortably off get to be brain surgeons and those in an economic rut get to sweep the floor. We know that a shooting star rises up occasionally from among the plebs and achieves a position of eminence, but as H.G. Wells pointed out, the waste of human talent and goodwill meanwhile is horrifying.

Not that it would be bad for brain surgeons to sweep the wards themselves from time to time. Then there might be some fundamental changes in easy - clean, self sterilising hospital floors.

The idea of all avenues being open to anybody who wanted to progress along them, amounts to pissing against the wind in the environment of the Market economy, but it offers interesting possibilities in the context of an economy aimed at satisfying needs ... Still, for me, I'll settle for sweeping floors indefinitely. I never could stand the sight of blood.

1. *Karl Marx : Theses on Feuerbach No. XI.*

2. *Karl Polanyi : The great Transformation, p.140.*

3. *J.M. Keynes: General Theory of Employment, Interest and Money, chapter 20.*

4. *Financial Times 23/02/87.*

5. *Economist 13/12/86.*

6. *Michael Harrington: The Twilight of Capitalism p.310.*

7. *Michael Barratt Brown : Socialist Register 1971 p. 193.*

8. Guardian 9/02/87.

9. Sunday Times 18/01/87.

10. Richard Carlson : Comparative Economic Systems (Macmillan USA 1973) p.330.

11. The motto caveat emptor (let the buyer beware) which could stand as the governing principle of capitalism, acquires ever more sinister overtones as the market economy spirals downwards. The whole-food sector is invaded by the junk-food multinationals, - Birds Eye (Unilever), Booker McConnell, etc. whose devotion to purity is suspect. And the nature-cure, healthy-life arena is swarming with schpronkel merchants, replete with armfuls of suspect degrees and diplomas: "Five food-allergy clinics are attacked today by the Consumers Association for charging up to £80 for alleged unreliable and dubious dietary advice .....One clinic run by a man with no medical qualifications even claims to be able to diagnose serious illnesses such as muscular dystrophy from dried blood samples sent through the post." (Guardian 8/01/87).

12. This subject merits a library to itself. For those with less leisure I recommend Peter Taylor's book: The Smoke Ring ; Tobacco, Money and Multinational Politics (Sphere 1984).

Chapter 17.

Doing Our Own Thing.

Centuries after being driven off the land, people are beginning to recover control of a little area of their lives once more. Not all. Some are like battery hens released by Animal Liberation, and are trying to get back into the cages again. But increasing numbers are questioning what they eat, growing their own vegetables and fruit; gardening has moved to the top of people's leisure activities, and for the unemployed, more than just leisure. At the same time that the fashion industry is becoming ever more shrill, many among the young and even more among the mature are rejecting the siren calls; they persist in wearing jeans and bomber jackets; middle-class kids insist in dressing from Oxfam shops. The shock to those of us who remember 'reach-me-downs' with the humiliation involved is difficult to convey.

Many are improving and converting their homes to their own needs;

everything from putting up shelves and the more ambitious Do It Yourself schemes to building their own homes through housing associations and Community Architecture projects led by architects like Ted Cullinan and Rod Hackney. There are said to be more than a thousand such architects working alongside slum dwellers all over the country on schemes to upgrade or in some cases build from scratch the house of their dreams.

Salubritas Et Eruditio.

In education a similar development can be seen taking place. At the same time that television, radio, and the tabloid newspapers are going downmarket, the number of people going to evening classes, joining cultural and artistic societies and reading books was never higher. Book sales have tripled in the last fifty years and now total nearly sixty thousand new titles each year. Many of them are pulp-stand trade, true enough, but the number of mind and consciousness-expanding books has increased enormously.

This has affected relations between social classes. Earlier generations of the poor were intimidated by the superior education of the rich. Their awe was not totally warranted. The rich were victims then and are even more victimised in todays' world by the complacent rubbish that passes for education in the public schools and older universities. In the Humanities, that is, not in Science which has rules for dealing with absurdity. But their History still treats of battles and treaties and great men. In religion, which has not moved far from Archbishop Ussher, the new school of bible scholarship - Don Cupitt, John Robinson, David Jenkins, are dismissed as cranks or Communists. In English literature they are resolutely middlebrow or middle class: Trollope rather than Dickens, Waugh rather than Joyce or Beckett. There is little awareness or even curiosity about what is being written on the Continent or in Latin America; parochialism if not xenophobia.

At the same time that ordinary people are discovering the world of ideas, many at the other end of the social and wealth scale are finding out that not only the hewers of wood and the drawers of water are deprived. Some perceptive members of the ruling class found this out long ago. Peter the Great worked in Deptford shipyard; Winston Churchill was a passionate spare-time bricklayer; the deposed Kaiser Wilhelm spent his exile at Doorn in Holland indulging his fantasy as a lumberjack, felling trees and sawing logs with an enthusiasm that confused the servants. Toward the end of the 19th century the 'Back to the Land' and Pre-Raphaelite movements prompted some of the wealthy, and more of the clerkly class to try working with their hands. Prompted by the writings of Carlyle, Ruskin, William Morris, Edward Carpenter, and many others, they sampled what they saw as the ennobling quality of manual work, with indifferent results. Coming from a world swarming with servants, many of them were barely pot-trained, and their efforts should evoke the caution: Don't laugh!

The survivors of that social group found themselves between the wars in a different world, where the servants had gone, and they had not acquired survival skills, like Indians from the Amazonian rain forest dumped in a modern city. Marganita Laski wrote a cruelly funny little novel called 'Love on the Supertax' in which the Duke and Duchess are in the basement of their house in Eaton Square during the blitz trying to fry kippers over a paraffin stove. You know they are never going to make it.

In a later generation the lucky ones are finding that the traditional view of life at the top involves deprivation too; deprivation of the sensual pleasures of wood and metal, of masonry and the soil; deprivation that is not entirely compensated for by fly-fishing or gun and dog, deeply pleasurable though those pursuits may be.

It must be said, however, that there are severe limits to the changes that we can make individually, crucial though they are. The Government, together with armies of middlemen, stand waiting to insert themselves between us and our fellows and slice the lion's share off any transaction where money is involved. This is where the Black Economy and any mutual help activity is enormously efficient in return for effort. But any larger scale economic activity involves carrying the usual cargo of free-loaders: taxes, money transaction costs, advertising and selling costs, etc, etc, so that the returns are often not worth the effort as, at another economic level, those on overtime frequently find out. We must have access to the machines and the raw materials to make any significant change.

Some people may find it difficult to imagine how we can organise ourselves to produce and supply everything for free, and I don't mean rationing, fair shares, or 'equality', whatever that could possibly mean. I mean a situation of help-yourself to yachts, cars, aeroplanes, and anything else we can think of; caviar, truffles, champagne. There is nothing that we cannot produce beyond the point where it ceases to be attractive solely on account of its scarcity, or because the glut itself repels. And this situation is not the result of recent technological developments or of the Industrial Revolution itself. It has always been like this. The only change has been the arrival of the Market economy to put a brake on production whenever there threatened to be enough of anything.

The mere mention of plenty has always been a signal for economic and financial panic in capitalist economies, so it is not surprising that through the last few centuries a great deal of propaganda has gone into stressing shortages. Things are short now they say, and they were even shorter in earlier times. Of course it is only a device for massaging, for talking-up the market. It has gone into the textbooks: "Economics is the science which studies human behaviour as a relationship between ends and scarce means ..." in Professor Robbins' famous definition. How awful if those means should turn out to be abundant; the Market would collapse!

In the late 1960s The Club of Rome, a group of economists, environmentalists, and other assorted academics, mainly American, were financed by Ford, Volkswagen, and Fiat, to produce a report which showed that the world was desperately short and getting shorter still of food, energy sources, metals and almost everything else that people or the economic system needed. Less than twenty years later the world's economy faced crisis because there was too much of everything listed in the Club of Rome's report. This was despite the fact that most of what was being consumed by the system was being squandered : forests being cut down for junk mail shots; cars being built for commercial reps; coal and steel being dug and made for tanks and submarines. The proportion directed at satisfying people's needs was, and is, tiny.

Of course, a great deal of what we consume is already 'free', on a help-yourself basis. The activities of most women as housewives and mothers, and husbands and fathers as handy-men about the house, - all work on this principle. Any doubts about whether they are economic activities are quickly dispelled when the mother goes out to work and has to pay for baby-minding, and the husband has to buy meals out. And the thousands of voluntary societies mentioned elsewhere, from St John's Ambulance to Meals on Wheels operate on the basis of need.

According to the Legal & General Insurance Company the services of a housewife with two children and a husband to administer to are worth £370 a week, or £19,240 a year. 'This represents the total cost of hiring replacement help at employment agency rates to cover the roles of a housewife during her 90-hour, seven-day working week.'[1] This is just about double the average male wage for a working week not quite half as long.

The wife's work creates use-values only; the goods and services are supplied on-demand. There are no on-costs to speak of. The wealth created is real, consumable. A husband's employment on the other hand consists of some 90 per cent aggregate on-costs. Where the husband stays at home and the woman works the position is exactly reversed. The role of the husband in spare-time work as handyman, helping with the chores, growing vegetables, mowing the lawn, is again as a creator of use-values, with scarcely any on-costs.

People have persisted in these social activities despite the relentless pressure of the Market to reduce every relationship to a cash nexus.[2] Indeed the Market economy has never achieved more than a minority status and never could, because of its contradictions. Fred Hirsch, echoing Sweezy and Baran, points out that Capitalism could never survive on its own, but relies upon the informal economy to deal with its contradictions (cf.Chapter 6) Thus in times of depression and unemployment, the Wage System relies upon the informal economy to look after the unemployed, feeding, clothing and housing them until they are wanted in the next upsurge of demand and production. Help from family and friends, and self help, the black economy, picking coal off the tip, a bit of window cleaning, picking blackberries and other wild fruit, totting (collecting scrap metal, rags, paper, etc), like so many seagulls on the beach, all of the million and one devices that unemployed men and women resort to when the Capitalist economy breaks down.

Another wheeze practised by thousands of youngsters is to use the unemployment pittance to support them in further education at polytechnic or university. And last of all, though this is strictly part of the heart of the Market economy itself; a bit of thieving to keep the home fires burning.

The services of the Army, Navy, and Air Force are free. Some people might say they could do without them, but that is neither here nor there. For those who want the protection of the armed services, they come free, they are supplied on the basis of need, real or imagined; they are not marketed. So are the services of the Police, but not Securicor nor Group 4.

The supply of paved roads and sidewalks and street lighting is also on the basis of need, not ability to pay. It was not always so. In earlier centuries the Army operated on Free-market principles, with rape and looting opportunities as the profit that secured the bottom line of the balance sheet; the Navy equally. In earlier centuries you could rent a man to walk in front of you with a lamp to light the street, and the streets or roads were paved in sections, and gated-off at suitable distances to provide a return on capital for the entrepreneur who had paid to pave them. Several of the new bridges: Severn, Humber, etc still operate on the same basis but not Westminster, or Battersea, or Barnes, or Hammersmith. Why ever not?

Europe has tended to temper some of the harsher consequences of the Market economy. Welfare systems have been more generous with the poor, the old, the sick, and the children. By contrast, much of the poverty seen in the United States seems to belong to the Third World; to Calcutta rather than California, to Ouagadougou rather than New York. Nevertheless health care, much more comprehensive than in the U.S., costs British employers less than half of American rates, currently twelve per cent of their Gross National Product. Other European countries show similar savings with even more generous treatment than in Britain. The difference is that American medicine is supplied on Market principles, with all of the on-costs involved.[3]

The ethos encouraged by a health service 'on demand' is illustrated by the blood donor system. There are about a million blood donors in Britain giving an average of two pints of blood a year - in exchange for a cup of tea! This in turn is supplied to the victims of accidents or otherwise in need of transfusions, also for free. But in the United States the donor is paid an average of 35 dollars per pint which is then multiplied according to Market principles to 350 dollars per pint for those in need of transfusions.

Inevitably, in such an ethos, those in the business of selling blood in the U.S. are from among the socially desperate: dope fiends, alcoholics, degenerates of every description, and the blood is frequently infected with hepatitis etc. The Thatcher administration, obsessed with the idea of putting the blood business on a thoroughly commercial basis, managed to buy a consignment of blood from the U.S. which was contaminated with the AIDS virus. This was then pumped into hapless leukemia and haemophilia sufferers, giving them and their nearest and dearest something else to worry about.[4] The Thatcher administration had blood on its hands in more senses than one. All of this arose out of its hatred of the idea of something-for-nothing and hence for the NHS. But the Economist scribes returned like dogs to lick their own vomit. Having recognised that the Thatcherites had deliberately sabotaged the NHS and the free blood service, they reported : "The latest issue of the British Medical Journal led with a vitriolic attack on the 'shambles' of the blood transfusion service in England and Wales ... written by the director of the Scottish service, Professor John Cash. When the dust settled, many English regional directors confessed to agreeing with the professors criticisms."

They then continued:

> "The quickest way to get more (blood) plasma would be to adopt a new technique called plasma-pherisis. This returns red cells to donors, which makes it possible for them to give blood as often as once a fortnight instead of the present limit of two or three times a year. If demand keeps growing, plasma-pherisis must be brought in - unless synthetic blood products arrive first. Because of the extra time taken, donors may well expect more than their present cup of tea. That should not mean worse-quality blood. Experts now agree that, unlike 20 years ago, America-which pays donors and uses plasma-pherisis-has better blood products than Britain, which does neither."[5]

What could be more characteristic of the Market economy than to create or allow a shortage to develop and then resort to crisis-management to deal with it. And that is assuming that the shortage was real and not invented. A few months earlier, the head of the Blood Products Laboratory, Dr Lane said that he might consider selling surplus products to Germany: subsequently, Department of Health and Social Security officials told him not to answer criticisms of his service. Meanwhile the Oxford area director Dr Colin Entwhistle had ordered his department to cut back on collecting blood: "There was no way we could justify collecting vast excesses of blood that nobody wanted." Meanwhile there was a shortage of more than 100 pints a day in the south London region.[6]

Clearly, blood given for free is not only cheaper, it tends to be of better quality.

The lifeboat and mountain rescue services also work on a voluntary basis and are, consequently, unbelievably low-cost operations. There is no stretch of coastline in the British Isles not covered by the 200 stations of the lifeboat service, and any craft in difficulties can be sure that the lifeboat will be launched within minutes of the alarm being raised, often into a storm raging in excess of force ten on the Beaufort Scale. Why do the men do it when the reward is the equivalent of no more than a couple of pints of beer? The answer is the same as the reason why a young constable can be relied upon to plunge into a frozen canal on a February morning to rescue a child - people are just like that.

The BBC 9pm TV news on the 12th April 1985 carried the item that in Arkansas, Kansas, USA, the firemen allowed a quarter of a million dollar business and several houses to burn down because the owner of one of the properties had not paid a twenty dollar local tax. In Britain the services of the Fire Brigade are supplied whether or not the rates have been paid, and in the smaller towns the firemen, called 'retained' men are paid a very modest stipend to continue in their job or business but to be ready to drop everything they are doing when the alarm goes and run like hell for the fire engine.

How much more costly would the lifeboat and mountain rescue and all the other voluntary services be if they moved onto Market principles? A factor of ten? Twenty? Wages clerks, wage snatches, taxmen collecting the taxes to pay for the services; all of the merry go round that has been mopping up much of the increase in productivity in recent centuries.

The Free-Marketeers argue that people only do things for selfish reasons, but that Adam Smith's famous 'invisible hand' converts their avarice into benefits for all. The state of the world proves that the last part is a lie, and a moment's reflection shows that the first part is not true either. Professor Milton Friedman asks:

> "If what a person gets does not depend on the price he receives for the services of his resources, what incentive does he have to seek out information on price or to act on the basis of that information? ... If your income will be the same whether you work hard or not why should you work hard?"[7]

Why indeed? That is a question the one hundred and ten thousand people saved by the lifeboatmen of Britain since the service started could well ask themselves. But apart from that Professor Friedman supplies his own answer:

> "The esteem or approval of fellow scholars serves very much the same function that monetary reward does in the economic market."[8]

Professor Friedman is clearly one of the Pharisees and not the Publican, smiting his breast and crying out: 'God be merciful to me a miserable sinner.' Still, it is good to hear him saying that he is not in Economics for the money. We never thought he was. He shows every indication of being a kindly man. Economics, or any other academic pursuit for that matter, is not for the greedy. There are lots of other activities they would be better off with if they sincerely wanted to be rich.

Meanwhile, alongside the vast spread of goods and services that people supply to each other for free, either in the family or out of neighbourliness or from the sheer love of their fellow humans; alongside the long list that local or national government supplies for free, from public libraries to defence, policing, street lighting, paved roads, piped water, sewerage, medicine, education, etc, etc, we have the irrational 'Alice Through the Looking Glass' side of the economy, from dog licences at 37 pence which cost more than one pound to collect, to cash benefits for the poor and old which cost £4 to administer for each £1 paid out. Other examples abound: the cost of collecting the entrance fee to the Victoria and Albert Museum is two thirds of the money collected; and elsewhere:

> "The cost of a car trip through the Dartford Tunnel at peak times is far more than the 60p toll fee.On the basis of the Department of Transport's own cost figures, used to justify road-building projects, a car with three passengers on a leisure trip wastes £8.45 per hour when it is caught in a jam, while a car on a business trip with only a driver is costed at twice that figure. A working truck with driver counts at £12.30 an hour on the same basis.
>
> At current peaks about 6,500 vehicles can be waiting to go through the tunnel in either direction, guaranteeing a delay of about an hour. This means that each is paying about £8.45 plus the toll fee and together they are wasting about £55,000 an hour yet contributing only £3,900

to pay off the cost of the tunnel.

Just over £1 million of the £19.6 million estimated income from tolls and break-down fees this year, will be spent on collecting tolls, £5.5 million on maintenance and improvements, and £5.7 million on interest payments. Only £7.2 million goes towards repayment of the current principal debt of £56 million."[9]

1. Times 28/03/87.

2. Richard Titmuss: The Gift Relationship (Pantheon Books NY. 1971) p.148

3. Economist 22/08/87. However thick the skull, some ideas have the penetrating power of cosmic rays. The skulls of Economist writers, for example: "Insurance based systems have coverage problems - nobody is keen to take on those likely to be ill. They also have higher administrative costs than the NHS ...Many observers abroad envy the NHS's ability to contain costs. Indeed, some are thinking of copying it. They argue that the NHS can use monopsony power to keep down staff wages and other costs; and they note that the United States often has worse health than Britain despite spending three times as much on health care (my emphasis).[3]

4. By the 12th August, 1987, 1,200 of these unfortunate people were infected with the HIV virus, 41 were dead and a further 57 had AIDS and were waiting to die. (Guardian)

5. Economist 10/09/87.

6. Guardian 12/08/87.

7. Milton Friedman : Free to Choose (Secker) p.23.

8. ibid. p.26

9. Guardian 22/08/87

Chapter 18.

Water is supplied to householders in Britain, as in most of Europe, on a free-access basis, with the exception of the tiny West Midlands town of Malvern, where it is metered. Sewerage services are also supplied on the basis of need to nearly ninety-six per cent of the population. The exceptions are remote country properties, where the householders have to build their own treatment plants to the requirements of the Building Regulations.

Nobody has yet proposed privatising the sewerage services of the country. They were built to deal with the cholera, typhus and typhoid epidemics of the last century. Both Queen Victoria and her prime minister W.E. Gladstone got typhoid and her beloved Albert, Prince Consort, died of it, leaving her to be tended by her stud groom, John Brown, and it was felt by loyal subjects in the know that he should be well hung for *lese majeste*.

The prospect of a repetition of those plagues following blocking-off the drains of non-payers has stifled any urge of the Free-Marketeers to put meters on the sewerage system. They have not shown the same reticence about the water supply.

Mr. Roy Watts, Chairman of the Thames Water Authority led a committee which recommended fitting water meters to all houses on the grounds that it is "not only right but almost inevitable."[1]

It was good that Mr Watts' committee arugued moral justification, that it was the 'right' course of action. The usual one is efficiency, cost benefit, may-hurt-but-it- will-do-you-good sort of argument. Let us be cruel-but-only-to-be-kind to his committee.

During the great drought of 1976 the correspondence columns of the newspapers were full of letters from enraged housholders complaining that their neighbours were using their lawn sprinklers and washing their cars and why wasn't something done about it, why wasn't water metered? Accountants from the water boards were kept busy during that long hot summer explaining that yes, water could be metered if the public wanted, but that it would raise the cost to the ratepayer by 400 to 500 per cent. These replies were invariably followed by a deathly hush.

Enter Mr. Watts' committee a decade later, once more floating the idea of metering water, at the same time conceding that metering was a more expensive way of collecting charges than through the rates. They estimated that savings for the average household would be between £2.50 and £6.50 a year because they would be more sparing in the use of water, while the cost of reading and billing would be an extra £4.75 a year. But the initial cost of installing water meters could be up to £140 per household.

If we accept these figures and set the cost of amortising the meters at 10 per cent, that yields a figure of £14 per year which added to the figure for reading and billing gives a total of £18.75 for a saving of, at the most £6.25 but perhaps as little as £2.50 per annum. This is the kind of commercial arithmetic that the greatest business expert of all time, Mr. Wilkins Micawber, warned us against: "Annual income twenty pounds, annual expenditure twenty pounds nought shillings and sixpence, - result, misery."

But let us heap on the misery. We have accepted the Committee's costing at face value. Would they personally guarantee any cost over-runs from metering, the way that local authorities were made personally responsible for spending over-runs by the Thatcher administration? This is not a criticism of that government; rather a suggestion that the Committee put its money where its mouth is. And we haven't finished yet.

According to official figures, between a quarter and a third of all water supplied is lost through leaky mains. This fact drove Mr. Fletcher of Glasgow to do some arithmetic of his own and write to the Times:

> "Sir, One quarter of water supplied to the mains leaks to the ground, so only 75 per cent is delivered. Of this 54 per cent goes to households (report December 12, page 3) that is, 41 per cent of the original supply to the mains. Of this 41 per cent, it is estimated that over one tenth would be saved by domestic metering of the whole country, i.e. a saving of 4.1 per cent of the original supply quantity.
>
> So householders are to be put to the expense of meters to save 4.1 per cent, whilst the water boards sit on their hands and watch 25 per cent going to waste.
>
> Someone in the UK is half witted and it ain't me."[2]

As the Times pointed out, some of the interest suddenly shown in the water industry had been generated by the Government's use of the utility to help the Treasury out with funds, and some had come from the

> "dubious promise that in the event of privatisation, there is gold in them there faucets. Yet such new-found interest in an old subject is misplaced if it exaggerates the financial importance of water supply. (It cost the average household just over £36 in 1984-85; industry's demand for water is declining). Here is a subject swimming in confusions. One arm of government, the Treasury, estimates the assets of a water authority at £4.4 billion and dictates a rate of return accordingly; the same officials apparently accept a merchant bank's estimate of assets at £1 billion and a completely different estimate of profitability for the sake of privatisation calculations. And consumers,

> motivated by no love for water authorities which since 1983 have not even had a vestige of local electorial accountability, are led to believe the way to get the water bureaucrats off their backs is to install a meter."[3]

The Times was right to minimise the financial importance of the water supply industry. Here we have the first requirement of 55 million people, before food, before clothing, before shelter, being supplied by a mere eighteen thousand workers or, if we include sewerage, treatment and disposal of same, and land drainage, a total of forty-five thousand. This is half the number employed in the gas industry which has to deal with a much smaller pipe network, and smaller amount of processing and purifying of the product.

May we not conclude that this disparity has something to do with the fact that gas is marketed, with all of the on-costs associated with marketing? Water rates were already much higher than they need be; they were being plundered by the 'cost conscious' Thatcher government to fund its rakes-progress. They were still only a fraction of the cost of gas to the consumer.

The gas industry spent £300 million advertising itself, a monopoly, to the private sector. It paid a billion pounds to the City of London for handling the sale. And who had to find that money? Why, the gas consumers, of course. And gas prices were already higher in Britain than in any other country in Europe, in a country which had more gas deposits that the rest of Europe put together. Gas costs the consumer some five times as much as water supply. Could this have anything to do with the cost, not of the gas, but of advertising, metering, meter reading, billing, chasing bad debts, countering meter fraud, etc, etc. The 46 per cent of water that is supplied to industry is metered, of course, but that only underlines the potential cost of metering to domestic consumers. Water is much cheaper if it is free.

The alternative is a water industry where the staff devoted to selling outnumber those devoted to producing by five to one or even ten to one. Add to the sales effort the cost of extra office blocks, tons of paper, telephones, postage, word-processors, computers, security men, - all earning far more than the men poking those long iron keys down holes in the road and turning taps on and off for some mysterious purpose.

The government is proposing to abolish the rates. Why not just leave it at that? You never know where it might end. There would be enormous advantages for any government moving significant amounts of goods and services out of the Market and onto a help-yourself basis. It would reduce costs of materials and labour overnight and on a scale to overwhelm its competitors, including the cheap labour advantages of Third World countries. In addition there would almost certainly be a reduction in home demand for the items so treated. People are seldom greedy about things that are so abundant they are for free.

Of course such actions would cause panic in the Markets of the rest of the world. Just a whiff of the laughing gas of abundance, and prices would collapse, to be followed by bankruptcies on a scale never known, not even in the worst of slumps. Such a government would be laying a trail in the same way that Britain did with the cheap goods from the Industrial Revolution, which in Marx's words, knocked down the Chinese Walls of feudalism.

Being first into the new world of Capitalism had some advantages, for the ruling class in Britain, at least. The rest of the world, still slumbering, had no reply to the cheap goods of the British exporters, and was soon in hock to the British merchant class. It should be added that the cheapness of the goods was as much due to the starvation of the dispossessed peasants who had been forced into the mills and mines, as to any division of labour. Peasants abroad who were still in possession of their plots could resist any efforts to get them to submit to such abasement.

There were disadvantages too. Being first in the queue meant that those following could profit from any mistakes that were made. Not many allowed developments that put little girls of four and five down the coal mines or which put little boys up the chimneys, together with the nauseating arguments in justification, that marked Britain's move into a commodity producing society. But none appear to have been able to avoid any of the major steps in the process.

> "No nation can, by legal enactments or bold leaps bypass the successive steps in its own development."[4]

Marx's deterministic language reads a little old-fashioned now. He was right but gave the wrong reasons for being so. Certainly, no country up to the present has been able to avoid altogether, the stages that Britain has passed through. From this we can pretty safely conclude that problems affecting us are likely to affect others in the future. Every country has cultural, geographical, and historical differences which call for special treatment, but the broad outline of development seems to have been followed by every modern power as W.W. Rostow demonstrated in his classic : 'The Stages of Economic Growth.'[5]

Notwithstanding the obvious advantages to everybody from moving the economy onto a 'help yourself' basis, are there any grounds for believing that the ruling oligarchy in any country might initiate it? Clearly not, despite the fact that the economy offers every good or service free to some sector of the population from free food - or the money to buy it - to the poor, the old, the children; to free cars to company employees, or free aeroplanes to executives. The economist Fred Hirsch points out that these latter 'positional goods' as he calls them, derive their attraction from their scarcity.[6] We can use the Massachussets Institute of Technology report on the future of the motor industry in confirmation[7] that a country quickly arrives at a saturation point where cars begin to have a negative value. Not many taxi drivers or thousand-mile-a-week reps go in for week-end rallying. In the developed countries people are beginning to drive less and walk more, - those who don't are soon dead and out of the way, in any case. And one does not have to imagine too many small planes in the air to scare off the dilettantes and leave the genuine enthusiasts.

It is too much to expect that politicians whose function is, after all, the art of government, might embark on a programme whose end will be the negation of government. People co-operating in small groups to supply what we all require will no more need governments than a hole in the head. They would be irrelevant, have no function to perform.

At the same time, those governments and the oligarchies they represent control the sources of information, the media, the education systems, the publishing companies. With these they control the admass, the immoral majority, the tabloid readers, the TV zombies, the voting cattle, and can claim the democratic mandate from now until the Bomb drops. Those who have any fundamental criticism of the system are marginalised, are condemned to the sidelines, and have so been since the inception of the bourgeois system.

The reaction of some, from the Fenians to the Anarcho- syndicalists, to the Red-Brigades, Action-Directe, Bader- Meinhof, has been violence, bombs, shooting. We can dismiss the moral outrage of governments to these events as hypocrisy of the most loathsome kind. They daily enact policies that kill and maim millions with no better justification than the direct-action militants could advance.

It could be that we have not seen the last of this phenomenon. Britain has been, or rather the British Government has been relatively lucky compared with Continental Europe and Northern Ireland as far as political violence is concerned. What little violence there has been has come mainly from the Government side. The Brighton bombing, when the Cabinet was almost wiped out, was a corrective to those who argue that nothing can prevail against the State Machine, and that it couldn't happen here. If a few dozen Irishmen could inflict such damage, what might the disaffection of a few tens or hundreds of thousands of miners, industrial workers bring about? There are the materials, the chemicals, to be found under every sink, in every garden shed, not to mention on every farm, that could produce mayhem on the streets which neither the Police nor the Army could control.

A half a century ago the French military expert General Duval pointed out in 'Les Lecons de la Guerre d'Espagne,' one of the conclusions to be drawn from the Spanish Civil War was that a resolute city population was more than a match for a modern army. The events in Beirut in 1984 which forced both the Americans and French to withdraw and obliged the Israelies to bomb and shell from a distance will not allow us to draw any different conclusion. Molotov cocktails, bottled-gas bombs, gas-pipe machine guns, weedkiller and ammonium fertiliser explosives; expert opinion is that a modest nuclear bomb is not beyond the capability of a hard-working and dedicated group. Clearly the future of city riots like Handsworth, Brixton, Tottenham and Toxteth, could be lively.

There are the strongest grounds for believing that the rage and frustration arising from impotence to make any serious improvement in the system will drive more people in the future than in the past to lash out, take hostages, subvert, sabotage. The increasing complexity of modern society and its artifacts make it much easier than in earlier times. To the secret police with their computer lists will be opposed an increasing number of non-persons - large numbers of people are not bothering to draw Social Security benefits but have gone to ground in the Black Economy. Large numbers of people pursued by creditors: banks, hire-purchase companies, and other loan sharks, have signed off 'over and out' and have changed their name, moved address, started a new life. They are not among the thirty million or so people on the police computer, or any other computer.

The rising tide of social protest and chaos from nuclear waste dump and nuclear power station protests among stockbrokers, to inner city riots among the totally alienated may cause concern among the ruling oligarchy and its servants; it will not bring the end of the Market- economy and the introduction of a 'help-yourself' system one day nearer. Even if governments had the will to change the system, they do not have the power. Government proposes but Capitalism disposes. The alternative does not lie with governments. You cannot free anybody. People can only free themselves. Voluntary co-operation cannot be imposed from above. That would be a contradiction. Either it would not be imposed or it would not be voluntary. The only contribution the Government can make is to get out of the business of governing, but if it just did that and people weren't primed, hadn't already started to combine in groups no bigger than necessary to accomplish the job in hand, the result would be a shambles. The situation would be like letting animals out of a zoo and leaving them to fend for themselves. People who have spent a lifetime getting up and going to work as they have been programmed to do would simply disintegrate mentally and physically. A disproportionate number of workers die within a couple of years of retirement. And that has nothing to do with old age. Unemployed men become listless, are much more frequent visitors to the doctor. The cure is occupational therapy, which is Latin and Greek for cure by work. The ultimate punishment in jail, after 'chokey', after bread and water, after solitary, is deprivation of work. The next step is that you go stir- crazy.

So what prospect is there of a change to a really 'free' system? We have been shunted into this siding of history by the Market economy, the wheels are screaming and grinding but we are up against the buffers with no hope of going anywhere. Has anything changed to allow us to believe we can get back onto the main line of history and resume our journey into the future? Indeed it has. After several centuries when only the mass of the poor were being driven to disaffection by their fate, the unpleasant consequences of the system are increasingly affecting everybody. The shit is hitting the fan and it is everywhere.

Noble lords in the Highlands and Cumbria and North Wales are looking out on their radioactive acres and their radioactive grouse and their radioactive sheep, thanks to Chernobyl. The President of The Country

Landowners Association, Lord Melchett, has been arrested for leading an anti-nuclear protest. In the stockbroker suburbs, residents, having had an exhausting drive home from the office cannot sit in their gardens because the roar of aircraft makes thinking, let alone conversation, impossible.

The very areas once thought to be remote from the more unpleasant aspects of modern life are now the very centres: missile convoys, atomic power stations, poison gas and germ warfare production, tank manoeuvres, bombing ranges. The roar of motorway traffic and the melancholy glow of sodium vapour lights cut through what was not so very long ago, a green and pleasant land. And the hoorays don't like it.

The hundreds of protest movements[8] which have sprung up in the last two or three decades are not working class initiatives. The latter continue to struggle for another penny on the hour and another hour off the day. If getting a nasty and dangerous factory closed down means a loss of jobs, no dice. If the products are designed to kill people, too bad.

The new protests are of a different kind, bringing into question subjects previously thought unquestionable like patriotism, employment, economies of scale, something-for- nothing, is-my-journey-really-necessary. Columns of the disenchanted, armed with evidence of the failure of the Market-based economic system are marching from every point of the ideological compass to a common rallying point. Many of them are non-political, although the point where they all integrate must be political: - the abolition of the wages system.

Peace movements, generals who have looked hard at the strategy of nuclear war, environmentalists, medical workers exhausted from the struggle against Market sponsored diseases, are all moving toward this rallying point. A few politicians, even, disgusted with the sleazy stratagems that governmental power forces upon the 'winners': secrecy, lying, public relations devices to overcome public scepticism, - 'the manufacture of consent' in Walter Lipmann's words. Salesmen of rubbish, much of it dangerous, suddenly aghast at their own bonhomie; workers waking up to the fact that more money meant more hire-purchase commitments and no time to enjoy the proceeds; employers wondering whether dealing with money in telephone numbers has much to do with the quality of life; those in revolt against the sheer ugliness of almost everything that is built or made today[9] who wonder what the hell we shall leave to future generations to show what followed the Cathedrals, the Bronzes of Benin, the Temples of Angkor Wat.

The former New York Times chief in London, Bernard Nossiter, signed himself off on his return to the U.S. in 1976 with a valedictory note expressing his pleasure with the knowledge that the British were showing decreasing enthusiasm for the goals of twentieth century capitalism:- acquisition at the price of reduced leisure, the might-and-main effort to keep up with the Joneses, the sales resistance to electric toothbrushes, dishwashers, and TV-in-every-room. Instead Social Trends reports that Britain is becoming a nation of environment addicts:

> "The National Trust has seen its membership quadruple from 315,000 in 1971 to 1.3 million while the Royal Society for the Protection of Birds has seen an increase from 98,000 to 466,000. Friends of the Earth records a 27-fold increase from 1,000 members to 27,000 over the period. People are also becoming more active. The Ramblers' Association membership has doubled to 44,000 over the same period. The number of volunteer members of mountain rescue teams has gone up by nearly 50 per cent over the same period to 3,408 - with the number of people helped rising nearly fourfold to 774. The number of volunteers in caving teams has fallen slightly but the number of people needing rescue nearly halved between 1981 and 1984. Volunteer workers with the National Federation of Young Farmers' Clubs have jumped by 2,000, while their membership is up by 9,000 since 1971."[10]

The fact that the system is producing consequences which alarm and disturb the people who have the power to manipulate the rest of the population is no guarantee of an alternative society. The oligarchy could not, of itself, create a regime free of the rising tide of horror; they call the shots but they do not execute them. But they do through the media, the education system, publishing, and all the other powers that wealth confers, have the ability to keep working people in a state of confusion, if not of submission. It is because of the enormous changes in recent decades that some are beginning to ask themselves whether their loyalty to the system is whole-hearted.

And when we have bulldozed the commercial centres, office blocks, banks, and shopping arcades, all that will conceivably remain is the supermarkets minus their cash- registers. If that is too difficult to swallow, we should consider that half the population today, pensioners and children, the handicapped and the unemployed, are given the money to go round the shelves and hand it over to the girl at the till. Nine tenths of the cost of the merchandise that they buy lies in the money transaction, not in the goods themselves. It would be so much cheaper to make them free!

As far as the industrial areas are concerned, we shall just have to start again. People with freedom to choose where they work, or indeed whether they work at all (there will be a desperate shortage of it, to begin with), will scarcely be content with the concrete-block barracks which house industry now. Perhaps the redundant bank buildings could be used, if only as a temporary measure. Industry, we, us, would be so much more at ease surrounded by mahogany panelling and carpeted underfoot.

Parts of the road system could become as superfluous as the phased-out railway tracks, or those miles of concrete aircraft runways which have littered the country, particularly the Cotswolds and East Anglia, since the Second World War. We could either rip them up and plant native trees and shrubs or simply let them crumble away, with weeds and wild flowers following the frosts and colonising them, so that our grandchildren will be able to point out a particular swathe of poppies or dog-daisies and say: I remember when that was jammed with cars; reps going north to sell soap powder and reps coming south to sell chocolate bars.

As people's control over their own lives strengthens so will the power of government weaken until it finally becomes simply a clearing house for co-ordinating group activity everywhere. And group activity is where power will, and can only be found. Voluntary group effort to produce what we want; agreement to share out fairly the small amount of work available to those wanting to do it. It will be the only thing in short supply. Our greatest task will lie in getting together to study the creation of meaningful activity to replace lost employment.

But all of the foregoing implies a political act for which there is no alternative. Failure to obtain political power would leave those in control of the status quo free to sabotage any social reorganisation that might be attempted.

Some eighty years ago a commune was set up on the Cotswolds at Whiteway, near Stroud. The land was bought, the deeds were burned (the settlers did not want to be 'landowners') and the members divided up the plots among themselves. They settled down to become as self-sufficient and free from the Market economy as possible.

But they reckoned without the local Council which wanted rates paid on the small houses they had built. They refused, or were unable to pay, had judgement entered against them, and arranged to go to jail in turn to deal with the debt. Today they would be thrown into the gutter and their properties sold to provide the rate money.

More recently a Quaker from Gloucester, Arthur Windsor, has gone to jail more than once for deducting from his taxes the proportion he calculates is being spent on armaments. But there is no escape from the powers of the State. It must be captured and its powers turned against itself. There have been many Whiteways and Arthur Windsors who have tried to resist the State Machine.[11] Their courage and independence of spirit have been no match for the policemen and bailiffs any more than the Jews in the Warsaw Ghetto were a match for the German Army.

The political act of taking power will lead immediately to the disappearance of the basis of power. The return of the land of Britain to the people of Britain will destroy the support that the oligarchy enjoys, that enables it to buy through suborning, patronage, control, and ultimately police and military violence, its continuing - but gravely diminishing-privileges. The paradox of obtaining power to abolish power becomes less paradoxical: power is only really sought by minorities.

All of those thousands of voluntary agencies mentioned earlier, all of the informal economy, all of the amateur cricket clubs, football clubs, dramatic societies, brass bands, all of the myriad forms of collaboration and cooperation that human society has adopted through the ages will become the model for the reorganisation of producing for our needs, but this time from the bottom up, and not the top down.

The answer to the major problems before us lies not in the impossible dreams, the Utopian schemes, of those who tinker with the Market economy in the hope that, after five centuries of failure, it could be made to work. The real answer lies all around us in the attitude of self-help, in the spontaneous groupings of mutual-aid, in the inescapable urges of sociability that have always characterised the human race.

To the incredulous we say that there is nothing unusual in the idea of something for nothing, of production for need and not for sale. The organisations, services, goods, are all around us to prove the point: health, education, roads, street-lighting, policing, libraries, water, drainage. Free-market madmen rise up from time to time with proposals to bottle the air we breathe and sell it back to us in the name of efficiency, but they are soon sedated and put back in their beds.

We are surrounded by mirror-images of what our free-world will look like, albeit distorting mirrors. It is foolish for sceptics to say it won't work; it already does. The only difference is that instead of waiting for an indulgent authority to hand things down to us, meanwhile retaining the power to take them back, we shall make and do them for ourselves. Then the enormous burden of control and regulation, of calculating and mediating, will fall away like the melting of ice, after the Siberian winter of the Market system. If we listen and look, we can already hear the cracking and see the fissures.

1. Economist 21/06/86

2. Times 15/12/85

3. Times 11/12/85

4. Karl Marx: Capital. Preface to the 1st German edition (1867)

5. W.W.Rostow: The Stages of Economic Growth (Cambridge 1967)

6. Fred Hirsch:Social Limits to Growth (Routledge Kegan Paul 1977)

7. MIT: The Future of the Automobile (Unwin 1985)

8. Among the many rich and powerful who are showing increasing signs of alarm at the way things are going are Godfrey Bradman, 'director of 17 companies mostly in finance, banking and property. His financial base is the Rosehaugh empire, the initiator of huge property deals in the City and at the Albert Docks.' (Guardian 1/07/87) Bradman moved from Chelsea to the country, concerned that lead from exhaust emissions was harming his young daughters and has bankrolled organisations ranging from CLEAR - the Campaign for Lead Free Air, - to the Campaign for the Freedom of Information, Friends of the Earth, Citizen Action and offered £2 million to the victims of the drug Opren to fight Ely Lilly, the manufacturers.

Another surprising entrant into the lists is Sir James Goldsmith, the Goldenballs of Private Eye magazine, whose political position appears to be a bit to the Right of Attilla the Hun. Sir James, who has demonstrated a strong support of nuclear weapons to fight World War III launched a violent attack on the French nuclear power industry through the pages of his magazine L'Express (15/03/87). Calling his article : The Arrogance of Man, he contrasted the claims of safety and economy of the French bureaucrats for nuclear power with the information available from other countries. While the French Embassy in Bonn put out the soothing news that there had been no increase in radioactivity anywhere in France after the Chernobyl catastrophe, the Environment Minister for the Saar, next door, commented that the Saar had registered a 2,000 fold increase. He cited the man considered the father of the French nuclear system : Georges Vendryes, who had written in 1986 in the journal of the industry : 'For forty years, the great decisions concerning the development of the French nuclear programme were taken by a very restricted group of persons occupying key posts in the government or the administration of the electricity industry and private companies.' In a subsequent battle in the columns of L'Express he took on Jean Pierre Capron, General Manager of the Commissariat a l'Energie Atomique and Professor Raymond Paulin, director of the Isotope Institute, and gave them a real rubbishing. Capron argued that whatever radiation there was in France, it was safe. Goldsmith pointed out that the scientists who in Capron's words had "from the beginning been right on top of the subject of radioactivity and its effect on mankind" had in 1931 affirmed that people were safe up to 75 rems per annum, then this had been reduced to 50 rems, then to 25 rems; in 1954 to 15 rems; in 1958 to 5 rems. Meanwhile, Professor Radford of the Behr Committee of the American Academy of Science suggests that the acceptable level ought to be reduced again by a factor of 5, or perhaps 10! As Goldsmith says, each time the scientists have pronounced the new levels with the same confidence.

He pointed out how fraudulent were the balance sheets of the industry and the claim by Capron that French electricity prices were amongst the lowest in the world, because the French paid twice over, once through their electricity bill and again through taxation, because the industry is subsidised up to the hilt. Goldsmith could have added that the French situation was paralleled by that in Britain with the added feature that the consumer here was being burdened with even higher prices to make the industry attractive for privatisation. But sceptics in the City were pointing out that no amount of frills on the hambone could conceal the stink of rotten meat from the decaying nuclear power stations. As Goldsmith pointed out, the Americans started into nuclear power stations ten years before France in the early 1960s. The last power station to go into commission was ordered in 1974. After that date 108 reactors were cancelled, many of them three-quarters constructed. In the late 1980s many of the utilities concerned had gone bankrupt.

9. Victor Papanek: Design for the Real World (Paladin 1974): "There are professions more harmful than industrial design, but only a very few of them. And possibly only one profession is phonier. Advertising design, in persuading people to buy things they don't need, with money they don't have, in order to impress others who don't care, is probably the phoniest field in existence today. Industrial design by concocting the tawdry idiocies hawked by advertisers, comes a close second. Never before in history have grown men sat down and seriously designed electric hairbrushes, rhinestone covered file boxes, and mink carpeting for bathrooms, and then drawn up elaborate plans to make and sell these gadgets to millions of people. Before (in 'the good old days') if a person liked killing people, he had to become a general, purchase a coal-mine, or else study nuclear physics. Today, industrial design has put murder on a mass-production basis. By designing criminally unsafe automobiles that kill or maim nearly one million people around the world each year, by creating whole new species of permanent garbage to clutter up the landscape, and by choosing materials and processes that pollute the air we breathe, designers have become a dangerous breed." p.9.

10. Guardian 9/01/87

11.Two and a half centuries before Whiteway, Gerrard Winstanley and his friends set up a similar commune in Surrey until it was destroyed by the military: "On 3 April 1649, two days after Winstanley and his comrades started digging on St George's Hill, Peter Chamberlen (The Poor Mans Advocate 1649) suggested using the confiscated lands of crown, church and royalists, together with common and waste lands, for a public bank. 'If you provide not for the poor', he declared, 'they will provide for themselves.' Such thoughts had indeed already occurred. A continual anxiety during the civil war had been lest 'the necessitous people of the whole kingdom' should 'set up for themselves, to the utter ruin of all the nobility and gentry.'" Christopher Hill, introduction to Winstanley, The Law of Freedom and Other Writings (Pelican 1973) p.22

INDEX